The Descriptive Phenomenological Method
in Psychology

The Descriptive Phenomenological Method in Psychology

A Modified Husserlian Approach

Amedeo Giorgi

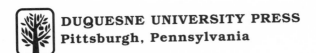

DUQUESNE UNIVERSITY PRESS
Pittsburgh, Pennsylvania

Published in the United States of America by
DUQUESNE UNIVERSITY PRESS
600 Forbes Avenue
Pittsburgh, Pennsylvania 15282

Library of Congress Cataloging-in-Publication Data
Giorgi, Amedeo, 1931–
    The descriptive phenomenological method in psychology : a modified Husserlian
approach / Amedeo Giorgi.
        p. cm.
    Includes bibliographical references and index.
    Summary: "Discusses the phenomenological foundations for qualitative research
in psychology which operates out of the intersection of phenomenological philosophy, science, and psychology; challenges long-standing assumptions about the
practice of grounding the science of psychology in empiricism and asserts that the
broader philosophy of phenomenological theory of science permits more adequate
psychological development"—Provided by publisher.
    ISBN 978-0-8207-0418-0 (pbk. : alk. paper)
    1. Phenomenological psychology. 2. Psychology—Research. I. Title.
BF204.5.G53 2009
150.19'2—dc22

                                                        2009008308

∞ Printed on acid-free paper.

Dedicated to the memory of my late,
dearly beloved and irreplaceable wife,
Barbro M. Giorgi (1957–2007)

Contents

I have been concerned about a proper qualitative method for psychology since 1962. I worried about the question even before that time but it became thematic for me in that year because I was hired by Duquesne University to develop such a method based upon phenomenological principles. However, my understanding of phenomenological philosophy when I first arrived was minimal, so I spent the first half dozen years simply acquiring knowledge about phenomenological philosophy. This was easy to do at Duquesne because at least two-thirds of the philosophy department consisted of philosophers with an existential-phenomenological orientation and there was a visiting professor program whereby European philosophers were invited to give courses on various specialties within phenomenological thought. I sat in on these courses and had discussions with these philosophers for some 24 years overall, but in the first six years I was primarily a learner. I learned what themes phenomenological philosophers pursued, and I was trying to see how phenomenological psychology could both respect those themes and yet differentiate itself from them. I wanted to base psychology on philosophical phenomenology because the notion of a human being in that line of thinking was not reductionistic and I was primarily interested in the psychology of humans. I also learned that philosophical phenomenology contained a method for investigating consciousness in a rigorous way, so I was motivated to see how that method functioned so that I could adapt it for psychological purposes.

From a few brief visits to Europe in the early and mid-1960s and from conversations with the European philosophers who visited the university I was told that there were in Europe psychologists who were already using the phenomenological method in their research. Some of the names mentioned were F. J. J. Buytendijk, H. Linschoten, J. H. van den Berg, and M. J. Langeveld, all of whom were members of the so-called Utrecht school in the Netherlands, plus C. Graumann of Germany. I also became aware of the Copenhagen school of phenomenology. Consequently, in the 1960s, in addition to learning phenomenological philosophy, I kept looking for someone who knew the method that was already being applied. However, I could never find someone who could articulate the method for me. I specifically asked Adrian van Kaam several times because he had founded the department at Duquesne and was Dutch, and I knew that he could read all of the pertinent literature. Probably because he was not a methodologist, he only gave me vague answers and kept referring me to the Dutch men mentioned above. Consequently, I was waiting eagerly for my first sabbatical so that I could go to Europe and investigate for myself just how the phenomenological method was being practiced by research psychologists.

My sabbatical semester began in January 1969 and lasted until July of that year. My home base was the University of Aarhus in Denmark, but I was free to travel extensively and I sought out every phenomenological psychologist that I could find. I visited Copenhagen, Stockholm, Utrecht, Louvain, Heidelberg, and any other place that had someone who might be doing phenomenological psychological research. To make a long story short, I did not find anyone who had a research program using a phenomenological method in psychology. There were certainly some psychologists who had interests in phenomenological psychology, but they were not carrying out research with a phenomenological method. What passed for phenomenological psychology was mostly a theoretical critique of mainstream psychology or else some interesting phenomenological analyses that failed to articulate a method. It almost seemed as though I were pursuing a will-o'-the-wisp.

When I returned to Duquesne University I decided to grab the bull by the horns. I realized that the phenomenological approach in psychology would never get off the ground if there weren't some constructive work done other than theoretical critique. Every theoretical critique should offer some sort of constructive alternative. So in January 1970 I first offered a seminar on applying the phenomenological method to psychological phenomena, but I was not at all sure how I was going to conduct it. I reviewed Husserl and Merleau-Ponty on the method and then tried to see how it could be applied with psychological interests rather than philosophical ones. I taught the seminar annually and groped my way to some degree of clarity, obviously, with some false starts, modifications, and even reversals until what emerged is the method presented in this work.

I have written some dozen articles relating to the phenomenological method as applied to psychology. Most of them were narrowly construed and dealt primarily with practical issues, especially the steps of the method. The actual steps of the method as presented in this book do not differ so much from the most recent articles, but I wanted to give the method some sort of historical context to show that qualitative analyses are not alien to scientific psychological practices. To meet this goal I stayed within the academic research tradition and did not appeal to any clinical literature. In addition, I wanted to give a broader phenomenological contextualization for the method in order to demonstrate that phenomenological philosophy is as rigorous as empiricism, if properly understood, and that it can serve equally well as a basis for scientific practices. My prior attempt (Giorgi 1985, 23–52) to justify phenomenology as a basis for psychology was much briefer.

Since I am a psychologist, I have written in this book about how to apply the phenomenological method to psychological phenomena. But the method described here is generic enough to be applied to any social science that works with human beings, with a few minor modifications. The key change is that researchers from other disciplines have to assume the attitude of their specific disciplines and show sensitivity to detecting their phenomena of interest even though they are mixed in with other sorts of phenomena. As stated in the main part of this book, the raw data consists of descriptions from the perspective of everyday life but the analyses take place within a disciplinary attitude as well as within the scientific phenomenological reduction and with a special sensitivity to the phenomenon being investigated. This means that nurses, sociologists, pedagogists, anthropologists, and scientists from other disciplines can use the method. The raw data should consist of concrete descriptions of specific experiences.

■ ■ ■

Given the fact that I always had teaching responsibilities while writing this book, it has taken me several years to write it. Nevertheless, it could not have been completed without the help of some other important persons. First and foremost, I owe much to my late wife, Barbro Giorgi, who encouraged me to continue working on the manuscript several times when I was discouraged with its slow progress. Moreover, since she herself was a psychologist, we had innumerable discussions about many of the issues discussed in the text that I am sure have led to clarifications that are too numerous to mention. So I thank her very much for all that she has given me, in life, first and foremost, but also in terms of scholarly contributions. I am most happy to dedicate this book to her memory.

I would also like to thank Richard Rojcewicz for reading and commenting upon an earlier version of this book, and I especially would like to thank John Scanlon, the man who has taught me more about Husserl than I could ever have gotten on my own, for his critical comments and for his patient tolerance for my interrogations about interpretations of Husserl's thought. I also have to add the usual disclaimer: These two philosophers have passed on to me certain pearls of wisdom that I have stubbornly refused to accept and so all errors and infelicitous expressions should be attributed solely to me.

ONE

Conceptual Framework

This book draws upon the intersection of three intellectual movements: phenomenological philosophy, science, and psychology. Obviously, when perspectives intersect with one another rather than function within their own comfortable frameworks, scholars must modify their expectations concerning mixed expressions within their disciplines. These modifications often alarm purists, but history shows that there is hardly a movement without dissidents or variable interpretations. Consequently, while all due respect is intended toward the actual history of the disciplines with which we shall engage, I have interpreted the modifications to be consistent with the basic values of each intellectual movement. As every scholar knows, new problems and different questions often tap into various dimensions of already established intellectual traditions. Very often, the new perspectives demand novel formulations.

The most familiar institution, perhaps, is science, which is a knowledge-producing enterprise. Whenever one encounters a phenomenon within the perspective of science, it is ultimately knowledge that one is seeking. One wants to understand the phenomenon or event more completely, sometimes for practical reasons and sometimes simply for its own sake. The curiosity of humans is such that whatever is encountered in the world can also be interrogated further in order to be better understood. Of course, access to phenomena depends upon how they present themselves to conscious human beings, and categories of phenomena can be classified depending upon their mode of presence. On the one hand, phenomena of the world are not so unique that there are no similarities across differentiable phenomena. On the other hand, differences among phenomena can also be irreducible to one another. It seems that the phenomena of the world and their possible variations are so rich that an infinite process is needed to sort them out and understand them.

Humans always have been attracted initially to phenomena that are distant from themselves. The ancients, for example, first became interested in the heavens and the forms of the earth and so cosmologies developed early on. Gradually, it dawned on us humans that there was a constant source to the curiosity about the world, namely, ourselves. Then attention shifted to philosophies of self-comprehension. The source of wonder, ourselves, was initially taken for granted, then became thematized and eventually became a problem. Thus, the knowledge of the world and of the questioner of the world did not develop evenly. To be sure, there were always religions or philosophies that tried to place an overarching order on all of the experienceable phenomena, but such superordinate schemas were usually highly speculative.

In the seventeenth century, science really began to grow in leaps and bounds with the work of Galileo and Newton, among many others. What differentiated genuine scientific work from philosophical speculation was a deep conviction that much could be learned from insightful observation. There was a growing awareness that the world did not follow logical deductions in a straightforward way but that the rationality of the world was more hidden and had to be extracted slowly and painfully from how things appeared. The sciences that were correlated with physical nature really blossomed during the last two centuries, and indeed so much so that they became intellectual models for knowing. The philosophy that supported the turn toward observation — empiricism — whether strict or liberal, also became dominant, along with its auxiliaries — logic, mathematics, and technology. As human curiosity turned from phenomena of the natural world to human phenomena, the same scientific strategies used to study nature understandably were carried over to the study of humans. Moreover, it is not surprising that some early successes were observed since all humans are embodied and the body offers the basis for the kinds of observations that lead to success with the phenomena of the natural world.

In the twenty-first century, advances in scientific knowledge are still pretty much determined by the same criteria as those over the last two centuries, even though technological advances have radically transformed what is given in appearances. However, the idea of the human sciences, perhaps coupled with criteria that are different from those of the physical sciences, has been progressively developing, and it is this notion that will be stressed in this work.

Psychology, as a discipline, began to adopt the criteria and values of the natural sciences during the latter part of the nineteenth century. It broke away from a philosophical style of investigation, and with great adaptability, sometimes with amazing ingenuity, it developed, during the course of the twentieth century, to become an almost exclusive practice that can be called a natural science approach to knowledge. Basically, this type of practice requires the following: the object of study, however defined, has to be present to the sensory-perceptual awareness of the researcher; some sense of reification has to take place; measurement processes have to be applied to the data; and some kind of public verification has to be demonstrated.

These criteria are hardly challengeable in themselves, and they are important in overcoming superstitions and private biases, but they can, at times, present a problem for the psychologist. They are very useful criteria where they are applicable, but I argue in this work that they are not applicable to the full range of phenomena that psychologists would be interested in studying. Consciousness is a prime, but not the only, example. Memories, images, dreams, hallucinations, and the like are other examples of phenomena that do not meet all of the criteria mentioned above.

Mainstream psychologists have frequently tried to reduce such phenomena so that their research strategies could meet the traditional scientific criteria; otherwise, they have to justify transgressing their criteria. Most alternative psychologists operating within the dominant mainstream tradition usually accept the transgression of acceptable criteria, but they often do so apologetically. I will attempt to modify the above-mentioned criteria without sacrificing rigor. However, I shall do so with the help of phenomenological philosophy. I attribute some of the earlier failures to the limits of an empiricist approach as the sole basis for psychological science.

Phenomenology is a philosophy that had its beginnings in the early years of the twentieth century and became explicitly aware of itself in 1913 (Husserl 1983). Husserl, the founder of phenomenology in the modern sense of the term, was a thorough and painstaking worker who constantly revised his work. During his lifetime, he published only about a half-dozen books, but he left around 40,000 pages in manuscript form for his followers to work on. One consequence of this state of affairs is that Husserl often had analyzed in some detail issues that were buried in the manuscripts that were not explicitly discussed in published texts, and as a consequence his critics often got wrong impressions of his views. In addition, Husserl kept revising his views as he saw limitations in his earlier writings and so critics were often attributing to him positions that he outgrew. In any case, these factors, plus the intrinsic difficulty of the philosophical problems that Husserl dealt with, have made a proper understanding of his thought very difficult, especially for nonphilosophers. However, even though difficult, the insights that Husserl was able to express are well worth the extended effort required.

Phenomenology as a philosophy seeks to understand anything at all that can be experienced through the consciousness one has of whatever is "given"[1]—whether it be an object, a person, or a complex state of affairs—from the perspective of the conscious person undergoing the experience. Thus, it is not interested in an objectivistic analysis of the "given," that is, an analysis that would exclude the experiencer, but rather in a precise analysis of how the "given" is experienced by the experiencer. The reason for this is that nothing can be known or spoken about that does not come through consciousness. If science is concerned about knowledge, knowledge itself is correlated with consciousness, and phenomenology is concerned with how any "given" whatsoever, including knowledge, is related to consciousness. Phenomenology also claims to have a method whereby it can access how "givens" appear to consciousness. The method, too, is often misunderstood, especially when judged by nonphenomenological criteria.

The major difficulty in attempting to present phenomenology is that there are many versions of it. It is doubly difficult when trying to present a version of phenomenology that would be directly relevant for human science practices since the version often involves modifications unfamiliar to philosophers and philosophical projects. Nevertheless, in this work I believe that the sense of phenomenology I employ is consistent with the basic tenets of phenomenological philosophy even as it moves toward scientific phenomenological understandings and practices.

At the level of scientific practice, phenomenological research tends to converge with qualitative research strategies, and the latter have been slow in making headway in psychology, although other human sciences have adopted such strategies more readily. Even though it is a minority perspective, qualitative research and its strategies have not been entirely missing, even in the history of psychology as a natural science. Since some of the resistance to a phenomenological approach is due to its qualitative emphasis, I shall first give a brief review of qualitative research strategies in psychology in order to indicate that it is not less scientific but only differently so. Phenomenology is not "anti-quantitative"; its position is neutral with respect to research strategies. If one asks a quantitative question, then one should use a quantitative method; if one asks a qualitative question, then one should use a qualitative method. The reason that phenomenology is often associated with qualitative research practices in this era of science is that it is a philosophy that offers a certain logic for legitimating qualitative discriminations with rigor. Not all philosophies provide such a legitimation as well as phenomenology does.

PSYCHOLOGY AS A NATURAL SCIENCE

It is no secret that scholars strongly desired psychology to become a natural science ever since the natural sciences in the modern sense were able to demonstrate their successful achievements. Of course, not all of the scholars interested in psychological phenomena or epistemological issues wanted this outcome, but a significant number did and there were, in Germany throughout the nineteenth century, multiple attempts to legitimate and demonstrate the achievement of this goal (Leary 1978). A consensus was arrived at and historians of psychology acknowledge that psychology as a natural science was firmly established by Wundt in 1879 when he established a lab for psychological research at the University of Leipzig. Even though competitive perspectives existed (for example, Brentano 1973; Dilthey 1977), the natural science viewpoint took off and outdistanced other perspectives; today it is known as "mainstream psychology" and is recognized as the established psychological standpoint.

Mainstream psychology adopted the framework of the natural sciences and has continued to evolve within that perspective. Its models were physics and chemistry even though physiology was the most proximate influence (Wundt 1904). To accept such a model meant that the experimental paradigm was the most desirable situation for research and that measurement of variables was a desideratum along with quantified expression of results.[2] Psychological phenomena were understood to be analogues of the physical phenomena that the natural sciences studied. In this view, the fact that a living person was being studied, or even the fact that certain living beings had a type of consciousness that was as sophisticated as that of the psychological researcher, only meant that modifications of the natural science paradigm were required as opposed to a radical rethinking of the research situation itself. Thus, statistical designs predominated in psychological research, including applied settings, and the application and development of tests grew in innumerable ways and always with the help of statistical procedures. There is no sign that such developments are abating.

However, the natural science paradigm is not necessarily hostile to qualitative research. Certain sciences, such as astronomy, botany, and geography, have necessarily used qualitative procedures over long periods of time. It is true, of course, that the desire to move to a more quantitative stage of scientific work is desired by many of these practitioners, but still, qualitative, descriptive work is taken seriously. It may surprise some contemporary psychologists that, however sparse, there is nevertheless a qualitative tradition within psychology conceived as a natural science. In the early days, it was taken for granted that such qualitative work was legitimate science, but over time the sophisticated analyses of newer statistical procedures and the alleged power they seemed to have made the direct qualitative analyses seem like impoverished findings. It soon became the standard interpretation that qualitative analyses were propaedeutic, or "soft science," or something one did only until the real scientific procedures could take over. While criticisms of the quantitative approach occasionally surfaced (for example, Brower 1949, Mauran 1998, Michell 2000), the development of qualitative strategies atrophied and practically disappeared from scientific psychology. They remained mostly in clinical settings where description was still essential, but, of course, such settings were not considered to be scientific and thus the power of description or qualitative analyses was never really acknowledged. Only at the beginning of the twenty-first century has psychology begun to acknowledge that qualitative methods may have scientific value (J. A. Smith 2003; Camic, Rhodes, and Yardley 2003)—long after almost all of the other human sciences have acknowledged the value of qualitative methods. Psychology is the last discipline to make such an acknowledgment. Of course, everything that I said above is true of psychology conceived within a natural science perspective. If a human science perspective toward psychology were to be adopted, the need for, and the power of, qualitative methods would be much more obvious and no apologies would be required.

As Spiegelberg, the chief historian of the phenomenological movement, demonstrates, the term "phenomenology" was in use in different senses before its current meaning emerged (Spiegelberg and Schuhmann 1982). Even the key terms of phenomenology underwent development, in Husserl and in the hands of other philosophical phenomenologists, and then the term was stretched even further when it was applied in the social sciences, including psychology and psychiatry (Spiegelberg 1972, Spiegelberg and Schuhmann 1982). Thus, it is not easy to give a comprehensive yet precise definition of phenomenology. (For a comprehensive understanding, see Spiegelberg and Schuhmann 1982.) I can, however, cite the thinkers whose phenomenological ideas I follow in this work: Husserl (1970a, 1970b, 1983, 1989), Gurwitsch (1964), and those aspects of Merleau-Ponty (1962, 1963) that are consistent with the Husserlian framework. Obviously, the latter two thinkers were philosophers in their own right and developed ideas not necessarily consistent with Husserl. Nevertheless, each has given Husserl credit for launching them into phenomenological issues even if contrary ideas sometimes were pursued.

Phenomenology, of course, is primarily a philosophy, but one that has consequential implications for psychology, as does empiricism. A big difference, of course, is that empiricism has been guiding the development of the natural sciences since the seventeenth century, and it has had a huge influence on the history of psychology since at least the mid-nineteenth century, whereas phenomenology (in the sense in which it is used in this work) is a distinctly twentieth century movement. It is also a movement of multiple perspectives and even contrary emphases, so to speak of the impact of phenomenology on psychology is still to make an ambiguous claim. My task here, however, is not so much to straighten out the phenomenological movement as it is to clarify the sense in which I am using it. For those familiar with phenomenology, I will follow primarily a Husserlian perspective with its major concerns about epistemology, the status of knowledge (especially theoretical knowledge), its foundations, and the types of science required to establish sound knowledge. I do not believe that empiricism is the best philosophy for grounding the science of psychology, and I will demonstrate that a phenomenological theory of science will permit a more adequate psychological development. It should be noted that phenomenology is not antiempirical so much as broader than empirical philosophy.

For Husserl, a more secure founding for knowledge would start with consciousness, because no knowledge can be achieved without referring to consciousness. Thus, Husserl desired to clarify how any possible object presented itself to consciousness, which led him to a series of complex analyses and deepening problems requiring solutions. Husserl distinguished between the act of consciousness that is directed toward an object and the object itself which is the focus of the act. He also distinguished between the object and the reflective grasp of the "act-object relationship," which reveals the meaning of the relationship. Husserl also specified that careful reflection upon the act-object relationship will also reveal that the act relates to an "ego" that subsumes the acts. Thus, phenomenology is concerned primarily with the "ego-act-object" or "ego-cogito-cogitatum" structure of consciousness. Psychology, of course, is also interested in the life of consciousness and in the activities that an individual projects toward others and the world. Initially, the overlap between these two modes of thought is easier to see than their distinctiveness.

I have made introductory remarks about phenomenology elsewhere (Giorgi 1976, 1977a, 1977b, 1983a, 1983b, 1992), but two notions should be articulated before starting—the idea of phenomenon and the notion of the "lifeworld" and its relationship to science. All other critical phenomenological concepts will be discussed as they are introduced.

The sense of phenomenon in phenomenology is that one must be present to the "given" precisely as it presents itself, neither adding to nor subtracting from what is "given." Moreover, one employs the attitude of the phenomenological reduction (more on this later) whereby the spontaneous positing of the existence of the "given" is not carried out. That is, the "given" is considered as something that is present to consciousness, but one refrains from stating that the "given" also exists in the way it is presented to the consciousness of the experiencer. The caution of limiting perception to only the claim of something being present is exercised because in everyday life, without fully realizing it, one automatically posits the object of perception as existing. Normally, we see something and we take it as existing. Husserl wants us first to see how the object presents itself. Thus, a phenomenon is anything that can present itself to consciousness, and it is considered to be just that: something that is present to consciousness. No existential declaration is made even if the "given" actually exists. If the "given" does actually exist, one's attitude is modified so that it is considered only as a presence. Phenomenology, then, in this context, is considered to be the study of the structures of such phenomena as they appear to consciousness. These structures include both the "given" that is present and the acts of consciousness to which the "given" is present. As Husserl (1983, 61) himself puts it, "I am exercising the 'phenomenological' ἐποχή which also *completely shuts me off from any judgment about spatiotemporal factual being. Thus I exclude all sciences relating to this natural world* no matter how firmly they stand there for me, no matter how much I admire them." This means that the natural attitude and all that belongs to it, including knowledge derived from all of the positive sciences, is put "out of play"; none of the assurances of the natural attitude can be used as valid bases for phenomenological claims. Implied with the notion of epoché or bracketing is the notion that past knowledge about whatever is presently given is also put aside so that unprejudiced attention can be directed to what is present in the current act of consciousness being considered.

Another key term developed by Husserl (1970a) in his later years is the notion of the lifeworld. In philosophical contexts this term takes on several meanings (Carr 1987), but I wish to emphasize only one of them here. By "lifeworld," Husserl wishes to designate the common, everyday world into which we are all born and live. It is usually a world of ordinariness. We get up, wash, have breakfast, go to work, come home, meet with friends and family, have dinner, relax, and go to bed. This is the world all humans initially encounter, however diversified.

Husserl's point is that this is the "ground world," the basic world from which all other specialized worlds emerge. The world of entertainment, the world of business, the academic world, and even the world of science are all derivations of the basic lifeworld and often the specialized worlds take the lifeworld for granted. Consequently, a complete understanding of our specialized worlds requires an understanding of how the specialized worlds relate to the lifeworld. We are interested in understanding science because that is the specialized world within which the phenomenological method will be applied even though it initially developed within the context of philosophy. However, Husserl did desire that philosophy should become a "rigorous science," and so he was always concerned with the formulations of scientific and theoretical knowledge.

Unfortunately, a thorough and consistent explication of the phenomenological theory of science is not yet a historical achievement. Certain viewpoints and perspectives on phenomenological science can be found scattered throughout Husserl's works (for example, 1970a, 1970b, 1980, 1983) and among certain commentators (Kockelmans and Kisiel 1970, Gurwitsch 1974, Harvey 1989, Hardy 1992, Ströker 1997, Reeder 1997), but a definitive articulation does not yet exist. Consequently, I will give my perspectives on the phenomenological approach to science as they are relevant to the issues that arrive in the practice of phenomenological psychology as a scientific discipline.

Husserl (1980, 1:37) provides a succinct definition of science: "A science: that means an infinity of systematically connected truths explorable in a systematic unity and naturally truths that do not lie at hand but rather are discovered only as fruits of arduous investigation." Thus, despite Husserl's reputation in certain circles for seeking absolute and universal knowledge, Husserl here acknowledges that gaining scientific knowledge is an infinite process. Moreover, he allows that the task is far from easy. In addition, when Husserl (1970b, 1:62) speaks about "systematically connected truths," he means that science "involves unity in the whole system of grounded validation," and this unity includes theories.

Husserl obviously acknowledged that there were many types of sciences, but also many levels. Husserl also maintained that the separate sciences were incomplete in the sense that very good practitioners of science could not always justify their methods or practices with clarified principles and thus satisfy theoretical questions. The sciences, said Husserl (1970b, 1:59), "as theories, (are) not crystal clear: the function of all their concepts and propositions is not fully intelligible, not all of their propositions have been exactly analyzed, they are not in their entirety raised above all theoretical doubt." This incompleteness is what calls for a theory of science or *Wissenschaftslehre*.

Husserl (1970b, 1:63) goes on to argue for, and demonstrate, that sciences require methods and "more or less artificial aids" in order to establish truths. Scientific knowledge requires evidence, or backing, in order to be acceptable by the community of scientists. Husserl warns that no one would put up with the disciplinary constraints of a method if truth were immediately shared by intimation or if the mere intention to arrive at the truth established it. Thus, methodical procedures in his view are required in order to transform knowledge into truths.

Husserl (1970b, 1:64–65) claims that scientific knowledge requires evidence or grounded validations. At the time he was writing, science was quite well established, so he was able to point to three general characteristics that grounded validations had in common. The first characteristic was that evidence had to have the "character of a fixed structure in relation to (its) content" (64). This means that content can vary quite a bit while the relationship of the content to the goal remains fixed. Secondly, he notes that "Connections of validation are not governed by caprice or chance, but by reason and order, i.e. by regulative laws" (64). A chance coming together of facts does not establish a rational understanding. Science seeks to discover the sense by which such facts hang together and the sense relates to some principle of unity. Randomly aggregated facts merely externally related do not constitute a rational mode of understanding. Finally, Husserl argues that forms of validation, expressed at the proper level of universality, are not limited to specific fields of knowledge (65). Thus, a form of correct reasoning as is found in the syllogism is applicable to both chemistry and mathematics. Consequently, a theory of science dealing with the articulation of such discoveries would be a positive development for acquisition of knowledge. Husserl concludes, "Research into the sciences as systematic unities is unthinkable without prior research into their validatory procedures" (70). Part of the task of a theory of science, for Husserl, is to distinguish valid from invalid demonstrations but also to critique invalid theories and sciences as well as to establish "methods of knowledge in the sciences."

Husserl also hierarchizes different types of science. For Husserl (1970b), the foundational sciences are the theoretical ones and they are the basis for the normative and practical sciences. Theoretical sciences are concerned with the coherence of the things themselves and in the forms of the objective coherence of the matters being studied. For Husserl, logic should be such a theoretical science even though in the tradition of science it is used as a normative science. A normative science, for Husserl, is one based upon a certain valuation such that its laws tell one what should be or should not be, whether or not the conditions that would make something be actually exist or not. A normative discipline, says Husserl (1970b, 1:86), "is therefore unambiguously characterized by its basic norm, or by the definition of what shall count as 'good' in such a discipline... and has its own basic norm which is in each case its unifying principle." Theoretical disciplines are not focused about a valuation but rather about "The inner laws of things... and their mutual coherence." A practical science is one where, based on a particular normative science's valuation, a practical aim is sought universally (87).

Psychology should, in part, be a theoretical science oriented toward a well-delineated subject matter, but it is not a well-developed theoretical science. In psychology there are many theories rather than a well-established single theory as is seen in the various schools of psychology that existed from the 1920s through the 1940s, as well as the historical switching from external perspectives to internal perspectives without proper integration and the different definitions of subject matter (behavior and consciousness). There are also the viewpoints of the dissenters from mainstream psychology that are not well known but often reward serious study. This state of affairs often exists in science because sciences do not develop logically and coherently. Rather, scientific development is sporadic, and it frequently takes a critical evaluation long after being initiated in order for a science to be organized in a logical way. Thus, in the prolegomena of *Logical Investigations,* Husserl (1970b) argues against the prevailing notion that logic was a practical discipline rooted in psychology rather than a theoretical discipline independent of psychological factors. His critique contributed to a better understanding of logic despite the fact that it came long after logic existed. Thus, a clarified understanding of the meaning of science may help psychology to progress as well.

Thus, I am about to launch a project in which a scientific phenomenological method will be applied to psychological subject matter. However, this model will not be the historically existing natural sciences that have already achieved much success. There already exists a natural scientific psychology, and in my opinion the model chosen has restrained the development of psychology. Consequently, based upon a phenomenological approach, I will follow a generic model of science, one broader than what guides the natural sciences. This model will allow for empirical objects as well as objects that are given in an expanded empirical sense; one that can easily accommodate theoretical matters as well as data; one that is open to qualitative as well as quantitative data; and one that can be tolerant of pararational givens as well as rational criteria. This model at the moment is an embryo, it does not come ready-made. Rather, it has to develop as it is being practiced. Thus, it is to be expected that false steps as well as correct ones may be taken and that corrections will ensue. It is an example of science as it is being lived rather than reflectively considered. It is a matter of doing, criticizing, clarifying, and then redoing.

Two

The Qualitative Perspective in Researching Psychological Phenomena

The first section of this chapter describes movements or general trends in the history of modern psychology that either emphasized the qualitative dimensions of phenomena or at least allowed for the presence of qualitative dimensions. In the second section, I will cover psychologists who have spent the greater part of their careers, if not exclusively using qualitative methods, then certainly making room for such methods in their work.

BRIEF GENERAL HISTORY

The proper history of the qualitative perspective in psychology since the introduction of experimentation has not yet been written. This section cannot substitute for that history, but it can at least demonstrate that an avoidance of the qualitative is not conducive to growth of psychological knowledge. Despite the great emphasis on quantification since the introduction of experimentation, and despite the habit acquired during those years of expressing qualitative characteristics in quantitative forms, the presence of qualitative data in modern psychology is still rather pronounced.

All psychological knowledge until about the middle of the nineteenth century was basically qualitative. In part that is because psychology was not yet an independent scientific discipline but under the aegis of philosophy, and so it was expected that its scholarly style would be philosophical. Thus, when psychologists wanted their field to be considered a science, they had to conduct and express themselves as the sciences did and this meant primarily experimentation and quantification, despite the fact that such a move was totally new for psychological subject matter. It went against the grain of the philosophical style that had been expressing psychological insights for centuries. Difficulties arose in trying to make psychological phenomena conform to natural science criteria (Fay 1939, Blumenthal 1980, Adler 1994), but by and large psychology succeeded (Boring 1953).

Perhaps the best description of the transformation required to join the camp of the natural sciences on the part of psychology is that provided by Morawski (1988, vii):

> The massive project to implement experimentation on mental processes necessitated the scrutiny and rejection of some deep cultural beliefs about personal experience and the extent to which they are accessible to others. The project also required substantial alterations in scientific work practices, since the laboratory had to accommodate human subjects, rather than gases, minerals, cells, molecules and drosophila. Few of the instruments and procedures from the biological or physical sciences could be adopted directly. Instead, researchers had to construct ways of observing psychological events, often redefining the very phenomena along the way. They likewise had to devise entirely new work procedures that could meet the practical problems encountered when the experimenters' subjects were fellow humans.
>
> Viewed in terms of its proper subject matter and work practices, experimental psychology can be seen as a transformative enterprise. Through the creation of laboratory instruments and techniques, the reeling cacophonous world of human experiences was transformed into discrete, feasible problems that could be analyzed in controlled settings. Human experiences were translated into a shared scientific language and increasingly sophisticated inscription (both numeric and graphic) of that language. This was necessary for the growth of a professional community defined by a common language and skills.

The very fact that such huge transformations had to take place supports a contention for which I had argued earlier, that the experimental model and human psychological phenomena do not mesh together very well (Giorgi 1970). However, despite the hegemony of the experimental paradigm, qualitative studies not following the criteria of the experimental paradigm still persisted within late nineteenth and early twentieth century psychology. This is the history I wish to track in a brief way in this chapter.

A point of departure is Edward B. Titchener's (1867–1927) designated critical year: 1874. In that year, Wilhelm Wundt (1832–1920) published his *Grundzüge der physiologischen Psychologie,* which outlined a different style of scholarship that included experimentation and the gathering of facts, whereas Brentano (1838–1917) in the same year published *Psychologie vom empirischen Standpunkt,* an influential work very much in the philosophical style to which scholars were accustomed. Titchener called Wundt's style "experimental" and Brentano's "empirical." Brentano, of course, was a philosopher and he did not claim to be initiating a new movement as Wundt was. Nevertheless, his whole approach was descriptive, evidence for his position being provided by and supported by arguments against opponents' positions. In this style, Brentano made some significant contributions toward the understanding of psychological phenomena. He took on the very foundational problem of the nature of psychological phenomena and how to discriminate them from physical phenomena. His solution was not fully satisfactory to all interested parties, but then the answer to that question is still not a historical achievement 125 years after Brentano offered his solution. It is very likely that some aspect of what Brentano said will be part of the genuine answer when it is forthcoming.

In addition, Brentano (1973) revivified the notion of "intentional inexistence," which he received from the Scholastics, and that notion was modified by Husserl (1970a) and is today known as "intentionality," and it is playing an important role in contemporary phenomenological psychology and in certain forms of cognitive psychology. A basic psychological understanding of intentionality refers to the fact that mental phenomena are directed toward objects other than themselves, and even themselves if a reflective act is undertaken. Brentano made many other distinctions, including those relating to classification of psychological phenomena. These results had their detractors and supporters, which means his findings fared no worse than those produced by the early experimental psychologists even though his method was descriptive and qualitative.

Wundt did indeed initiate experimentation in psychology (although Fechner is credited by many) and looked for facts that could be expressed quantitatively, but he never proclaimed that the experimental method was the only method (Blumenthal 1985). Wundt believed that the experimental method had limited applications, and he spent the latter part of his life using the historical method to study social and cultural phenomena; that method produces qualitative results (Blumenthal 1975, 1985; Graumann 1980). Greenwood (2003) disputes these interpretations, but there is plenty of evidence in Wundt that he set limits to the use of the experimental method. Of course, Wundt did not extol the use of nonexperimental methods since they were not as innovative as the experimental ones. The quantitative findings were the novelties that were prized by the emerging natural scientific psychologists.

There were even those who opposed the very idea of an experimental approach to psychological subject matter, and one of those thinkers was Wilhelm Dilthey (1833–1911), who proposed a wholly different approach to the study of the psyche. His method was based upon descriptions and understanding and was completely qualitative but not identical to the previous psychological understandings that were parts of philosophical systems (Dilthey 1977). Another psychologist who spanned the years of those already mentioned, the Frenchman Alfred Binet (1857–1911), is known mostly for his work with intelligence tests within educational contexts, but he also argued for the importance of qualitative dimensions on intelligence and in psychological work in general (Binet 1903; Wolf 1966). In England, Sully (1842–1923) published his *Outlines of Psychology* (1884) and Ward (1843–1925) his famous Encyclopedia Britannica article (1886), the first time that the encyclopedia included an entry for psychology. Both of these works were very much "empirical" in Titchener's sense of the term. That is, they covered the history of the field, made discriminations, argued for various positions, and then presented their systems. Indeed, Ward had spent time in Germany and was influenced by Brentano. His final statement on his sense of psychology was published in book form over 30 years later (Ward 1918). Experimentation came late in England, and G. F. Stout (1860–1944) continued the empirical tradition with his textbook writing (Stout 1903). All of the writings by these three British men were philosophical in style and thus qualitative. Among Americans, William James (1842–1910) and E. B. Titchener also allowed for a qualitative perspective, but I will discuss them in more detail below.

Around the beginning of the twentieth century in Germany, the introspective method underwent some radical changes at the hands of the members of the Würzburg school. The Würzburg school, led by Oswald Külpe (1862–1915), sparked both a content and method controversy. The content controversy was concerned with the possible existence of "imageless thoughts." Experimental subjects were given certain tasks to perform and then they were to describe how they performed the task. Many subjects claimed that they were aware of certain ideas, "directions," or "tendencies" without any empirical content. These results flew in the face of all of the contemporary theories of conscious elements. All other researchers claimed that the contents had to be palpable, that is, sensorial or empirical even if only in an imaginary way. The question was never resolved because the type of data provided by the subjects led to methodological controversies that were also not theoretically resolved, but practically so, because the controversy led to the demise of the introspective method. Wundt severely criticized the Würzburg method because the introspections were not closely tied to experimental conditions (Humphrey 1963, 107–12). Everyone lost confidence in the method because different schools of thought could only come up with findings consistent with their own theories, despite the so-called "objective experimental procedures." Behaviorism came along at the beginning of the next decade to help seal the fate of introspectionism. Whether the cessation of the introspective method was theoretically justified is a wholly different and complex issue that cannot be pursued here. The point is that after the demise of introspectionism some descriptive work still continued, but it was no longer called introspection (Boring 1953).

Around 1912, there was an explosion of psychology's subject matter. Until then, the theme of psychology was consciousness, and the approach to it was contested among functionalism, Titchenerian structuralism, and Wundtian voluntarism. But, around 1912, Gestalt theory made its appearance with its emphasis on given, experiential phenomena (Ash 1985); behaviorism announced itself with John B. Watson's (1878–1958) original manifesto (Watson 1913); and between 1911 and 1915 psychoanalysis, with its emphasis upon unconscious factors, also began to creep into academic teachings (Ross 1978, Gifford 1978). Thus, experience, behavior, and the unconscious were all affirmed as psychological subject matters, sometimes at the expense of consciousness, and sometimes along with consciousness, but in any case, consciousness, in the long run, was never wholly eliminated from the subject matter of psychology.

While two of these movements remained experimental in approach, they were not excessively quantitative. Gestalt psychology, of course, very much depended upon descriptions of experiences in order to communicate how the phenomenal world of an individual appeared. Kurt Koffka (1886–1941) even distinguished between functional concepts, defined as "Facts which anyone can determine (and pertain to) *actual* or *real* things or processes" and descriptive concepts, which are applied to "*experiences* or *phenomena*" (Koffka 1928, 8). Koffka hastened to add that experiential givens or phenomena are not less real than those pertaining to functional concepts, but descriptive accounts can only be given by the experiencer, not by anyone. Furthermore, Koffka advocated the use of three methods: "1) a purely objective method; 2) a combined objective-subjective method, called psychophysical; and 3) a purely subjective descriptive method, depending altogether on the observation of experience" (Koffka 1928, 25). For the Gestaltists, everything involving experience or description purported qualitative work, even though experimental situations were employed. One could almost say that the use of quantification in Gestalt psychology was pretty close to ideal. It was properly conceptualized and never simply done for its own sake.

Behaviorism was the second new movement and it, too, was essentially experimental in approach. Watson (1913), its originator, worked primarily with animals, or infants, and so he was forced to be more descriptive in order to discriminate relevant responses since he could not depend on the subjects' verbal responses. Moreover, since Watson had done mostly field studies with animals up until the publication of his manifesto, he had to be qualitatively descriptive because he took a protoethological perspective (Dewsbury 1994). Indeed, Watson was not even against verbal reports. He writes:

> The notion has somehow gained ground that objective psychology does not deal with speech reactions. This, of course, is a mistake. It would be foolish and one-sided to an absurd degree to neglect men's vocal behavior...the verbal report or response is put down in our records of the results of the experiment and is used exactly as the conditioned reflex responses would be used had we adopted that form of experimentation in our test. (Watson 1919, 38–39)

Watson was largely experimental and descriptive in his approach, sometimes linguistically descriptive, and, where possible, statistically descriptive. In fact, several years after he left academic life, he lamented the fact that psychology was still "largely at the descriptive level" (Watson 1928, 16). Consequently, it seems to have been pervasively practiced.

Not all behaviorists were satisfied with descriptive approaches. Hull (1943), for example, actively sought mathematical formulas. However, the other major behaviorist of the twentieth century, B. F. Skinner, was strictly descriptive in his approach and often even qualitatively so. As Salzinger (1994, 155) points out, behaviorists preferred to work in depth with a small number of animals and then depict results in terms of visual displays (tables and graphs) as well as words (L. D. Smith 1995). Skinner was a Machian positivist, which meant that he wanted to stay as close to the given facts as possible without any appeal to theoretical, inferential, or hypothetical entities (L. D. Smith 1995; Skinner 1938, 1950). Skinner's position is a descriptive positivism, which is not the same as logical positivism, and his behaviorism was radical behaviorism and not methodological behaviorism. As early as the *Behavior of Organisms,* Skinner (1938, 5) wrote that a "directly descriptive science of behavior" was needed and that, in terms of scientific method, this entailed a method that was "positivistic. It confines itself to description rather than explanation. Its concepts are defined in terms of immediate observations; . . . they are not hypotheses, in the sense of things to be proved or disproved, but convenient representations of things already known" (44). Again, Skinner was not against statistical description or depiction by graphs and curves, but he thought that the least erroneous way of communicating scientific findings was by means of description of facts. This procedure does not eliminate the qualitative dimension.

The third and final movement, psychoanalysis, is neither experimental nor quantitative, but qualitative, descriptive, and theoretical. While psychoanalysis can be said to have begun in 1900 with the publication of the *Interpretation of Dreams* (Freud 1938), historians of psychology noted that it took over a decade for psychoanalysis to impact academia. Sigmund Freud (1856–1939) described the project of psychoanalysis (1966) as a natural scientific project, but basically his scientific expressions were based upon his clients' descriptions of their experiences and on his theoretical interpretations of them. In fact, Bettelheim (1984) claims that Freud should be understood to be a worker in the field of the *Geisteswissenschaften* rather than the natural sciences, despite what Freud claimed in his "Project for a Scientific Psychology." In any case, Freud's *Interpretation of Dreams* is entirely descriptive, reflective, and qualitative. Indeed, the entire psychoanalytic tradition works in the same way, and if one were to deny legitimate scientific status to this tradition, psychological knowledge in the area of psychopathology would be significantly diminished.

It is rarely noted that during the 1920s in Germany, at the time of the Weimar Republic, there were five holistic schools of psychology:

Gestalt psychology (the Berlin school); the personalistic psychology of Wilhelm Stern (1871–1938); the *Ganzheitspsychologie* of the second Leipzig school led by Felix Krueger (1874–1948); the phenomenological experimental work of David Katz (1884–1953); and finally, the *Verstehenpsychologie* represented by Eduard Spranger (1882–1963), a follower of Wilhelm Dilthey. All of these movements or schools worked extensively with the qualitative dimension of psychological phenomena. The Nazi government ended the development of the majority of these movements by forcing exile on most of its members.

Also in the 1920s, in France, Georges Politzer (1903–42) made some significant critiques of the experimental approach endorsed by Wundt, and he argued for a concrete psychology based upon description and the analysis of meaning (Politzer 1968, 1973). This movement did not last long in part because Politzer was killed during the war years by the Nazis for refusing to collaborate with them and in part because Politzer himself aborted his whole idea when he realized that allegedly sympathetic others were merely projecting their own ideas into his notion of "concrete psychology" rather than listening to his articulations of the sense of concrete psychology. Still, his criticisms of Wundt and Freud were sharp and they impacted a whole generation of philosopher psychologists in France. His work was almost exclusively qualitative.

In Switzerland during the 1920s and 1930s, Jean Piaget (1896–1980) was pursuing his interests in genetic epistemology and in the process conducted many experiments that eventually came to be evaluated as landmarks in developmental psychology. Piaget was interested basically in the world of the child and how the structures of cognition varied with development. Thus, he explored language, thought, reasoning, judgment, and moral understanding (Piaget 1926, 1928, 1932) as well as the child's conception of the world and his or her understanding of causality (Piaget 1929, 1930). All of these studies were basically qualitative in nature even though he was not in principle opposed to quantifying results (Flavell 1962). Ironically, in pursuit of his understanding of the child's understanding of quantity, he also used a basic qualitative approach (Piaget and Inhelder 1941).

Piaget's research methods were counter to the prevailing norms of experimental research, and this fact delayed general acceptance for his work in the United States for at least a generation. Flavell's (1962) book contributed greatly to the acceptance of Piaget among American psychologists.

As mentioned above, experimental psychology got a late start in Great Britain. A laboratory was founded at Cambridge University in 1913 and was headed by C. S. Myers (1873–1946), assisted in the early years by Frederic C. Bartlett (1886–1969), who took over the directorship of the lab in 1922 after Myers died. Bartlett was appointed professor of experimental psychology in 1931 and remained in that position until he retired in 1952.

Bartlett was as much an experimentalist as a psychologist could be but his mode of experimenting was quite different. Bartlett (1995) stated that he was aware of the work that Hermann Ebbinghaus had begun and tried to conduct his work in that mode but found it unsatisfactory. He was more interested in memory studies that were more "realistic," or as we would say today, had greater "ecological validity." No statistics were used and the analyses were basically qualitative. Bartlett (1958) also initiated studies of thinking at the same time, but because of the Second World War these studies were not published until about 25 years later. The works on thinking were also entirely qualitative. Except for a very few followers, Bartlett had little influence initially, but after the cognitive turn in psychology that took place in the late 1950s and early 1960s, his mode of experimentation and his theoretical contributions were more readily appreciated.

Throughout the 1930s, many psychologists were involved in the war effort and with the practical tasks of selecting, training, and fitting young men for various military responsibilities as well as taking care of the wounded and psychologically disturbed veterans. However, early in the 1940s, Gordon Allport (1897–1967) prepared a report sponsored by the Social Science Research Council on how to use personal documents in the science of psychology (Allport 1942). This book is a significant contribution, unfortunately only rarely referred to, but I will cover it in some detail below. However, since most personal documents are written documents, many implications for qualitative research are contained in Allport's report. Toward the end of the decade, Robert MacLeod (1907–1970) wrote a classic article on the phenomenological approach to social psychology (MacLeod 1947). The article was based on his experience in Germany, but a small phenomenological movement in America was already taking shape prior to the impact of continental philosophy.

Even though phenomenology in the modern sense of the term first appeared in 1900 in Europe with the work of Husserl (1970b), a case has been made by Hans Linschoten (1925–64) (1968) that William James (1950) had anticipated many phenomenological themes even though it would be anachronistic to actually call him a phenomenologist. However, James's depiction of the difference in experience between his own perception of a woods near campus as restful and peaceful as opposed to that of a child who finds it dark and scary is precisely touching upon a key phenomenological theme because it shows how the same "objective situation" can be taken up differently by different persons, and even differently by the same person at different times. The role of subjective experience in constituting the appearance of the world is what James was, and phenomenologists are, concerned about.

Remarkably, without any apparent direct connection to James, or anyone else, the phenomenal world of an individual is what Donald Snygg (1904–67) (1941) emphasized in the early 1940s. Later, Arthur Combs (1912–99) and Snygg (1959) published a fuller systematic exposition of their phenomenological approach and this book was modified again (Combs, Richards, and Richards 1988). The approach of these authors has been labeled "grassroots American phenomenology" because it sprang up spontaneously without philosophical guidance.[1] Interesting variations within this approach are given by Kuenzli (1959).

MacLeod's (1947, 1951, 1964) version of phenomenology was influenced to some extent by continental approaches because he learned it from David Katz while the latter was still in Rostock, Germany. MacLeod was an advocate of the phenomenological approach, but he saw it as propaedeutic to psychology rather than as a psychological method per se (MacLeod 1970). He felt that after phenomenological analyses one ought to conduct typical psychological experiments. Cloonan (1995) provides a thorough description of this phase of phenomenological psychology in America. A more radical understanding of phenomenological philosophy happens in the late 1960s and early 1970s. While phenomenology is not in principle against quantitative analyses, all of the work cited above is primarily qualitative.

Another movement that is relevant for our concerns took place within mainstream psychology beginning in the late 1940s and lasted until the mid-1960s. The so-called "New Look" in perception emerged, was promoted and criticized, and finally dissipated in the mid-1960s. Allport (1955) summarizes the pros and cons of this movement, as has Wertz (1982, 1983), from whom I will draw. For a long time, perceptual experiments were in the hands of psychophysicists, and the assumption underlying their research was that perception was due only to phsycial factors rather than social or cultural influences. The subjectivity of the perceiver was basically ignored and it was easy to overlook the subjective factor as long as the perceiver's attitude was kept passive. Despite their holistic approach, the Gestaltists were criticized by the New Look researchers, but the Gestalt view was defended by Luchins (1951) in his countercriticism of the New Look studies. However, for many psychologists interested in personal issues the understanding of perception was unsatisfactory, not to say unsuccessful as well, with the psychophysical approach, so, as Wertz (1983, 224) summarizes it, "The New Look therefore, set forth three implicitly interrelated aims: to bring the study of perception close to everyday life, to include the person as a whole in the study of perception, and to begin to heal the dangerous wounds of fragmentation in the discipline by unifying the study of perception with other subfields of psychology."

Since experimentation was the privileged mode of establishing facts in psychology, the New Look chose that form of research. Most of the research was conducted with ambiguous stimuli so that personal factors in perception would have the chance to show themselves. While there were differences among New Look researchers, they all wanted to account for concrete perceptions in terms of factors that went beyond stimulus characteristics. Werner and Wapner (1950) relied upon organismic factors, others upon central, nonperceptual factors derived from other subfields of psychology (for example, Bruner and Goodman 1947 relied upon the social values of the stimulus; Beams and Thompson 1952 used the desire or lack of desire for certain objects; Cowen and Beier 1950 employed the role of anxiety as a blockage to recognition of words), and finally, explicit personality factors such as rigidity (Frenkel-Brunswik 1950) or tendencies to accentuate stimulus characteristics (for example, Klein 1951) were used to account for the results.

The reason the New Look movement never got integrated into mainstream psychology is that it was severely criticized on method-ological grounds. It turned out that the variables that the New Look researchers wanted to investigate were difficult to control according to the established means of the time. How could one stay close to the lifeworld and be accurate, or include the whole person and measure accurately, or overcome psychology's fragmentation with a precise sense of unity? As Wertz (1983, 232) points out,

> While [the New Look's] examples of percepts include such proper-ties as clarity, friendliness, threateningness, and seductiveness, we find [with the experiments] such properties as size, brightness, weight, and distance.... Since it is impossible to measure or precisely manipulate such qualities as friendliness and seductiveness, what is studied is not the percept in its full everyday reality but only its manipulable and mathematizable characteristics.

Perhaps for the first time a clear tension manifested itself between clearly defined experiential psychological variables and the strategy of using differences in quantitative dimensions to measure the experi-ences. It could possibly have shown itself earlier, but with the New Look studies there is a clear case of the inadequacy of the measure to fit the subjective characteristics of the experienced phenomena adequately in order to clarify lived experience. Size may be a factor for the experience of friendliness, but it is far from being the sole deter-miner of friendliness as such. Clearly, what was lacking was a strategy of qualitative analysis that could answer more specific questions. Previously, the qualitative understandings of psychology were empirical in the sense of Titchener — generic analyses, arguments, criticisms, and then resyntheses according to the perspective of the writer. However, there was very little appeal to qualitative data collected in research settings. Only specific methods of that type could have resolved the New Look issues. Instead, the basic natural science framework that developed in dialogue with things and physical processes was used, rather than looking for new strategies to study qualitative relationships rigorously. The former framework could not adequately provide the proper distinctions and discriminations to resolve the questions raised about holistic, experiential phenomena. A need for a different framework, or for a complementary set of strategies, presented itself, but no one took up the challenge. The New Look movement quietly faded away and was interpreted as another fad or fashion rather than as the failure of the natural scientific framework as applied to experiential phenomena rich with complex qualities.

In the late 1950s and early 1960s, another movement got started, still extant today—the humanistic psychology movement. It was also known as the "third force" because it was a reaction against the limitations of the other two dominant forces in psychology. The first force, behaviorism, was primarily concerned with animals and limited to an external perspective on "organisms," and the second force, psychoanalysis, focused on a perspective that emphasized instincts and drives from below that determined behavior and concentrated on pathologies. The humanistic movement wanted to be person centered and to emphasize the positive and creative activities of human beings. Practitioners of that movement wanted to study the upper reaches of human beings as well as restore dignity to the sense of the human person. However, the humanistic perspective was sustained more by clinicians, personality theorists, and practitioners rather than by academicians, and so radical methodological innovations were not forthcoming. There were certainly criticisms of the limits of traditional psychology's methods and the undue emphasis they assumed in conducting research, especially by Maslow (1966) and Matson (1964), but few different qualitative methods were introduced. Indeed, one of the criticisms of the humanistic psychology movement was that it simply inserted the human person into the same research designs as used by mainstream psychology (Giorgi 1987). They seemingly believed the rhetoric that said that the methods were "neutral." What the humanistic movement did do was increase the awareness that different and better qualitative methods were required to truly investigate the higher faculties of the human person.

The 1950s and early 1960s were also the years that the cognitive perspective reemerged. It is sometimes referred to as a "revolution," but in my view that is an exaggeration since psychology from the beginning was defined as the study of the mind or mental phenomena. While the behavioristic movement precipitated a great decline in the study of consciousness, such an interest never quite disappeared altogether. Moreover, the ascendancy of cognitive psychology, which dominates the field today, did not really shake up the primary frame of reference for psychology. Thus, it is not a revolution because it is simply a change of content within the natural scientific framework. Indeed, the theory behind most of cognitive psychology is precisely the way to approach cognition as the theme of psychology without changing the basic assumptions of natural scientific psychology.

There are two streams within cognitive psychology, one that is dominated by information processing theories and that draws heavily upon computer analogies and the other that seeks careful descriptions of how humans actually function—that is, think, perceive, attend, and so on, so that better understandings of the processes can ensue. It is in this latter stream that one can find an argument for qualitative analyses. In fact, Ericsson and Simon (1984) wrote a book justifying and articulating the use of "verbal reports." The more objectivistic expression for the desire for, and use of, descriptive data is probably a concession to the times, although logic plays a heavy role in the analysis of these reports. Thus, even within the movement that dominates today, there is an acknowledged role for qualitative data and analyses.

Finally, also beginning in the late 1950s, another small movement began to influence psychology, and while it never grew very large, it still exists today as a minority perspective. I am speaking about the impact of existential phenomenological philosophy on psychology. In 1958, Rollo May (1909–94) edited and contributed to the volume entitled *Existence* in which he and other contributors highlighted the value of existential and experiential factors for the proper under-standing of the human person and the role such factors played for proper psychological analyses (May, Angel, and Ellenberger 1958). In effect, this movement stressed the need for a better anthropological philosophy of the person than was provided by either behaviorism or psychoanalysis. This idea motivated Adrian van Kaam (1920–2007), a Dutch immigrant, to found a department dedicated to the goal of formulating and making explicit the psychology implicitly contained within existential-phenomenological philosophy. The graduate pro-gram of this department also began in 1958, and basically remained true to the original vision for about 30 years or so, when external pressures and internal disputes finally watered down the vision to a more eclectic perspective. While such single-mindedness for a whole department is not unheard of, it is rare, especially when the department defines itself at odds with the psychological establishment. And it is even more rare on the American scene, where a general eclecticism is preferred to specialized perspectives.

In any case, with the help of phenomenological philosophy, a methodological perspective was introduced that concentrated on the qualitative dimensions of experience. To be clear, as I noted above, phenomenology is not intrinsically against quantitative methods. If one asks a quantitative question, one uses a quantitative method. However, if one asks a qualitative question, then a qualitative method is appropriate. However, a phenomenological approach would be against the arbitrary imposition of quantitative approaches to intrinsi-cally qualitative questions.

Psychology as an independent science, especially in its nonclini-cal areas, has operated mostly under the hegemony of experimental situations and quantitative approaches. Perhaps this was a sure way of showing its independence from its philosophical heritage since the philosophical style of scholarship was exclusively reflective and qualitative. In any case, now that psychology is securely established as an independent discipline, it is beginning to show signs of openness to qualitative strategies, although much more slowly and reluctantly as compared with many other social sciences.

SOME HISTORICAL EXAMPLES OF QUALITATIVE RESEARCH STRATEGIES

Even though experimentation and quantitative procedures domi-nated the studies performed by psychologists since psychology's found-ing as a science, such strategies were not the whole story. Below I will examine in a bit more detail the procedures used by those psychologists and researchers who favored a qualitative approach.

William James (1842–1910)

William James ended up preferring to be called a philosopher rather than a psychologist, and his writing style is more philosophical than scientific, but he was conversant with the contemporary psychology of his time, including experimental studies. After all, James had set aside a room for experimental work at Harvard in 1875 or 1876, a few years before Wundt's official founding in 1879 (Linschoten 1968, 27). However, James was not of the temperament to do experimental research himself, nor was he inclined to review experimental work and its criticisms. His dismissal of such work in the *Principles* (James 1950, 192–93) is fairly well known.

However, James was interested in researching issues that concerned him deeply, although the style of research he advocated was different from experimentation. Perhaps the best example of his original research, other than theoretical or philosophical analyses, was the research that appeared in his *Varieties of Religious Experience* (James 1902). After finishing his magnum opus in 1890, James reacted even more strongly against the narrowing of the field of psychology to laboratory studies, and he began to explore what he called "exceptional mental states" (Taylor 1982). These states included phenomena such as dreams, hypnotic states, hysteria, automatisms, and the like. James's interest in religion was allied with his curiosity about exceptional phenomena, and he never wanted to be so exclusively scientific that religion would disappear (Taylor 1982).

My interest in the *Varieties,* of course, is in the strategies that James used to study religious phenomena. Basically, James went to the many sources that claimed religious experiences, and he drew out the implications of all of the expressions of those experiences. As is well known, he did not limit himself with respect to denominations, gender, or even types of religion; he was inclusive of all of them. Nor did he make it a task for himself to interview religious people. Rather, he drew upon diaries, autobiographies, journals, letters, or whatever sources expressed a religious sentiment. These documents were written for other purposes, which James acknowledged, but he read them all with the explicit purpose of trying to determine the meaning of the religious experience based upon the experiencer's verbal expressions.

While James was not patently as rigorous in his methical concerns as some of his experimental counterparts seemed to be, he was not without some guidelines in his pursuit of the understanding of the psychological aspects of the religious experience. In the preface of his book, James announces a primary principle of his approach: "In my belief that a large acquaintance with particulars often makes us wiser than the possession of abstract formulas, however deep, I have loaded the lectures with concrete examples, and I have chosen these among the extreme expressions of the religious temperament" (1902, xvii). Here, James articulates two principles: a turn to the concrete as much as possible and a selection of extreme examples of religiosity. He must have learned the principle on value of concrete cases from his association with Louis Agassiz, since James writes: "One must know concrete instances first; for, as Professor Agassiz used to say, one can see no farther into a generalization than just so far as one's previous acquaintance with particulars enables one to take it in" (213). Exposure to, and contact with, concrete instances was a much desired starting point for James.

With respect to the selection of extreme cases, James writes:

It is a good rule in physiology, when we are studying the meaning of an organ, to ask after its most peculiar and characteristic sort of performance, and to seek its office in that one of its functions which no other organ can possibly exert. Surely the same maxim holds good in our present quest. The essence of religious experiences, the thing by which we finally must judge them, must be that element or quality in them which we can meet nowhere else. And such a quality will be of course most prominent and easy to notice in those religious experiences which are most one-sided, exaggerated, and intense. (45)

In responding to a potential critic of this criterion, James states, "I reply that I took these extreme examples as yielding the profounder information" (476), and "we learn most about a thing when we view it under a microscope, as it were, or in its most exaggerated form" (39).

James declares throughout his lectures that his method is descriptive and empirical. He does not elaborate much on what he means by description, but clearly assumes that it can be implemented and is productive. He does provide a strategic insight with respect to description when he tackles the problem of mysticism:

Phenomena are best understood when placed within their series, studied in their germ and in their over-ripe decay, and compared with their exaggerated and degenerated kindred. The range of mystical experience is very wide, much too wide for us to cover in the time at our disposal. Yet the method of serial study is so essential for interpretation that if we really wish to reach conclusions we must use it. I will begin, therefore, with phenomena which claim no special religious significance, and end with those of which the religious pretensions are extreme. (373)

James's interest in the range of phenomena is probably a correlate of his belief in pluralism. Always inclusive in his approach, he dismissed no bit of experiential reality. His radical openness prevented him from absolutizing the scientific approach or belittling the most subjective of experiences. James acknowledges that "Science...had evolved by utterly repudiating the personal point of view" (ibid., 481). He affirms that the scientific viewpoint is one legitimate point of view and that it should be pushed to its limit; however, it is not the only point of view. James goes on to write,

> In spite of the appeal which this impersonality of the scientific attitude makes to a certain magnanimity of temper, I believe it to be shallow, and I can now state my reason in comparatively few words. That reason is that, so long as we deal with the cosmic and the general, we deal only with the symbols of reality, but *as soon as we deal with private and personal phenomena as such, we deal with realities in the completest sense of the term.* (488–89)

James admits that our experience always consists of two parts, an objective and a subjective aspect, and while he concedes that the former may be much more extensive, he also avers that the latter can never be surpassed, however insignificant it may seem to be:

> the inner state is our very experience itself; its reality and that of our experience are one. A conscious field *plus* its object as felt or thought of *plus* an attitude towards the object *plus* the sense of a self to whom the attitude belongs — such a concrete lot of personal experience may be a small bit, but it is a solid bit as long as it lasts.... That unsharable feeling which each one of us has of the pinch of his individual destiny as he privately feels it rolling out on fortune's wheel may be disparaged for its egotism, may be sneered at as unscientific, but it is one thing that fills up the measure of our concrete actuality and any would-be existent that should lack such a feeling or its analogue, would be a piece of reality only half made up.... To describe the world with all the various feelings of the individual pinch of destiny, all the various spiritual attitudes, left out from the description — they being as desirable as anything else — would be something like offering a printed bill of fare as the equivalent for a solid meal. (489–90)

James implies that it seems to be absurd to study personal or subjective reality by means of a rigorous impersonal attitude. Some dimensions of the personal may be captured in such an attitude, but there is plenty left over for a personal perspective to deal with. Indeed, James argues that both science and "mind cure" philosophies basically follow the same procedure: experiment and verification (ibid., 116–20). Science declares, "If this law is truly universal, I should be able to predict the outcome of this study"; the person who believes in mind cures would say, "If I truly believe that minds can cure, then my leg should heal." James gives examples of the latter claim.

Thus, even though James was seeking to understand a type of phenomenon that science hesitates to touch, he could easily justify his own approach in the study as being scientific. He modified a botanical approach that he learned from Agassiz, he modified a physiological strategy as a basis for selection of phenomena, and he accepted the evidence of "experiment-verification" as declared by others. Yet, James remained descriptive and qualitative throughout his entire study of religious experiences.

Edward B. Titchener (1867–1927)

Not many present-day psychologists are aware of it, but Edward B. Titchener (1901a, 1901b, 1905a, 1905b) wrote two manuals of experimental psychology in the early years of the twentieth century, one on qualitative experiments, and the other on quantitative experiments, and each manual had two parts, a manual for students and one for instructors. These manuals were not only a set of instructions and helpful hints to the students and instructors, but they also contained a summary of the most recent literature on the topics the students were to experiment upon as well as pertinent historical and background information.

How does Titchener conceive of the qualitative experiment? In his qualitative exposition to students, Titchener (1901a, xiii) writes, "a psychological experiment consists of an *introspection or a series of introspections made under standard conditions.*" In the qualitative book, student's manual, Titchener starts off by distinguishing the qualitative experiment from the quantitative one:

> The object of the qualitative experiment in psychology is—if we may sum it up in a single word—to *describe;* the object of the quantitative experiment is to *measure.* In the former, we seek to gain familiarity, by methodically controlled introspection, with some type or kind of mental process; we live through, attentively and in isolation, some special bit of mental experience, and then give in words a report of the experience, making our own report, so far as possible, photographically accurate. Numerical determinations, formulae, measurements, come into account only in so far as they are necessary to the methodical control

of introspection; they are not of the essence of the experiment. The question asked of consciousness is the question "What?" or "How?": What possibly do I find here, in this attentive consciousness? How precisely is this fusion put together? In the quantitative experiment, on the other hand, we make no attempt at complete description: it is taken for granted that the mental processes now under examination have become familiar by practice. What we do is carry out a long series of observations, under the simplest and most general introspective conditions. Then we gather up the results of these observations in mathematical shorthand, and express them numerically by a single value. The questions asked of consciousness are, in the best analysis, two only: *"Present or absent?"* and *"Same or different?"* (1905a, v)

Some aspects of these quotations are worth highlighting. Note, for Titchener, there is no contradiction in speaking of a "qualitative experiment." Somehow that has developed into becoming an oxymoron in the contemporary vernacular, but the alleged contradiction is not intrinsic. Moreover, we see from Titchener that description is a legitimate goal of science and it is not identical to measurement but equally important. Both procedures or perspectives are necessary for a full science. That there is a difference between them is further evidenced when Titchener points out that there may be some "measurement" aspects in a qualitative experiment, but they are not the essence of such research, but introduced only as means of supporting methodical control in the experiment. Implicitly, Titchener also asserts that the qualitative experiment seeking accurate descriptions is basically discovery oriented. He says that the basic question to be asked of consciousness in such an experiment is "What?" or "How?" — the latter in the sense of "How did this memory come about?" or "How did this brightness present itself to me?" Examples of Titchener's (1901b, xxi) own questions are "How does one idea call up another?" and "What are the characteristic processes of the attentive consciousness?"

In the quantitative experiment, Titchener makes clear, a complete description is lacking. Rather, a long series of observations are undertaken and the responses required from the participants are highly truncated and generally dichotomous: "Present or absent; same or different; stimulus starts or stops." Note, it is taken for granted in these experiments that the mental processes or sensations being sought had become familiar through practice. This condition hardly exists in many modern forms of experimentation.

Titchener (1901a, xiii) further defines an experiment not as "a test of power or faculty or capacity, but a direction of consciousness, an analysis of a piece of the mental mechanism." Given the perspective of introspectionism that Titchener upheld, this dissection implied for him the necessity to "split a complex whole into simpler parts, and so ultimately to reduce it to its elements, the very simplest factors of which it is compounded" (1). Wherever the experimenter found an obscurity, he was to question the observer and tell him to report his experience definitely and concretely. An additional benefit of this procedure for Titchener was that he believed that the observer would gain practice in the description of his or her mental processes (xiv).

Titchener said that the qualitative experiment was a situation of complete description, and he meant it literally. He instructs the observer to tell the experimenter everything about his mood or status at the time of the experiment. He instructs the observer (today, participant) in the following way:

> Tell him everything that you are aware of, by introspection, as affecting the experiment. If, e.g., you are working on an "illusion" and you are conscious of a tendency to correct the illusion, mention the fact to him early in the experimental series; he has to explain your results, and may spend much time in puzzling over a matter that a little care on your part would have cleared up at once. No piece of true introspection is too trivial to speak of. Notice slips of attention, insistent memories, outside disturbances, variations of mood, etc., etc. (Ibid., xiv)

Basically, Titchener was demanding a constant frame of mind from his observer, and he suggested that about three-quarters of an hour was the most that observers could work in one stretch.

Titchener also cautioned against making suggestions to the observer or in any way communicating to him or her expected results. Training is also required because Titchener realized that students also had to be trained to give up the "popular psychology" they brought with them from everyday life (1905a, viii). They were required to adopt an entirely new attitude toward the mind and to learn to examine consciousness by introspection. This attitude and this method were not to be found outside of psychology. Students had to learn to psychologize (Titchener 1901b, xix). On the other hand, in the training of description, beginners had to learn the difference between wording conscious processes definitely and concretely and "picturesque or pictorial phrasing.... [The] picturesque report—a report which may seem, at first reading, to reproduce the warmth and intimacy of the experience as no other form of words could do—will generally be found, on deeper study, to rest upon some superficial analogy, and to contain no more of real introspection than the most arid and abstract sentence" (xxix–xxx). Titchener concluded that impressionism was as bad as formalism; photographic depiction is what he sought.

Titchener asserted several times over that doing introspective work was not easy. Moreover, he insisted that introspection could not be learned from books (1901b, xix). For him, the "understanding of the introspective method either comes by way of the laboratory or does not come at all" (xix). Titchener was aware that the learning of introspection could happen in various and unpredictable ways. On the one hand, it could be preceded by long periods of "blind work," or success could come with barely a period of training. On the other hand, taking a laboratory course in introspective training was no guarantee that the participant would learn how to use the method. Nor, once it was learned, was that fact a guarantee that it would always be used correctly. One may introspect inadequately. Thus, Titchener strongly advocated that instructors in psychology teach from their own knowledge of the processes of consciousness and not just from book knowledge. The method, in other words, demanded practical know-how as well as theoretical knowledge.

In the volumes on qualitative research, Titchener often went to great lengths to acknowledge that qualitative research was as legitimate as quantitative strategies. However, it is especially in the volume addressed to instructors that Titchener (1901b, xx–xxi) makes this point. He clarifies that the term "qualitative" does not mean that the experiments are "rough and inexact" and so should be considered merely "approximations" to the quantitative ideal, an attitude often found expressed today. Nor should qualitative experiments be considered indefinite, and their methods should not be regarded as inferior, as though they were incapable of mathematical formulation. Basically, Titchener argued that there is a logic intrinsic to qualitative research and that such research should be evaluated in terms of that logic and not in terms of the criteria of quantitative research. Titchener did not work out qualitative logic to a great extent in part because he was also developing quantitative strategies, but he fully appreciated the distinction. It is also possible that the logic of qualitative research got intertwined with his defense of his own school of introspectionism. Titchener even admitted (1901b, xxii) that one of the German labs at the time of his writing had almost left quantitative work behind and was doing almost exclusively qualitative work (presumably the Würzburg school).

I want to make clear that Titchener was not arguing for the development of qualitative research to the exclusion of quantitative approaches. Quite the contrary is true. Titchener clearly states that the two approaches are not mutually exclusive because a completely full experiment requires both aspects: "We cannot turn our introspective data to account for the 'How?' of sound localization unless we have the errors and the directions of error expressed in numerical terms. On the other hand, if the work is quantitative, it must still be supplemented by qualitative introspection, or the figures and formulae are barren. Reaction times are worth very little without the accompanying analyses of action-consciousness" (1901b, xxi). At base, Titchener was aware of the reciprocity between the qualitative and quantitative dimensions of a concrete situation. Use more than one participant or take more than one description and quantity is involved; discriminate an aspect of the mental process from the whole in order to count its appearances and quality is involved. So, ultimately, for Titchener, the line between the two types of research is relative. Still, what is thematic is different. Perhaps the best summary statement is provided by Titchener:

> The experiments are complementary, each sacrificing something and each gaining something. The qualitative experiment shows us all the detail and variety of the mental life, and in so doing forbids us to pack its results into formulae; the quantitative experiment furnishes us with certain uniformities of the mental life, neatly and summarily expressed, but for that very reason must pass unnoticed many things that a qualitatively directed introspection would bring to light. (1905a, vi)

It is also important to note that Titchener devoted several paragraphs concerning the issue of laboratory partnerships. Danziger (1990, 49–52) established that Wundt's laboratory manifested a collaborative style of interaction among its participants. Whether one was experimenter, participant, or conceptual developer, one saw oneself as participating in a common enterprise and the specific role that one fulfilled did not matter so much. Since all were also acquaintances or friends, the relationships obviously extended beyond the confines of the lab. It seems that Titchener wanted very much to continue this style of scientific research.

While Titchener (1901a, xiii) acknowledged that there were some "experiments best performed by oneself on oneself," he definitely preferred partnerships, especially in the process of training young scientists. He encouraged students to remain together throughout the year if the partners were basically compatible. He was explicit in his instructions for the roles of observer and experimenter, and he encouraged partners to be punctual, considerate, and polite. It was helpful if the partners were sympathetic to, and had full confidence in, each other. That a close relationship between partners existed as a context for the data of early psychological research is an important fact to remember when one reads about the difficulties in obtaining confirmatory data in introspective studies when the data from different laboratories were combined. Titchener (1901b, xxv–xxvi) even used data of "student types" published by Stern and Bolton to help instruct students on the proper roles and relationships for laboratory partners.

Finally, Titchener insisted again and again that each experiment should not be experienced as an entity in its own right, but in appreciation of its place in the system of psychology. No experiment should stand alone, but should be related to other experiments and psychological theory. Titchener (1901a, xvii) encouraged thinking along investigative lines, in terms of a series of experiments, rather than in terms of a single, decisive experiment.

Sir Frederic C. Bartlett (1886–1969)

Frederic Bartlett was an experimental psychologist whose work was almost exclusively descriptive and qualitative. His major works were in the areas of memory and thinking, and in each case he basically selected his own problems and designed an independent approach. With respect to memory, he was fully aware of Ebbinghaus's (1964) work, but as Bartlett states,

> Long before this, Ebbinghaus had introduced the "exact methods" of nonsense syllables into the laboratory consideration of memory. As in duty bound, I followed his lead and worked for some time with nonsense material. The result was disappointment and a growing dissatisfaction…the upshot was that I determined to try to retain the advantages of an experimental method of approach, with its relatively controlled situations, and also to keep my study as realistic as possible. (1995, xvii)

Bartlett was critical of Ebbinghaus's strategy even while he acknowledged that it was another legitimate approach. He saw Ebbinghaus's strategy as being based upon the "simplification of stimuli and the isolation of response" (Bartlett, 1995, 2), but points out that the consequences Ebbinghaus hoped for did not follow from this strategy. Bartlett was also aware of the work of his countryman Francis Galton and the statistical tradition Galton initiated, but he also criticized the statistical approach and then flatly stated, "In this book there will be no statistics whatever" (9). He stated that this was not due to disrespect for the power of statistics, but because he was interested in tying the relations of the subjects to the conditions of research as specifically as possible.

Bartlett described his own approach as a "method of description." Basically, this meant that the participants in the study were to answer questions about certain stimulus cards after different intervals since their initial perception of them. The new data consisted of the verbal responses of the participants, and the data were analyzed in terms of the various interests that the experimenter brought to bear upon the raw data. Bartlett also states that he used a "Method of Repeated Reproduction" (1995, 63), a "Method of Picture Writing" (95), and a "Method of Social Reproduction" (118). The difference between the first and third method is that in the first the same participant related a story to different individuals after certain lapses of time, and in the third method the same story was related across several individuals. The picture writing method required the participants to draw a sign or symbol connected to brief linguistic expressions presented visually after proscribed delays. Again, all of the analyses were qualitative and the concept of meaning played an important role in his analyses.

Hilgard makes an important observation concerning the type of naturalistic experiment conducted by Bartlett:

> The usual order of science is to go through a naturalistic stage, in which observations are classified and some apparent causal connections detected. Eventually knowledge is based on propositions according to a theoretical system. Here [the study of memory] the order was reversed. As the new conceptualization developed, it was discovered that psychologists had been so pleased that they could bring some aspects of learning and memory into the laboratory that they had not taken seriously enough the naturalistic scouting of the terrain with which a science usually begins (Craik, 1979). Therefore, in order to make an appropriate theoretical advance, it was necessary at the same time to do some of the psychologizing of the sort that William James had done and to retreat to more common sense observations made in a richer and more natural context. (1987, 217)

The above statement is a significant concession that in many areas experimental psychology began by leaping into a more mature experimental phase rather than beginning descriptively and with situations closer to those of everyday life. Unfortunately, holding out the hope of more rigorous experimentation is still prevalent in psychology, as exemplified by Kintsch (1995), who declares that the weakest part of Bartlett's studies on memory are his naturalistic settings and his casual mode of research. Bartlett (1995), however, justifies his strategies, in my view, in an acceptable way.

It was not until 1958 that Bartlett was able to publish his research on thinking, even though he states that he began to contemplate experimental research on the thinking process as early as 1932 (Bartlett 1958). He distinguished between situations described as "Thinking within Closed Systems" and situations wherein "Adventurous Thinking" could take place. Adventurous thinking was exemplified by three different types: the thinking of the experimental scientist, everyday thinking, and artistic thinking. Bartlett even used reflections on his own thinking processes while designing his memory research as the bases for insight into experimental thinking. Such a strategy could easily have been considered taboo among experimentalists at the time that he did it. For everyday thinking, he presented participants with descriptions of concrete social issues that were not resolved, sometimes individually and sometimes in groups, and the participants were asked to continue the arguments to a plausible conclusion. For differentiating artistic thinking, Bartlett used diaries, biographies, and other texts by the artists themselves or those near to them to discriminate among the variations peculiar to artistic differences. This strategy is similar to what James had done with religious experiences. This whole book contains only descriptions and various sorts of qualitative analyses. Yet Bartlett's work on thinking and memory are both considered to be seminal works well worth reading because of the insights contained in them.

Gordon Allport (1897–1967)

If Gordon Allport's quest in psychology could be reduced to a simple issue, it would probably be: "How shall psychological life history be written?" (G. Allport 1968, 377; Hevern 1999). While he respected the nomothetic work being done in psychology, and often contributed to such an approach, Allport was always equally concerned with the psychology of the individual. His pursuit was always for a "meaningful psychology" or, in his own phrase, "a full-bodied psychology" (Pettigrew 1970). After getting his degree, Allport spent time abroad in Germany and England in the early 1920s and thus was influenced by the various holistic views being promulgated in Germany at the time, especially by Spranger and Stern. Allport mentions that he was interested in personality before it became a well-known area of study in psychology, and this interest even earned him a rebuke from Titchener and his experimentalists at one of their meetings. However, Allport states that he continued with his "maverick interests" in psychology, and eventually the field caught up with him.

Allport did conduct some empirical studies in the quantitative tradition, but the desire to study personality *as a whole* was always an important goal for him. His idiographic interests were also very strong, which meant that he was always looking for new ways of understanding individuals psychologically. Allport knew that tapping into the subjective was important if we were to understand *minds,* and he realized that the use of the personal document would be helpful for this enterprise. Thus, Allport (1942) wrote a report for the Social Science Research Council on the use of personal documents in psychological research, which contains the majority of his contributions toward qualitative research.[2]

In *The Use of Personal Documents in Psychological Science,* Allport makes a thorough analysis of the types of personal documents and of the uses that psychologists could make of them. He lists the individuals' motives for writing and then distinguishes among types of personal documents, such as autobiographies, diaries, letters, verbatim records, questionnaires, and artistic and projective documents. He discusses the difficulties involved in conceptualizing about, and generalizing from, such documents and explores both nomothetic and idiographic types of results.

Allport also lists and responds to the many objections voiced by psychologists against the use of personal documents in the science of psychology. The list is long:

- personal documents are unrepresentative examples;

- the document writers are more fascinated by style, so it could easily be the case that "art [takes] precedence over sincerity and fact" (G. Allport 1942, 126);

- the documents are intrinsically subjective and therefore non-objective;
- it is difficult to estimate the documents' validity;
- the problem of deception, including self-deception, exists;
- writers are not necessarily aware of, or open to, their genuine motivations;
- writers tend to simplify complicated issues;
- documents are likely to be unreliable since they are often dependent upon words and attitudes, which vary greatly;
- errors of memory cannot always be easily checked;
- the conceptualizations formed by writers are often implicit and arbitrary and not always available to readers;
- documents are scarce and expensive to multiply; and
- personal documents can never be the basis of a scientific endeavor because they are single cases.

Allport dismisses some of these objections, accepts a few of them, and compromises with many others. In the end, however, Allport does argue for the use of personal documents. He contends that psychologists should be interested in the phenomenon of subjectivity, and all personal documents are replete with subjectivity. Moreover, Allport points out the advantages for idiographic research that the documents provide as well as the fact that they could be used to advance nomothetic research as well, insofar as typologies could be developed on their basis. Finally, Allport posits three criteria for meeting scientific standards—understanding, prediction, and control—and shows how personal documents could meet those criteria.

In any case, in his use of personal documents, Allport was advocating qualitative procedures, although he rarely used the term "qualitative research" itself. He was especially desirous to use qualitative procedures for idiographic research. His interest in personality and the individual motivated him to seek alternative methods. Another difference I have with Allport, then, is that I believe that all of psychology should use qualitative methods in any area or subfield as long as a qualitative question is being asked. I agree, however, that the qualitative question seems most pertinent when one is concerned with the study of a given individual. However, this fact does not in and of itself prevent adequate generalizations.

Jean Piaget (1896–1980)

Even though Piaget called himself a genetic epistemologist, many psychologists perceive his work to be valuable for developmental psychology.[3] Piaget wrote that where strict experimentation is not possible within the human sciences, research "can only be replaced by systematic observation based upon factual variations and the analysis of those variations in a functional—i.e. logical and mathematical—fashion" (1974, 39). It seems that Piaget was keenly interested in seeking structures, and he believed that it was impossible "to dissociate the qualitative and quantitative aspects of any structure, even one that is purely logical" (42). Despite this theoretical conviction, Piaget seemed to have worked mostly with qualitative strategies correlated with behavioral tasks or demonstrations.

More precisely, however, Mayer (2005) investigates the background of Piaget's "clinical method" and concludes that Piaget synthesized three traditions of research: psychometrics, naturalistic observation, and the psychiatric clinical interview. Although he was participating in psychometric situations early in his career because of his work with Simon, Piaget did not follow the rules of psychometric testing in a strict sense. Ginsburg and Opper (1969) relate that it was during his work with Simon that Piaget's interest in the development of intelligence received a new impetus:

> although in intelligence testing, attention is usually focused on the child's ability to produce correct responses, Piaget discovered that, on the contrary, the child's *incorrect* answers were far more fascinating. When questioning the children, Piaget found that the same wrong answers recurred frequently in children of about the same age. Moreover, there were different kinds of common wrong answers at different ages. Piaget puzzled on the meaning of these mistakes. He came to the conclusion that the older children were not just "brighter" than younger ones; instead the thought of younger children was *qualitatively different* from

that of older ones. In other words, Piaget came to reject a quantitative definition of intelligence — a definition based on the number of correct responses on a test. The real problem of intelligence, Piaget felt, was to discover the different methods of thinking used by children of different ages. (3)

Ginsberg and Opper also observed that Piaget knew how to track the important dimensions of a child's experience: "If the child said something interesting, then it would immediately be pursued, without regard for a standardized procedure. The aim of this method was to follow the child's own line of thought, without imposing any direction on it" (4).

Thus, having as a goal the discovery of qualitative differences in the thinking of children Piaget was not satisfied to simply determine whether the children's responses were right or wrong. In Binet's lab, follow-up interviews were permitted, and when Piaget saw that similar errors occurred with several children of the same age, he wanted to know why (Mayer 2005). Consequently, Piaget learned that the interviews could give him the type of information he wanted, which was, "what are the thinking processes of the children like?" Thus, Piaget used careful observation and interview procedures to get the relevant qualitative data he needed. He systematically manipulated certain variables but recorded mostly the statements of the children and sometimes the interpretations the children made of their actions or perceptions. Consequently, Piaget's style of research was primarily qualitative.

Robert Coles (b. 1929)

A psychiatrist well known for his work with children living through times of significant social change, Robert Coles charted his own way through the field of research with human beings. Coles was educated in medicine, psychiatry, and psychoanalysis, but perhaps due to a strong familial exposure to literature, he gravitated toward work that revealed a strong literary perspective (Coles 1967, 1989). As his biographer Ronda (1989) points out, Coles reacted negatively to his professional training and wanted to seek a way of understanding people that was not jargonistic, abstract, distancing, or generalizing in a categorical way. He also shied away from strong conclusions and was happy to merely describe impressions and make suggestions.

In the fifth volume, which deals with privileged children, of his series *Children of Crisis,* in the chapter "The Method," Coles states that "Any reader of my previous volumes may skip the following account of the way I work. It is never really different, never very dramatic or surprising" (1977, 51). All the books in this series have a chapter entitled "Method," but they are unlike any method section that one typically encounters in scientific treatises.

The first two chapters, or 36 pages, of the first volume (Coles 1967), were written to convey Coles's method. It almost seems as though Coles presents a context and an apology. The first chapter is entitled "The South," and basically Coles describes what it was like for him, a Northerner, to be appointed to do service duty in a hospital in Mississippi. He describes his prejudices, his perceptions, how he fit in, and the difficulties he had accommodating himself to the South as well as the problems he saw. The second chapter is called "Observation and Participation," but it is not really the typical understanding of "participant-observer" as regular sociologists use the term. Coles attempts to encounter his phenomenon, "individuals living under continuing social stress" (1967, 17) without a design and without a specific plan. The research project grew on him as he interviewed whomever he encountered and added grown-ups, friends, family members, teachers, and so on. He also admits that he is strongly present in the data in the sense that he asked the questions, he organized the data, and he reduced and transformed it in various ways. The projects were long-term ones—sometimes extending to 20 years. Basically, Coles's strategy was to be brutally honest about what he saw, heard, and did, including his own presence and participation.

But matters are even more complicated. As Ronda (1989, 35–36) points out, Coles did not want his method chapters to be isolated from the rest of his work. One has to conclude that Coles would want the entire narratives to reflect his understanding of method. Because of his own deep involvement in all that he did, including the presentation of his findings, Coles retreats from making any strong statements about his results. He recoils from the typical social science generalizations, but he values "direct observation." His goal was to ascertain as authentically as possible what the individuals thought and felt about all of the issues confronting them (Coles 1967, 21). His broad, personalistic, intuition-istic approach is complemented with an understatement concerning his findings. The results are clearly intended to be idiographic rather than nomothetic. Nevertheless, some generalizations slip through. For example, Coles states that he had "to read and edit the statements of others, and make sense of my own. More important, I had to extract what I thought to be the significant part of the material" (1967, 33). Moreover, Ronda notes,

> He (Coles) has altered names, places, family situations; he has put "some (by no means all)" of these interviews into familiar (middle-class) gram-mar and sentence structure. He has combined the insights of several different people into one narrative, and has taken a series of interviews with one person and condensed them into one or two paragraphs. Despite all this restructuring, this shaping and reshaping, Coles insists that he has been faithful to the tone, the mood, and the characteristic gesture of his subjects. (1989, 41–42)

Coles appreciates that his involvement in organizing, editing, and interpreting what his participants said based on his long and variegated interactions with them were done in order to bring his mind and heart "nearer to what I guess has to be called the essence (words simply fail here) of particular lives" (1971, 36). To speak about the significance of the particular narratives based upon insights in order to try to cap-ture the essence of individuals implies the findings have value beyond merely idiographic or particular domains. Ronda affirms that "Coles's re-presentation of the reality of these children and adults in crisis is persuasive and compelling. Despite all the changes he has made in the organization of the material—changes in names, situations, number of interviews, change in the logic and coherence of speech—his devotion to the full and authentic humanity of these people is power-fully evident" (1989, 42). Obviously, Coles is clearly a strictly qualitative researcher.

QUALITATIVE RESEARCHERS

I have discussed six thinkers since the beginning of modern psychology (that is, since 1879) who have clearly made contributions to psychology and who valued the qualitative perspective. The list is not exhaustive and is only meant to establish the fact that qualitative work in psychology was taken seriously even though it does not quite conform to the norm that most graduate schools in the United States prescribe. The persons briefly covered in this section are not insignificant contributors. William James is often described as America's most famous psychologist (G. Allport 1943); Edward B. Titchener was second only to Wilhelm Wundt in popularity while he was alive, and he was important in history because of the view of psychology that he upheld (Boring 1950, 419–20); certainly Gordon W. Allport was a well-known and respected psychologist with a worldwide reputation and a significant contributor to the field (Evans 1970, xvii); Frederic C. Bartlett got knighted for his work and is experiencing something of a revival since the so-called cognitive turn in psychology, and his work on remembering was called one of the three most influential works in the psychology of memory (Kintsch 1995, xi); Jean Piaget has often been called one of the most significant thinkers of the twentieth century (Callaway 2001); and Robert Coles has received more awards for his work with children than it is convenient to enumerate, and *Time* magazine once called him America's most influential psychiatrist (Ronda 1989). One may consider these men mavericks — and only three of them were psychologists — but there is hardly a psychologist who would deny that their work contributed to psychological knowledge.

Of what did their research consist? James, Bartlett, and Coles were descriptive in the narrative sense and probably the most open ended in their approach. They either described phenomena as they confronted them or else presented descriptions from others about their encounters with phenomena or events. After they presented the "raw data," they reflected and commented upon the descriptions and drew out implications. Their purpose in doing this was to help the reader see the significant points that they discerned in the data. For example, in the *Varieties,* James (1902, 213–26) presented a few examples of instantaneous conversions and then, admitting that many more examples could have been provided, proceeded to draw some generalities from the descriptions by stating that such experiences are "real, definite and memorable" to those who have them, that the experience of such phenomena "seems to himself a passive spectator or undergoer of an astounding process" and that there is the belief that "an absolutely new nature is breathed into us" (222) in such experiences. James is here highlighting aspects of the conversion experience that he believes it is important for the reader to know, but he describes the highlights in his own words and in a way that will heighten the psychological understanding of the phenomenon.

Coles operated almost exactly as James, except that he interviewed people in order to get his original data, whereas James utilized previously published accounts that had appeared in books, journals, and diaries. But Coles's presentations vary more. Primarily he is interested in revealing the unique worlds of the children he studies. Consequently, he describes the child, the environment within which the child lives, the family members and friends of the child, as well as every person who is significant in the life of the child (for example, their teacher). Basically, Coles interweaves his impressions and the key points he wants to make with the narratives that the children give him. Thus, in *Privileged Ones,* when he is writing about the "willful Delta girl," Coles first articulates one of his observations and then provides the supporting data: "The only hope is stubborn survival, as the girl of nine has been told and in her own way firmly believes: 'You can't stop people from doing what they're going to do; that's what my Daddy says, and he is right'" (1977, 65). All of Coles's works proceed pretty much in this integrated fashion. The distinctions among observations, data, and interpretations are not sharply presented, but they are all there in an interwoven way. Coles undoubtedly feels that sufficient evidence for his interpretations is provided in the integrated narrative itself. His priority seems to be to present a unified story line.

While Bartlett has specific differences in his series of experiments, they all have more or less the same basic structure: materials are presented to participants, they are given a specific task to perform with the materials, and they are then to report their experiences as well as they can. For example, in one of his memory experiments, in which Bartlett uses the method of serial reproduction, the task calls for a participant to repeat a description read by one person, and the one who hears the description is meant to relate it to another person, and so on. The reproductions given by different persons are the actual data, and they run from 10 up to 15 or so different reproductions. Bartlett then draws out the psychological implications of the unwitting changes made in the process. Thus, Bartlett (1995) speaks about a bias for the concrete, the loss of individual characteristics, and the nature of the abbreviations used. Significantly, Bartlett states that "In every single case, except that of the cumulative stories, the final result, after comparatively few reproductions, would hardly ever be connected with the original by any person who had no access to some intermediate versions" (171). In other words, the qualitative transformation of the story was great enough to be unrelatable to the original, and such a result could only have been detected by a qualitative procedure. Bartlett leaves it to the reader to make the connection between the findings as presented and the conclusions he draws from them.

Piaget's work is similar to Bartlett's in the sense that he also presented participants with materials to perform a task or to answer questions about manipulations that Piaget performed. The difference is that Piaget used children (including his own) of different ages because he was interested in intellectual development. A simple example is the level of water experiment performed by Piaget:

> The child is shown a glass three-quarter full of water and a pebble. We say: "I am going to put this pebble into the water, right in. What will happen? What will the water do?" If the child does not immediately say: "The water will go up," we add: "Will the water stay at the same place or not?" Once the child has given his answer, the experiment is done,

the child is asked to note that the level of water has risen and is asked to explain the phenomenon. (Piaget 1930, 164)

Piaget worked with variations of this type of experiment across age groups. His data consisted of the children's responses to his questions and the explanations they offered. Piaget then formulated principles or general conclusions about the development of intelligence on the basis of his data. In this case, for example, Piaget says that three stages can be distinguished concerning the displacement of water level, the first two of which are incorrect in qualitatively different ways, and the third stage being a correct explanation (165). These three stages are given elaborate comments and supported by the actual "raw data" that the children provided. Again, it is taken for granted that the reader can see the relationship between the data and the conclusions that Piaget draws from them.

As mentioned, Allport was not as uniquely a qualitative researcher as some of the others we have been considering (for example, his role in helping to transform Spranger's [1928] theory of types into the Allport-Vernon-Lindsey Scale of Values test [Allport and Vernon 1931]), but when he was qualitative, he worked pretty much as the scholars listed above, and he argued strenuously for the inclusion of qualitative data. First of all, as already mentioned, Allport (1942) wrote a theoretical work defending the use of personal documents in psychology. He was cautious and fair in his approach and pointed out the limitations of the use of qualitative materials as well as the constraints required to deal with such data properly. However, the best example of how Allport worked qualitatively is his *Letters from Jenny* (G. Allport 1965). First, Allport describes how the letters were obtained by him; he then provides a description of Jenny and her concerns, and then the letters themselves are reproduced in chronological order.

Allport begins by describing how daunting the task of analysis will be, and he is apologetic about psychology's desire to probe further, but he also justifies the endeavor. Then, unlike the other qualitative researchers covered so far, Allport takes up various explicit psychological perspectives (such as existential, psychoanalytic, and the like) and approaches the data contained in the letters from those broad but different psychological perspectives. Regardless of the psychological perspective adopted, the research strategy is the same: Allport makes some psychological observations and then turns to the data in the letters to support his claims. The fact that the data quoted supports the theoretical claim is taken to be obvious, or at least verifiable, by the reader.

Finally, we come to Titchener, whom I considered last because he worked most closely within the experimental tradition. Nevertheless, as indicated above, he wrote a laboratory manual for qualitative research as well as one for the quantitative perspective. Titchener's style was closer to that of Bartlett and Piaget except that he rarely had his participants perform tasks with his materials other than simply comparing and describing what they experienced. But the task was not really that simple because, as we have seen, introspective reports were intrinsically difficult and required extensive training. The reports produced by the participants were the basic data and Titchener used the data to throw light upon the object that was experienced, and he used that knowledge for theoretical purposes. Here, too, the description was accepted as produced by the subject. However, Titchener was always concerned that the describers might be guilty of the "stimulus error," that is, they might describe the physical characteristics of the stimulus rather than the experiential qualities that were actually experienced. This is why he believed in extensive training. But his straightforward reading of the observers' descriptions enabled him to determine whether or not the stimulus error was committed. He expected the reader to follow the reasoning based upon the data he provided.

All six thinkers used an empirical approach that was followed by a process of induction that allowed for some generalization. They all began with particular data but then used induction from the particulars to come up with some generalities, which science would require. None of these thinkers spoke about eidetic data, even though imaginative possibilities may have been used implicitly by some of them. Phenomenology, I would like to point out, explicitly utilizes an eidetic approach that strengthens the generalized claim, as subsequent chapters will demonstrate. Because of the phenomenologist's eidetic intuition into essences, the generalized findings are more substantial, and thus, provides qualitative analyses with stronger intersubjective findings.

THREE

The Research Process

From a philosophical phenomenological perspective, research on psychological phenomena can meet the standards of scientific practice. I have indicated in earlier chapters a general understanding of science, but before going into detail, I would like to present a global description of the process of conducting research. Psychologists follow this global process regardless of the specific philosophy adopted when conducting research with humans; research that follows either empirical or phenomenological criteria would have to consider the main points about to be discussed. Each of the steps to be considered in the global process is basically a choice made against the background of alternative possibilities. The diagram in figure 1 is a schematic presentation of the process. Even though this process is not always lived out in a logical, longitudinal way, I will follow the chronology as outlined for the sake of simplicity.[1]

The research interest of the psychologist has to be hammered into a researchable problem, which means that the researcher has to take into account the lifeworld situations where the phenomenon occurs spontaneously and yet design a research situation where the phenomenon can occur with some degree of control. The context of the research situation is lived complexly, but at the end of the data collection process the researcher deals only with the data that is correlated with the method chosen. The possibilities of implications of the data

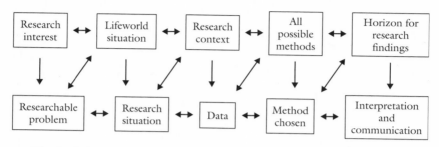

Fig. 1. Schematic presentation of essential factors for conducting research.

are broad, but the researcher has to give a limited number of inter-pretations as well as meet the criteria of journals for communication. All the way through the research process, the possibilities contained in the top line are greater than the choices represented in the bottom line of the figure.

Almost all individuals who study to become professional psycholo-gists, whether clinical or academic, carry within themselves certain interests that made them choose psychology as a career. Usually associated with those interests are questions or curiosities concerning psychological phenomena. Sometimes the answers to such questions can be found in the psychological research literature or other such sources, but sometimes the answers simply are not available. It is at such times that one may have recourse to research. The very first step in the process is that a research interest or even multiple interests have to be hammered into a researchable problem. This always means accepting limits. Our interests are usually so large that even a lifetime of research would not fully answer the questions involved in our unformulated interests. Almost all experienced researchers acknowledge that there is no end to the questions we can put to the world, and Edmund Husserl did describe scientific work as an infinite process.

Our unformulated or implicit interests are usually general, but all research is conducted with particular situations and concrete individu-als, even if our interest is an abstract dimension of particular situations (for example, if one were interested in how good therapy takes place or how learning happens). However, good therapy and learning are abstract dimensions or perspectives on particular situations. Thus, as a researcher moves from his or her general interest to the design of the particular research situation, he or she makes specific decisions that enable the research to be executed, but the decisions also influence and limit the nature of the outcome.

In making decisions concerning the particularization of the research situation, the researcher has to keep in mind the lifeworld situation wherein the phenomenon of interest happens spontaneously. On one hand, the research situation can never be exactly identical to its lifeworld counterpart, but on the other hand, it cannot be so different that the relationship to the lifeworld situation is merely contingent. Phenomenologists would describe the balance by stating that the research situation, in dialogue with the purpose of the research, would have to respect the essential characteristics of the lifeworld event. Thus, a research situation could look very different from the lifeworld analog but still be faithful to the essential characteristics of the situation in the light of the purpose of the research.

The number of variations possible in implementing research design criteria is almost infinite, but it may be helpful to consider some examples, including extreme ones. For example, it is possible to place a hidden camera in a room where therapy is taking place. Thus, one would have a record of a session in which therapy takes place spontaneously. However, such a procedure would be unethical. Both the therapist and the client would have a right to know that the session was being recorded. If there is foreknowledge concerning the recording of a session there is a good chance that the session might not be quite the same as an unrecorded session, which is one reason (but not the most serious one) why the recording has to be announced beforehand. From a research perspective, the very idea of observation introduces a modification in the lifeworld situation.

In mainstream experimental psychology, learning is often studied in laboratory situations involving maze learning, with humans or animals, or the learning of nonsense syllables or other verbal materials. The learning that takes place with mazes and nonsense syllables is quite different from what happens in everyday life in academic situations. However, both examples involve what would be essential to learning: something is produced by the participant, either verbally or behaviorally, that he or she could not spontaneously do before participation in the research situation. Thus, however impoverished such situations seem to be, most laboratory situations do respect the essence of learning, and so a certain fidelity to everyday world learning is honored.

Psychophysical experiments can provide different examples of how artificial situations may be useful. They often seek to discover threshold values for various sensory modalities. In such situations the purpose of the research is the primary determiner of the characteristics of the situation. For example, in the lifeworld, one does not discover the absence of sound or light. Consequently, researchers build artificial environments — soundproof rooms and dark rooms — so that a genuine minimum value of energy can be determined for hearing and seeing. Without artificial restrictions, environmental noise or light masks the true minimum amount of energy required to hear or see. In those and similar situations, the artificial conditions or inventions still respect the essentiality of the research. One must eliminate distractions as much as possible in order to come up with certain optimum findings, even if such conditions do not exist in the lifeworld. After determining the results in more or less ideal conditions, one can always return to conditions as they actually exist and either modify the conditions to improve performance or else mediate the ideal results in order to have them coexist better with actual conditions.

Other examples of the difference between research situations and the lifeworld can be provided by turning to social psychological experiments. In Asch's (1956) famous experiment, he employed confederates to respond according to instructions rather than spontaneously. The research situation called for the participants to judge whether two objects were of equal length or not, and even though the objects were obviously unequal, all the confederates said that they were equal; the purpose was to see whether the uninformed participant would also change his mind. The aim of this study was, in part, to determine if individuals would yield to social pressure or if they would stick with an obvious fact based upon individual experience. Obviously, in the life-world, if all participants spoke truthfully the social pressure would not even have been created. Thus, the results of the study weighed heavily on the design, and some persons played a role and spoke according to instructions given to the role-players. This is not unlike creating a dark room to discover visual thresholds where none can be found naturally in everyday life. While situations involving social pressure can be found spontaneously in the lifeworld, it would be difficult to wait for them to happen and then attempt to study them. Consequently, artificial situations are created in order to study how individuals might respond. In addition, in the artificial situations, no real physical danger exists for the nonconfederate participant, although that does not necessarily rule out genuine psychological stress for the selected individual. It is interesting to note that this study was conducted long before institutional review boards were created; I wonder if its design would be approved today.

These examples demonstrate how certain issues get resolved as a researcher takes into consideration how a phenomenon is spontaneously lived in the lifeworld, the possibilities of a suitable research situation, and the specific purpose of the study as formulated in the "researchable problem" step in figure 1. All of this is done against the horizon of the other steps that are yet to come. Under the heading of "Research Context" the researcher still has to specify every detail, from the instructions to the participants to the arrangement of the physical setting to the presentation of the task and the recording of the participants' responses. And yet after all this organization, the researcher basically comes away with data, and once the data are acquired, he or she rarely goes back to the site of the original data collection. Thus, it is critical that the researcher makes sure that none of the contingent factors that played a role in the original data collection contributed unfairly in a significant way to the quality of the data. Factors include the presence of the researcher (or the lack of one) as well as any other seemingly innocent factor. One has to ascertain that the data were primarily determined by the performance of the participants on the designated task. Once the data are collected and properly organized, the researcher continues to work only with the data, and the whole process lived through up until that point recedes into the background, even if its influences never completely disappear.

Once the researchable problem has been formulated and the research situation has been decided upon, the researcher has to worry about the method to be used and the constitution of the data. These two issues cannot be separated. The choice of method has to be made against the backdrop of a number of possible methods. It would be very difficult to argue that one and only one method can be used in research. Thus, the selection of method is a choice, sometimes of necessity, but far more frequently it is a preference that, in either case, has to be related to the basic research question and the purpose of the research. One key decision is whether the question is fundamentally quantitative or qualitative. Clearly the quantitative question and its various procedures have dominated research in psychology since the inception of psychology's independence as a natural science. The prior existence of the natural sciences with their developed quantitative methods have no doubt played a great role in influencing research psychologists' decisions. However, as chapter 2 indicates, the qualitative perspective also exists in the history of mainstream psychology even if it never reached parity with quantitative procedures. In any case, quantitative procedures basically answer two questions: "How much?" and "How many?" Thus, if the research question is basically motivated by the matter of frequency or magnitude, then quantitative methodologies have to be used. However, if the research question centers upon questions like: "What is it like to experience such a phenomenon?" "What can it mean that someone behaves in such a way?" then qualitative procedures are called for.

In contemporary academic psychological settings, until very recently, students or practitioners of research too often thought that the basic research question was: "How do I measure the phenomenon I'm interested in researching?" This has led to many studies involving questionnaires, surveys, and standardized tests that lead to either a quanti fication of human experience or else an a priori compartmentalization of such experiences yielding basic measures even if some interpretive statements are permitted. The problem here is that the quantified or measured phenomenon is not the best access to the lived phenomenon when the question motivating the research is "What was it like to live through that experience?" or "What is the basic meaning, psychologically speaking, of what the person has lived through?" Consequently, a more basic question should be asked at the beginning of the research process, namely, "What is the best access to the phenomenon I am interested in researching, given the question I am seeking to answer?" For example, will a measure of the intensity of the experience give a rich understanding of what it was like to live through a given phenomenon? Will the measure of intensity differentiate between anxiety and happiness—or should other modes of interrogating be utilized? Of course, quantitative methods will always provide some information about the phenomenon being researched. To know that the experience of a given phenomenon was either, in general, more intense or less intense is to gain some knowledge, but it is minimal if the research quest was driven by a search for the meaning of the phenomenon or a sense of the particulars of the experience. The same amount of effort, or perhaps less, qualitatively driven, could yield a much richer depiction of the phenomenon.

My point, then, is not that quantitative procedures used to research the qualitative dimensions of phenomena are totally useless, but rather that they are not best suited to research the qualitative aspects of phenomena. The information gained is relatively impoverished, given the effort and the genuine data sought. However, these conventions (not necessities) developed in large part because it was often assumed (wrongly) that measurement in and of itself was the sign of a scientific approach. The deeper relationships between the questions posed by the researcher and the phenomenon to be studied were not brought to the fore. The specific operations of the natural sciences were copied, but the logic behind the operations was not clarified sufficiently so that relevant, rather than ad hoc, modifications in procedures could ensue, or radical reformulations of the questions could have introduced very different but equally rigorous procedures.

Thus, when a researcher follows the schema presented in figure 1, there is a necessary correlation between the method chosen for research and the type of data to be obtained. If the quantitative dimension of the phenomenon is to be explored, then a method yielding numbers as basic data is required, and the assumptions upon which the statistical procedures are based would have to be clarified and met. If the qualitative dimension of a phenomenon is to be explored, then one has to be sure that the data obtained express the qualitative dimension of the phenomenon (usually linguistic expressions but not exclusively) and that the assumptions underlying the use of the qualitative procedures are met. Again, the researcher should be clear as to why he or she chose a certain method and not one of its possible competitors. Very often a range of methods can satisfy the purpose of the research, and there may be a degree of freedom in the selection of the method. But still, some sense of legitimization for the method chosen should be offered.

Finally, a research report is ineffective unless it is read. In order to be read, it has to be written and then published, and that is where the dynamics of the last box of figure 1 come in. The first problem concerns the interpretation of the findings, which, first of all, implies that there is a difference between results and their meaning. There is a tendency today to imply that even results are interpretive, but I adhere to the classical distinction between results and their interpretation. Rarely does one get results in a study that lead to a univocal interpretation. Yet the process of going from results to their meaning is rarely discussed in the training of psychological research practitioners. The interpretation is assumed to be directly accessible, but it often takes theoretical, descriptive, or interpretative skills to correctly articulate the meaning of results. Most psychological researchers know how to use statistical procedures to determine that differences in results are statistically significant. But such procedures do not determine the psychological meaning of the differences—only that what happened was most probably not due to chance. Phenomenologists, when they use the phenomenological reduction or the method of free imaginative variation, are using strategies that help precisely in clarifying the meaning of the results.

The specific journal chosen for publication and its audience are the final determiners of the report. In a discipline as complex as psychology, where certain subfields scarcely read the results of other subfields, the audience that the researcher has in mind is at least as important a co-determiner of how the results and their interpretation and discussion are written. If one is working within a very specific research tradition on a well-researched topic and speaking to an audience familiar with the specific tradition, then the task becomes rather straightforward. However, if one is reaching out to another tradition or conducting research on a problem in a way that is different from its habitual context, then difficulties can emerge because assumptions are usually not shared. Reaching across disciplines complicates this issue even more. The research writer has to be mindful of these factors when writing up his or her final report.

The choice of journal and its publication policy is also an important determiner. It is inevitable that journals will have their own editorial style and certain seemingly arbitrary conventions. The researcher simply has to learn these constraints and try to present the best picture of what he or she wants to present within such constraints. In scientific writing, nothing is better than a clean, straightforward presentation with minimal rhetorical flourishes. The presentation of the method should also be lucid so that other qualified researchers can reproduce the study.

There is, however, a special problem with qualitative research today that has not been fully addressed. Most existing research journals were initiated with the idea of publishing quantitative studies. In such studies tables and graphs summarize a lot of data so that efficient communication of findings is possible. With qualitative research, the value of the findings often depends upon the richness of the data, and a proper convention governing the presentation of such data has not yet been established. Too often, editors want contributors to present findings in a reduced manner, the way tables and graphs do, and as a consequence a lot of the valuable richness of the findings does not get communicated. Facts can be more easily reduced. The meanings that are the heart of phenomenological research, at least, require more space to be communicated fully because of the implicating nature of their findings. Qualitative studies that emphasize empirical facts may not face quite the same difficulty. In any case, a proper convention for communicating qualitative results is still needed.

The above commentary on the research process schema presented in figure 1 clearly indicates that there is a logic guiding the research process, whether it is quantitative or qualitative. I want to emphasize this point because it is often asserted that qualitative analysis is permitted as exploratory or as preliminary, but not as a legitimate research method. Certainly this claim has been made for phenomenological analyses (MacLeod 1964, Henle 1990). However, my position is that qualitative procedures are legitimate procedures that are guided by logic from first reflection upon a research problem until the writing of the report, just as quantitative procedures are. The difference is simply that quantitative research has a longer history and is better established because of its beginnings with the natural sciences.

In addition, the above schema and commentary are presented at a high level of abstraction. The differences in logic between quantitative and qualitative approaches begin to show themselves as one moves from this high level toward implementation of the research strategies. It is possible to follow different strategies while remaining faithful to the logic of psychological research, whether quantitative or qualitative. Differences are introduced in part because of different philosophies and we claim to remain faithful to phenomenological philosophy as we implement the logic of qualitative research.

FOUR

Scientific Phenomenological Method and Its Philosophical Context

This study is guided by a phenomenological philosophy of science and not an empirical philosophy. While I have already referred to the precise meaning of "phenomenon" in phenomenology and the sense of the lifeworld, others aspects of the phenomenological method must be explained to further understand its approach.

First of all, the phenomenological approach is not against the empirical perspective; it is more comprehensive than empiricism insofar as it allows for irreal objects as well as real or empirical ones. For Husserl (1983), any object is real that is in space, time, and is regulated by causality. An object that would lack any one of those characteristics would be irreal. Ideas, for example, are given to individuals in time but not in space, and for phenomenologists they are not causally determined. Meanings are also not spatial and so would not be considered real objects. Dreams, memories, and images are other phenomena that would not be considered real in the strict sense, but they are experiential in the sense that they can only appear in the consciousness of individuals. A broadened sense of "empirical" is required to appropriate them adequately. Real objects can exist independently of consciousness, but experiential phenomena cannot. Traditional empiricism actually bases its criteria for knowledge on the characteristics of real objects rather than strictly experiential ones.

Second, I am operating within a phenomenological theory of science that has not yet been systematically articulated. It is implicit in the writings of Husserl (1970b, 1983), and other phenomenologists (for example, Gurwitsch 1974, Merleau-Ponty 1962, 1963), but a full-blown, articulated exposition does not yet exist. Authors have spoken about it in passing and have treated specialized themes, but not systematically and comprehensively. This means that at various critical junctures in this work, I will fill in what is missing or inadequately discussed in such a theory. Unfortunately, an exposition of my own understanding of a phenomenological theory of science would require a book-length manuscript, which is not possible within this book on method.

Third, philosophical phenomenology makes explicit that it considers everything to be studied from the viewpoint of consciousness (which can exist at many levels) or subjectivity (which also has levels). Consequently, there is a certain priority given to consciousness because it is the medium of access for any knowledge whatsoever. Nothing can be spoken about or demonstrated without its being given to someone's consciousness. A corollary of this thesis is the understanding that the meaning of what is "given" to consciousness is influenced by its manner of givenness. Consequently, phenomenology is interested in describing both—what is given to consciousness and how it is given. However, this study makes no other presuppositions concerning the given, and thus the perspective is as open as possible to whatever may appear. I acknowledge, however, that many types of objects can be given to consciousness.

Fourth, phenomenology values possibilities and horizons and finds them to be vital for the determination of meanings. In a way, this point simply joins together the first and third above. Entities do not have to have physical existence to be given in experience, and phenomenology wants to be as open as possible to any object that is experientially given.

It is the experienced as experienced that interests phenomenology, and this includes the horizon of possibilities that surround the given.

There are two principles that might be considered as points of departure for a phenomenological approach to science. The first is what Husserl terms the principle of all principles: "*that every originary presentive intuition is a legitimizing source of cognition, that everything originarily* (so to speak, in its 'personal' actuality) *offered* to us *in 'intuition' is to be accepted simply as what it is presented as being,* but also *only within the limits in which it is presented there*" (1983, 44). Thus, Husserl is respectful and trusting with respect to experience. It is not the case that experiences cannot be illusory, it is just that illusions and other sorts of error are also corrected by experience. One goes along with experience unless there is some reason to doubt its unfolding. Note, too, that Husserl says that what is presented is a "legitimizing *source* of cognition" (my emphasis). It does not mean that potential errors cannot occur in the process of elaborating what was given. The other caution Husserl states is that what is presented has to be accepted "only within the limits in which it is presented." The implication of that instruction is that nothing is to be added to or subtracted from what is presented. If what is presented is incomplete, at variance with expectations, or unlike any known reality, it nevertheless has to be described just as it is. No aesthetic or theoretical additions are permitted.

A second key principle that guides research is the method of free imaginative variation, which Husserl illustrates with respect to the discovery of essences (Husserl 1983, 157). Husserl makes clear that the point of departure for philosophical investigations does not have to be factual, but could also be fictive. Moreover, an active imagination is helpful when trying to discover the essence of a phenomenon or attempting to clarify the meaningful structure of an experience. Free imaginative variation requires that one mentally remove an aspect of the phenomenon that is to be clarified in order to see whether the removal transforms what is presented in an essential way. If the given appears radically different because of the removal of a part, it is leaning toward being essential. If the given is still recognizable as the same after the removal of a part, it is most likely a contingent part. Obviously, each of these decisions has to be critically evaluated by the researcher through further imaginative effort before a final assessment can be made.

Thus, the approach offers both openness and rigor. Openness because anything experienced as experienced is considered a legitimate topic for investigation and the process of free imaginative variation gives a wide scope for determining the relevancy of the given. Rigor because whatever is given is described precisely as it presents itself. Further analyses are also required to adhere to the same criteria.

SKETCH OF A HUMAN SCIENCE PERSPECTIVE

At this point, it would be best to articulate minimally, at least, the vision of human science that is guiding us. By "human science" I mean an approach to human phenomena that respects the essential characteristics of humanness throughout the research process, from the conception of the design to the writing of the report. The primary implication of this statement is that a radical nonreductionistic approach is adopted. The point is to get stable knowledge about human phenomena by any reasonable means possible and not necessarily to follow the specific ways that the natural sciences gain their knowledge since their stable knowledge is based largely upon things and their processes. When this task is deemed impossible, it is because such thinkers are adhering too closely to other definitions of scientific knowledge as historically constituted by the natural sciences.

At the beginning of the development of an alternative method for working with humans from a psychological perspective I attempted to set up a polarity between the sciences of nature and the human sciences, although I wanted both sides to adhere to scientific criteria in general. Since the natural sciences preceded the human sciences in their development, I listed first the strengths of the natural sciences. But instead of simply accepting the criteria that were established by that approach, because physical nature was mostly the subject matter,

I asked an analogical question because the human sciences worked with persons and relationships. That is, instead of imitating in a direct way the criteria that the natural sciences established, I asked a question such as the following: "What will do for the human sciences (that is, for persons and their relationships) what 'X' (that is, analysis, measurement, and so on) will do for the study of things and processes?" In other words, the differences that the object of study introduces had to be taken into account in developing strategies and procedures for the human sciences (see table 1).

Table 1. Criteria for implementing scientific research according to natural science and human science approach priorities

Natural science criteria	Human science criteria
Experimentation	Other research modes
Quantity	Quality
Measurement	Meaning
Analysis-synthesis	Explicitation
Determined reactions	Intentional responses
Identical repetition	Identity through variations
Independent observer	Participant observer

I want to emphasize again that this was my point of departure. I had to dialogue with my own background as an experimental psychologist trained in the natural science approach. I did not want to reject science, but I knew that it had to be modified to deal with human beings as humans. Humans could not be reduced to the level of things, however implicitly. If one strictly followed procedures designed to deal with things and applied them to humans, an implicit reductionism would be involved. When such historical scientific strategies are interpreted as "absolute" scientific criteria rather than being seen in their proper context, the inevitable result is that humans are reduced to meet such criteria. It was never part of the scientific ethos to use approaches that distorted the phenomena it was investigating.

It is no secret that the ideal setting for gaining knowledge within the perspective of the natural sciences is the laboratory. The lab is a cultural institution created by humans that will enable them to have maximum control over a research situation. There is nothing intrinsically wrong with a lab, and indeed, it has been a boon to continual increasing knowledge about the phenomena of nature. The question is: Must all precise knowledge be laboratory based? A corollary question is whether experimentation, which goes hand-in-glove along with a lab, is the only procedure that will allow precise, stable knowledge. An obvious answer is that it depends upon the nature of the phenomenon being investigated. It is hard to study certain aspects of "lived language" in a lab as well as the social habits of primitive tribes, and certain religious experiences may be hard to evoke in such an environment. Clearly, the lab lends itself in a privileged way to certain phenomena and it alienates others.

Of course, experimental procedures can be applied outside the lab, as certain types of astronomical and botanical research projects testify. But as one moves away from things that can be controlled one sees that the rigor of research becomes more conceptual than physical. For example, research in naturalistic settings is minimally intrusive but conceptually rigorous because the researcher usually has clear ideas about what he or she expects to see. In such situations, not every detail is recorded, but rather a certain hierarchy is established and discriminatory values are placed upon what is to be keenly observed and recorded. This, too, is a type of rigor even though no quantitative expressions are used — or only rarely so.

The stronger argument for breaking from experimental procedures and quantitative expressions comes from the experience with researchers in fields where the latter procedures are clearly stretched — for example, history and anthropology. Of course, if one wanted to prove that *some* knowledge could be gained by viewing historical and anthropological phenomena quantitatively, I'm sure that it could be done (and has been done). (However, the same could be said about qualitative discoveries in traditionally hard-nosed quantitative areas.) In other words, historical issues cannot be replicated in a lab simply because what has taken place historically cannot be undone; it can only be understood. In the study of primitive tribes anthropologists try not to be so intrusive as to modify the existing culture even while trying to study it. This is closer to the mode of operating of naturalistic research than to the manipulative style of laboratory work. There are not only ethical reasons for not interfering with the culture of another society, but even scientific ones. One wants to understand the culture as it is for itself and not how the culture responds to outside interferences. Finally, political science, as the name implies, claims to get stable knowledge about the political process and yet manipulation by the investigator is something that is ruled out, and legal and power relations within society prevent the use of many intrusive procedures. Yet, all three disciplines claim to be sciences that get stable, reliable knowledge. How do they do it and how do they justify their claim?

Usually, these are efforts where language and meaning play pivotal roles. In history, one looks up written records, documents, reports, and the like and reads them and tries to determine their significance for the issues being researched. In politics, one might add interviews and other public speeches or pronouncements made by government officials, politicians, and so on, and the researcher usually tries to establish their sense and draw out the implications for policies. In other words, in both cases the assumption is made that communications are intelligible, meanings can be ascertained, and implications can be logically drawn out. Of course, historians and political scientists each bring a special perspective to bear upon the data that will heighten the sensitivity to each discipline's specialized viewpoint. However, scholars who have access to the original data and who can follow the purpose and method of the original researcher and know the rules of logical inference accept such labor as qualifying as scientific in the sense of gaining secure or stable knowledge (along with critical challenges from the relevant scientific community). Psychology as a human science has to follow a model more like other human sciences, rather than physics and chemistry, as the natural science approach to psychology attempted. Consequently, rather than posit laboratory settings and experimental procedures that the natural sciences prefer, I would simply assert that other, more open settings and procedures should be sought. I would encourage scientists to think freshly and differently, and I would

recommend that we not spend too much time looking for something else to imitate, but rather should think about science from
scratch and try to come up with methods that are uniquely suited for
psychology.

The second polarity in table 1 is that between quantity and quality.
Much has been and can be written about this polarity but I will limit
myself to a few pertinent remarks. First of all, every phenomenon in the
world has a quantitative aspect and a qualitative aspect. Second, there
is even certain reciprocity between the two. Exploring the quantitative
aspect of a phenomenon does reveal something about the qualitative
and vice versa. Finally, it should be repeated that phenomenology
is not in principle against a quantitative approach. Husserl, after all,
was a mathematician and logician and he was a strong believer in the
value of both. Rather, phenomenology is against an improper use of
quantification in the human sciences, or of an improper extrapolation
of quantification. It tries to set limits to the use of quantification in
science so that quantification is used properly.

The first bias to be overcome is the idea that quantification is the
only mode of being rigorous in science. To be sure, there is a certain
privilege with mathematics in the sense that relationships among
numbers are exact and unequivocal whereas, with words, the senses
communicated are often not univocal and highly dependent upon
context. The precision achieved with numbers is focal and specific, but
with words it is far more contextual but still attainable. However, it is
not just the relationships within the numerical system or language that
have to be considered but also the relationship between the numerical
system or language and the object to be described by such a system.
One has to be sure that the relationship between the system to be
used and the object to be described properly supports the interest of
the researcher. It is usually when this relationship is improper that
criticisms of quantification ensue.

This is where a proper understanding of Husserl's work is helpful.
Husserl understood that a sheer description of the flow of mental
experiences could not offer a sound basis for stable knowledge (Husserl
1983, 160–61; Zahavi 2000). The description of the flow would have

to be raised to an eidetic level, that is, to the level of a series of ideas, essences, or invariant meanings whose primary achievement would be to capture a great number of the variations of which the flow consists. Then Husserl asserts that once the notion of eidetics is introduced most scholars would turn to mathematical disciplines because they are the most well-established eidetic sciences. Eidetic sciences (such as geometry, logic, and so on) are those that deal with possibilities, but not factual givens even though the terms of eidetic science can be applied to real events. But then Husserl states that a search in the direction of formal eidetic sciences (again, such as math) would be an error. The conditions for the establishment of mathematical eidetics and the requirements for an eidetics of experiential processes do not match. In order to demonstrate this point Husserl first makes a distinction between formal and material eidetic disciplines, and he eliminates all the formal eidetic disciplines, which automatically eliminates many mathematical disciplines because the formal disciplines disregard content, and the content of the experiential flow is important for understanding it. Consequently, Husserl was seeking a material eidetic discipline to help found a science of mental life.

Husserl (1983, 162) also distinguishes between concrete and abstract sciences. This distinction is based upon whether the range of phenomena are made up of concrete objects that can stand on their own (real things) or abstract objects, those that are dependent on concrete objects, (spatial shapes, visual qualities). We find that psychology spans this distinction. It is concrete, for example, when observing a human being behaving in a specific situation, and it is abstract when studying color vision thresholds. Also, at a certain level of generality the stream of mental events can be understood as concrete, and specific perceptual experiences could be seen as concrete, but their emotional aspects, for example, as abstract.

In any case, Husserl makes the argument that the historically existing mathematical sciences should not be models for phenomenology. Husserl writes:

> It is only a misleading prejudice to believe that the methods of the historically given a priori sciences, all of which are exclusively *exact*

sciences of ideal objects, must serve forthwith as models for every new science, particularly for our transcendental phenomenology — as though there could be eidetic sciences of but one single methodic type, that of "exactness." Transcendental phenomenology, as a descriptive science of essence, belongs however to a fundamental class of eidetic sciences totally different from the one to which the mathematical sciences belong. (1983, 169–70)

The reason for this conclusion is that Husserl shows that the mode of operating of the mathematical sciences is not descriptive. Geometry, for example, Husserl notes, does not go about describing the many shapes that actually exist in the world as botanists do when describing plants. Rather, Husserl asserts,

> Geometry fixes a few kinds of fundamental structures, the ideas of solid, plane, point, angle and the like, the ones which play the determining role in the "axioms." With the help of axioms, i.e., the primitive eidetic laws, it is then in a position to derive purely deductively *all* the spatial shapes "existing," that is, ideally possible (shapes), in space and all the eidetic relationships pertaining to these shapes in the form of exactly determining concepts which take the place of the essences which, as a rule, remain foreign to our intuition...geometry can be completely certain of dominating actually by its method all the possibilities and of determining them exactly. (1983, 163)

Husserl states that such mathematical eidetic sciences have a fundamental logical property that he calls a "definite manifold," by which he means "that a finite number of concepts and propositions (can) completely and unambiguously determine to totality all of the possible formations belonging to the (region) so that, of essential necessity, nothing in the (region) is left open" (163). Moreover, the mathematical scientist then proceeds by way of deduction from the finite number of concepts and proportions. Because the manifold is definite, Husserl holds that it is exhaustively definable.

Having made the procedures of mathematical sciences clear, Husserl then wonders whether the study of mental processes could proceed in the same way. He asks the question: "Is the stream of consciousness a genuine mathematical manifold?" (Husserl 1983, 165). To answer this question, Husserl raises exactly the question we raised above in specific form: Does the phenomenon of consciousness lend itself to analyses in terms of definite manifolds? To answer that question, the phenomenon of consciousness would have to offer "exact essences" to be intuited. For him, descriptive sciences produce descriptive concepts that are not identical to exact sciences and their ideal concepts. The ways that descriptive and exact sciences function are different. Husserl notes that the geometer does not search for all actually existing indubitable shapes (166). Rather, the geometer's point of departure are ideal concepts, like square, circle, rectangle, and the like, and for Husserl these exact concepts have as their correlates essences that are like "ideas" in the Kantian sense. They are not based upon intuitable, sensuous givens. Consequently, with the help of a few axioms, a deductive procedure can take place and certain discoveries can be made.

However, since phenomenology is conceived by Husserl as a descriptive science based upon intuitions of concrete givens, it cannot proceed in the same way as formal, exact, eidetic sciences. Rather, those following a phenomenological procedure have to intuit (in a phenomenological sense, "be present to") all of the concrete manifestations of experiential phenomena, and they have to be carefully described. Further discoveries about such phenomena are determined by unfolding and describing the senseful implications within the horizons of the concrete phenomena and not by deduction. As noted above, deduction requires a "definite manifold" with exhaustive determinations within a closed system. However, the descriptive task involving senseful or meaningful implications is an open, indeterminate system. Nor does the phenomenological procedure involve induction because that would involve generalization after encountering a certain number of concrete manifestations. This is true even if every concrete instance of the phenomenon contains a manifestation of the dimension generalized. For phenomenology, the essential characteristic has to be intuited ("seen") and described. This "seeing" is aided by the use of the method of free, imaginative variation. As an eidetic manifestation, it is intrinsically general and so it can be fully described in its generality.

Finally, within a descriptive framework, the essence is not interpreted, but precisely described. Interpretation in this context implies bringing in a nongiven factor (such as hypothesis, theory, assumption) to help account for the essential presence. The descriptive phenomenological attitude neither adds to nor subtracts from what is "given," regardless of how it presents itself. For example, if I am presented tachistoscopically two sides of a triangle, but I experience a "triangle," then I have to say that "I experience a triangle based upon the two-sided figure presented to me for a brief period of time." I cannot say that "I experienced a complete triangle" (adding on), nor can I say that "I experienced a two-sided figure if a triangle was actually experienced," even if it was not fully given (subtracting).

Husserl (1983, 166–68) acknowledges that the concrete phenomena of mental life are vague and inexact, and he calls the essences derived from them "morphological essences," meaning that they are, in principle, inexact, but essences nevertheless. He writes:

> The *vagueness* of such concepts, the circumstances that their spheres of application are fluid, does not make them defective; for in the spheres of knowledge where they are used they are absolutely indispensable, or in those spheres they are the only legitimate concepts. . . . The most perfect geometry and the most perfect practical mastery of it cannot enable the descriptive natural scientist to express (in exact geometrical concepts) what he expresses in such a simple, understandable, and completely appropriate manner by the words "notches," "scalloped," "lens-shaped," "umbelliform," and the like — all to them concepts which are *essentially, rather than accidentally, inexact* and *consequently* also non-mathematical. (166)

Husserl further admits that exact and descriptive sciences may combine and interact, but they cannot take each other's place.

Quantification performs two tasks exceedingly well: it can elaborate and make precise magnitude and frequency. Whenever a researcher directs a question toward these dimensions of reality, he or she should use quantification. But in elaborating those two dimensions, quantification abstracts from the content of the phenomenon being studied. Counting frequencies and measuring magnitude can be applied to any phenomenon once it is perceived that a discrete entity can be discriminated for counting and that size differences are also perceivable and a unit of magnitude is constructed. But the wholeness of the entities either plays no role in the two procedures, or else only the minimal role that guarantees that the constructed units of measurement can be applied. In other words, a certain formalization takes place that gives measurement its strength. But psychology, like botany, depends upon the apprehension of content in a penetrating and systematic way, which is why essential descriptions are sought, at various levels of generality. The essences are intended to differentiate the multifarious phenomena that keep streaming forth in consciousness. One can measure the fact that one is intensely happy or intensely anxious, but the intensity dimension tells us very little about the difference between happiness and anxiety. Usually psychologists let an everyday level of understanding or personal experience fill in where more precise and systematic understandings and relationships should be considered. This is the gap that qualitative research tries to satisfy. Of course, ultimately the quantitative approaches will have to be integrated, but that can hardly happen where qualitative approaches do not exist.

In summary then, with respect to the quantitative-qualitative tension, on the qualitative side, phenomenology a manner of describing the contents of experience in a stable way through description of essences or invariant meanings (material eidetics), and a way of making the study of the quality of phenomena more rigorous by systematically differentiating descriptive sciences from formal sciences and demonstrating how descriptive sciences function. Although I am using phenomenological philosophy to justify qualitative research, it could just as easily be used to justify quantitative approaches for studying quantitative dimensions of reality, or even integrated approaches. Its perspective is sufficiently comprehensive to be the basis for a complete philosophy of science. It is simply a matter of having someone work out these developments.

The next polarity in table 1 is that between measurement and meaning.[1] Measurement is the elaboration and specification of the quantitative dimension of reality. Meaning emerged in the next column in answer to the analogical question: What will do for quality that measurement does for quantity? The determination of meanings is a way of penetrating and elaborating the qualitative dimensions of phenomena. Meanings basically answer questions such as: "What is the phenomenon or the experience like?" "What is it like to be anxious?" "What is it like to be depressed?" Concrete descriptions by the experiencer lead the researcher to the inner dimensions of the experience, and the facts therein get transformed into generalized meanings that reveal the situation as it is for the experiencer, and from such meanings essential descriptions can be obtained.

For Husserl, meanings are originated in acts of consciousness and they consist of a determinate relationship between an act of consciousness and its object. Meanings are usually discussed in phenomenology within the context of intentionality, which refers to the fact that many acts of consciousness are directed toward objects that transcend the acts in which the objects appear. Thus, at least three terms have to be involved: the act of consciousness, the object toward which the act is directed, and the meaning of the object. Conscious acts are directed toward objects, and upon reflection one can discover that the directedness toward the object was determinate and specific or particular and that particular quality is the meaning. Note, one lives the relationship to the object directly and the meaning is, so to speak, attached to the object and can be discerned upon reflection. The key point is that the meaning is not a "third term" between the act and the object but the particular way that the object is experienced. While Husserl (1970b) demonstrates that the intentional matter and intentional quality of the act help constitute the act's directedness and its meaning, the meaning transcends the act just as the object does and so its identification can be established and repeatedly referred to. This means that meanings can be objectively understood even if they are subjectively established. Of course, partial and less than adequate meanings also exist, and these have to be discriminated from adequate meanings and a proper sense of subjectivity and objectivity has to be understood as well. In Husserl, what is subjective belongs on the side of the act of consciousness; objectivity refers to the proper manner in which an object of consciousness is constituted. Intentional content refers to objective meanings that are ideal and objective. So, meanings are the determinate relations established between an act of consciousness and its object. Below I will make a distinction between philosophical ideal meanings and psychological meanings. One can see that these analyses have helped us, presumably, to understand why meaning can aid in penetrating and examining the qualitative aspects of experiential objects.

The next item in table 1 is that between analysis-synthesis and explicitation. It is a classic strategy to break down a complex entity into its component parts and then put it back together again. It is also a rather straightforward process when the component parts to be separated can exist independently of each other and can be discriminated on the basis of their physical contours. What complicates the analysis of experiential phenomena is the fact that the parts to be discriminated are dependent on each other, that is, they cannot stand alone independently of the entire conscious stream and they are fleeting, rather than static, and so cannot be held steadily before an act of without the help of retention or memory. Furthermore, the contours that separate different moments of the experiential stream are not as evident as physical ones and are often embedded in marginal states that contribute to the meaning of the significant moments. Following Husserl (1970b) here, the parts of the experiential stream are identified as "moments" and not pieces. That means that they cannot stand alone. Thus, the standard strategy of breaking down the major "entity" of interest becomes complicated. Moreover, it is not so much the intrinsic characteristics of the major entity that is of value when meanings are being sought (although their knowledge can be helpful) as the role of the entity (the phase of the experiential stream under scrutiny) in the segment of the experiential stream relevant for its understanding. This is where the idea of explicitation enters. As I stated, following Husserl, meaning is a determinate relationship between an act of consciousness and the object toward which the act is directed. In order to clarify the meaning of a certain phase of consciousness, one has to know its role in the segment of the stream that is relevant to it. Its role is not usually explicit, but implicit because the basic thrust of the act of consciousness is toward the object, not toward the act itself. Consequently, the task is understood as that of making as explicit as possible the assumptive network that is required in order for the act to be enacted. In addition, the act thematizes the object toward which it is directed and leaves the horizon of the object unthematized, which means that clarification also depends upon making explicit relevant aspects of the horizon. Consequently, explicitation refers to the process of making explicit the assumptions and horizonal features of the intentional act so that a more explicit and clarified understanding of the experience can be obtained. This procedure is quite different from taking the main moment as a whole and breaking it down. Rather, the main moment (entity) is seen as a part of a larger whole, and the task of explicitation is to understand the moment's role in the larger context.

The next contrast in table 1 is between determined reactions and intentional responses. In the typical experimental study advocated by mainstream psychology, the assumption is that all extraneous factors are held constant and the results of the experiment are the consequence of the effect of the independent variable on the dependent variable. The cause-effect relationship is presumed to be operating, so one can speak of determined reactions on the part of the participants. There is surely a partial truth to this interpretation, but there are difficulties when one tries to account for the totality of the experiential-behavioral response on the part of the human participant from a strictly causal perspective. Once the consciousness of the participant is involved and the intentional relation between the act of consciousness and its object is enacted a strictly causal explanation seems to be insufficient. I have already noted that the intentional relation is an irreal relation and cannot be accounted for in terms of causal factors. With human subjects, all experimentation requires a set of instructions to be read to the subjects; otherwise, placing them in the experimental situation would leave them guessing with respect to what is required of them. Instructions direct subjects to the key parts of the experimental situation and they imply that the participants understand what is demanded of them. The instructions do not cause the subjects to become coopera-tive participants, but rather they reach that desired attitude through communication and intelligibility. Similarly, when subjects respond to a task imposed on them in an experiment, their responses are mediated by the conscious understanding of the task. The role of conscious-ness, or the meaning of the experimental situation for the subject, is neglected when one seeks a total causal explanation of the responses of the subject. Consequently, "determined reactions" is a misnomer. Yes, there are effects of the stimuli, but these effects never act solely on normal subjects. Rather, even in simple threshold experiments, the meaning of the situation and the role of consciousness are critical for the proper understanding of the experimental results. The expression "intentional responses" is meant to convey that the meaning of the situation for the subject elaborates whatever physical effects are also taking place and therefore must be included in the interpretation of the experimental results. This point is easily demonstrated any time a subject misunderstands instructions and thus does not perform according to the experimenter's expectations. The experimental model presupposes a passive reactor with neither spontaneity nor initiative and such a model does not reflect human beings as we know them in everyday life.

The contrast between identical repetition and identity through vari-ations is more of a contrast of styles than substance because both types of science affirm identity but by different means. Within the empirical tradition of experimental science, a discovery made by a researcher with one experiment is never taken as absolute. Too many contingencies are involved in experimental situations for the results not to be considered as somewhat tentative. Replication of the experiment must be sought by the community of researchers. That is, another researcher in another setting has to replicate the experiment and if the same results emerge, then one has greater confidence in the findings. Replication here means that the second researcher has to duplicate exactly as possible what the first researcher did so that no extraneous influences could account for possibly different results. Thus, the strategy is one that signifies that identical conditions should lead to identical findings. Of course, in this context, identical findings mean identical facts.

Within the phenomenological perspective, what matters is the discovery of an identical sense that covers multiple factual variations. Everyone knows that particular situations contain numerous contingencies, not all of which are critical for a true understanding of what is typical about such situations. Thus, the empiricist wants to study various instances in order to see which facts systematically stand out and can be truly counted on. The phenomenologist approaches such situations in terms of discovering an essence — or invariant structure — that can comprehend multiple situations. Very often, a rather stable essence or invariable structure can be discovered by a careful analysis of a few cases that are richly described. Such structures are derived from the varied meanings that every concrete and detailed description contains, which in turn are correlated with facts that are also expressed in the description. In Husserl's view, essences are eidetic discoveries that appear with the help of the method of free imaginative variation. They express what necessarily must belong to the phenomenon if it is to appear as a phenomenon of a given type. Thus, the research strategy and design of phenomenological research reflect this different goal.

Merleau-Ponty (1964b) gives a perfect example of such an eidetic intuition. In discussing the notions of behavioral lability (persons with highly varied behavior in similar situations) and behavioral fixity (persons with fixed behavior in varied situations), he writes:

> One says that a type of behavior is labile either when it is reproduced without any change under very different conditions — that is, when it is not flexible — or when it changes or disappears in a way that is wholly unpredictable.... One could compare the relevant psychological facts as much as one wishes without finding anything held in common. What is there in common between a stereotyped mode of conduct and one that is ever ready to disappear?...The lack of centering is the meaning held in common by modes of behavior which are absolutely episodic and others which are invariable and monotonous.... The connection between the situation and the response is wholly external, so that the situation does not guide the response. (71)

In order to see that a "lack of centering" is what is essential between lability and fixity one must go beyond the facts, as Merleau-Ponty says. One has to have an eidetic intuition, with the help of imaginative variation, that enables one to be present to a type of invariant meaning that not only accounts for the many disparate facts but also clarifies them in a deeper way. This is why various situations contribute to a deep, meaningful structure rather than identical conditions.

The final polarity in table 1 is that between independent observer and dependent or participant observer. In the physical sciences it really does not matter who the researcher is with respect to the relationship with the object of study. The object of study does not have consciousness and so a genuine intersubjective relationship cannot be established. In the human sciences, however, every mode of presence will have some impact on the human person who serves as a participant in research. Thus, the very structure of the research situation in the human sciences is quite different from that of the natural sciences.

Mainstream psychology has noted this fact under the rubric of "the social psychology of the psychological experiment" (Orne 1962). It is noted in this subfield that special attitudes prevail in such situations. Sometimes there is the authority of science that induces persons to do strange things and sometimes it is the presence of the researcher that dominates the situation rather than the variable that is being manipulated. In this tradition, the researcher is therefore acknowledged as another variable, as though his or her mode of presence is simply something to be controlled. However, accounting for the presence of the researcher has to go deeper than this. This type of thinking is a hangover from the natural science mode of thinking about research. It keeps the same structure as the physical sciences and adapts for the consciousness of the participant, whereas acknowledgment of the consciousness of the participant and his or her humanness should be the point of departure for rethinking the research situation for the human sciences. This is why the ethical perspective inserts itself more quickly and differently than in the natural sciences. In the latter, the ethical question revolves around the use of the discoveries that are made. Will atomic energy be used wisely or for nefarious purposes?

But in the human sciences (or medical sciences that use humans or even animals), the question is more direct: Will the very participation of the person in research injure or scar the person in any way? If so, then the research should not be conducted in the proposed manner. Thus, the social dimension of the research situation in the human sciences ought to have been the basis for rethinking how to conduct research with humans.

In following the logic of the dichotomies presented in table 1, the idea of how to probe the qualitative dimensions of reality emerge. This approach clearly reflects my background and training as a natural scientific psychologist interested in basic (as opposed to applied) research.[2] Not that such a logic cannot be used in applied situations. It is just that the development of the logic was motivated primarily by the desire to understand psychological phenomena as such and not directed toward any particular usage. The assumptions were (and are) that once certain knowledge was gained, applications for it would emerge.

FIVE

The Phenomenological Method

Phenomenology was initiated as a philosophy concerned with epistemological issues and it never lost its concern with these issues even as it expanded to cover many other philosophical areas. Another quick definition of phenomenology is its identity as a method for investigating the structures of consciousness and the types of objects that present themselves to consciousness. Since, for Husserl, phenomenology was never less than a philosophy, the method he articulated was intended to be a philosophical one and so I will present his version of the method first even though I will add modifications to it in order to have it serve scientific purposes.

Assumption of the Transcendental Phenomenological Attitude

The first step, for Husserl, is that the researcher has to assume the phenomenological attitude. Although Husserl struggled with further specification of this attitude early on, he finally specified that a transcendental phenomenological attitude had to be assumed. First of all, the very idea that a phenomenological attitude had to be assumed means that the philosopher has to break from the natural attitude. The natural attitude is the attitude of everyday life, the attitude that one displays in the everyday world, where most things are simply taken for granted. To assume the phenomenological attitude means to regard everything from the perspective of consciousness, that is, to look at all objects from the perspective of how they are experienced regardless of whether or not they actually are the way they are being experienced. For example, a child may see a department store Santa Claus and believe him to be the real one who will bring him toys on Christmas. Phenomenologically, one would examine that "perception-belief matrix" even though one knows that there is no real Santa in the sense that the child believes in him. That is, the object may not be real, but the perception-belief complex is an experiential given. To assume the transcendental phenomenological perspective means to view the objects of consciousness from the perspective of pure, essential consciousness, which means a consciousness that is not limited by any existing forms of it. Thus, transcendental consciousness is not a human consciousness. It is pure, flowing, essential consciousness, and Husserl claims that this mode of consciousness is capable of being intuited, that is, actually experienced with the proper attitude. This attitude is a consequence of the application of a severe criterion of ultimacy and universality, often a desideratum with philosophical modes of thinking.

Search for the Essence of the Phenomenon

Once having assumed the transcendental phenomenological attitude, the philosopher focuses on an example or a specific instance of the object of study, which may be something real or imagined. Then he or she applies the method of free imaginative variation, described above, to the object in order to determine what is essential about it. That is, the philosopher wants to know more precisely how to articulate what makes the object a specific example or instance of the type of phenomenon it is.

The example that Husserl provides within a transcendental perspective is that no consciousness can perceive color if there is no extension of it in space. No matter what the shade of color, it is impossible to even imagine any type of consciousness perceiving it if it has no extension. The color has to be at least the size of a dot in order to be perceived. Thus, color perception is essentially tied to extensiveness or spatiality because if extension is removed, color disappears. On the other hand, one can vary intensity, hue, or size of the extension and there would still be some form of color. While varying all those factors would have an effect on the specificity of the perception, it would not affect the very perception of some color and so each of these variables is contingent with respect to the essential relationship of color and space.

Description of the Essence

Once the philosopher believes that he or she has determined the essence of the phenomenon or state of affairs he or she is researching, the next obligation is to describe it as accurately as possible. This means that the researcher must neither add to nor subtract from what is present, although co-present absences should be included if they are constitutive of the essence. Depending on the nature of the object being described, co-present absences refer to horizonal aspects of the given that may be referred to but are not actually present. These aspects may be determinative of the essence of the given.

The major implication of this step is that description is favored rather than other philosophical alternatives. Description is the use of language to articulate the intentional objects of experience. This sense of description is contrasted with interpretation, which, in my view, is the use of language to articulate the intentional objects of experience with the help of some nongiven factor, such as an assumption, hypothesis, theory, or the like. Description is also contrasted with construction, which is not satisfied to stay strictly with the given, but uses imagination or other nongiven factors to either present or account for the objects of experience. Finally, description is contrasted with explanation, which attempts to account for what is presented, usually by employing factors that are not necessarily given or in terms of other known but nonpresent events (for example, causes). But its goal is not simply to exhibit what is given. All of the above alternatives are legitimate philosophical strategies for *accounting* for phenomena, but they follow from other philosophical criteria, not those of Husserlian phenomenology. In phenomenology, the exhibition of the given is the basis of its accountability.

To be more precise, the above description actually refers to two reductions: the transcendental phenomenological reduction and the eidetic reduction. The transcendental phenomenological reduction sees the object from the perspective of a generalized, pure conscious-ness. The eidetic reduction is a process whereby a particular object is reduced to its essence. Moreover, the whole procedure is undertaken with philosophical goals in mind. As Stapleton (1994) observes, "What evokes philosophical questioning is a sense of the infinite, the absolute, the unconditional, and in particular, a sense of these as under siege" (234). Husserl was seeking to defend the acquisition of knowledge against skepticism and relativisms. Thus, he was seeking criteria and procedures that would admit of no exceptions.

What also needs to be clarified is the idea of the phenomenological reduction liberated from its transcendental criterion because Husserl (1977, 1983) allows for a number of levels of the reduction. The first primary meaning of the reduction is that the object presented to consciousness must be understood as something that is present to consciousness exactly as it is experienced and one does not claim that it exists exactly the way it is experienced. That is, one does not posit the existence of the object but sees it simply as a presence to be explored. Husserl (1983) points out that the perception of an object in the natural attitude often includes the positing of the existence of the object. When I walk into a restaurant and see tables, chairs, wait-resses, and other customers, I simply take them to be real things and people who are sharing that particular space and time with me. Analysis shows, however, that there is a difference between the perception of the objects or persons and the positing of them as real things or real others. Ambiguous situations expose this quick double-step process because the positing is slowed down. This happens when one is trying to determine if a figure in a store window is a person or a mannequin, or when one sees a person who might be an old friend or perhaps is simply someone who resembles the friend. We then recognize that there is a difference between merely "being present" to an object and positing it as really being thus and so. The speed and habituality of such acts often make us ignore presentational aspects of the given that are important or make us posit as existing certain characteristics that do not warrant such positings. Therefore, Husserl recommends that in the phenomenological attitude, where care and precision matter, one should separate the act of perceiving from the act of positing and systematically consider what is presented in the act of perceiving. One can always posit later if it is called for. The withholding of the positing leaves us with presences, not existences.

While this meaning of the phenomenological reduction implies a certain lack—hence the term "reduction"—it is actually a heightening of the experiencer's presence to the activity of consciousness. It makes more available to the researcher the contributions of consciousness to the constitution of the object or state of affairs being presented. It also helps to make visible the manner in which the object is given, and the availability of these dimensions helps to clarify the meaning of the experience of what is given. In other words, insofar as phenomenology thematizes consciousness as its field of study, any action that increases the manifestation of consciousness is a help to its exploration. (The same would be true of psychology.)

The second major attitudinal shift that the phenomenological reduction induces is the bracketing of past knowledge or nonpresented presuppositions about the given object. (This attitude is also known as the "epoché," and it is sometimes considered a separate step and sometimes as part of the reduction. I favor the latter interpretation.) Again, in the natural attitude we are constantly evaluating our present experiences in terms of our past experiences. It is important that we do so (and of course, we probably cannot help but do so); otherwise, every experience would be a new experience and our lives would become unduly burdensome. However, in allowing such a role for past experience we often diminish the present experience by interpreting it as being identical to the past ones, whereas it is more frequently similar rather than identical. Practically speaking, there is often no consequence to this slurring over of the present. However, once one assumes a rigorous perspective, then one wants to account for the differences between the present and the past as well as the similarities. That is why Husserl was motivated to introduce the "bracketing" of past knowledge *about* the phenomenon being researched so that critical attention could be brought to bear on the present experience.

Many researchers have difficulties with this concept because certain erroneous interpretations are brought to bear upon it. Sometimes potential practitioners of bracketing believe that they have to forget everything about the phenomenon they are investigating, but that is not the case. It is not a matter of forgetting the past; bracketing means that we should not let our past knowledge be *engaged* while we are determining the mode and content of the present experience. Indeed, quite often one is very aware of the past as one tries not to let it influence an ongoing experience. This task can be difficult at times, but it is not impossible. Indeed, other walks of life make the same demand. A juror in a criminal trial may hear a judge say that a piece of evidence they just heard is not admissible and so they are not to consider it when they begin to discuss the guilt or innocence of the defendant. A scientific researcher running a crucial experiment may have high hopes for his or her pet hypothesis, but then notes that the results are not supporting it. The researcher may even strain to try to give as sympathetic an interpretation of the data as he or she can, but ultimately the demand is to remain open to the recalcitrant data and all of its contrary implications. The same is true of the phenomenologist practicing bracketing. One may very much be aware of past personal experiences relevant to the ongoing experiential encounter or favorite theories leading to comfortable interpretations about the ongoing experience, but the demand to be followed is that one puts aside all such temptations and systematically notes and explores the ongoing occurrences as they are unfolding. Of course, there is no a priori way of guaranteeing that one has bracketed successfully. One can only judge from the results, and even then assessment of the results may not be perfect.

A second difficulty researchers often have with the procedure of bracketing is the assumption that no one can execute a complete reduction. This claim probably stems from Merleau-Ponty's statement, "The most important lesson which the reduction teaches us is the impossibility of a complete reduction" (1962, xiv). Perhaps this is true within a philosophical context where ultimate things are sought. But within psychology, it seems that all that is required is a circumscribable task. What is required is a shift in attitude so that one can be fully attentively present to an ongoing experience rather than habitually present to it—or, perhaps better—be present to it as we are in the natural attitude. A certain heightening of the present is being called for, not an obliteration of the past. Indeed, this shift in attentiveness may even highlight the role of past experience in constituting the meaning of the present experience, and the use of imaginative variation in relation to the specific role of past experience may even deepen our understanding about how it works. But to do that means that one is already distinguishing the past from the ongoing experience.

One has to remember that Husserl always recommends something that is doable. He never claims esoteric or exotic status for the practice of phenomenology, even if some difficult steps are implied. Thus, to bracket never means to become a "new Adam or Eve," as though we lost our linguistic ability and are trying to invent language for the first time. This would be using a *reductio ad absurdum* strategy, where one pushes the meaning of the demand to an extreme and then says it is impossible. A principle of relevancy is involved. If I am examining a specific instance of learning in order to determine its meaning structure, and let us say that the example has to do with learning how to use a computer, do I have to bracket my preference for Beethoven over Brahms? Does such a prejudice even arise? I do not see how, unless through some imaginative leap from the data my preference comes to my awareness, in which case it is my responsibility to note that the preference is my bias and then I return to the data in order to see what was stated there that made me think of my bias. Bracketing means "holding in suspension," keeping a tension between the past and the present in order to discern their respective roles.

Basically, the employment of the phenomenological method has for its purpose the examination of any experienceable object as a phenomenon, that is, the object as it exists for consciousness, not as it is in itself. That is the precise meaning of phenomenon in phenomenology: any object whatsoever considered insofar as it is viewed from the perspective of consciousness. The method of free imaginative variation is then applied to the object so that its essence may be discovered. Finally, when that essence is determined, it is carefully described, which includes, when possible, the relationships the essence has with other phenomena.

The Scientific Phenomenological Method

If one followed the method as described above, one would be doing philosophy. However, as a psychologist, I want to perform phenomenological analyses that are relevant for psychology. This implies two attitudinal changes: (1) I want to operate at a scientific level of analysis and not at a philosophical level, and (2) I want the analyses to be psychologically sensitive, and again, not philosophically so. Consequently, based upon scientific and psychological perspectives, modifications will be introduced into the above method, but I will still claim phenomenological status for the method.

Thus, in terms of criteria, my method is responding to a synthesis of philosophical phenomenology, a human science perspective, and psychology. Furthermore, the three disciplines from which the criteria are being drawn are unsettled and constantly undergoing development. As a philosophy, phenomenology in its modern sense is fairly young and is notorious for the fact that practically all of the major philosophers in the movement differ substantially from one another. While the natural sciences are fairly well settled, the human sciences are not, and many competing movements exist within that framework. Finally, psychology has a one-hundred-year-old tradition as a natural science, but it still has not been able to define its subject matter in a way that is acceptable to all practitioners and theoreticians in the field. As a human science, psychology is very young and a marginalized movement in the field. Consequently, the synthesis that was produced in this work had to be done against the horizon of all of the above-mentioned uncertainties. Nevertheless, the development of phenomenological psychology must proceed so that it can be seen as a viable project capable of growing and being corrected. When Sartre was confronted with this dilemma, he wrote:

> We will not quarrel with psychology for not bringing man into question or putting the world into brackets. It takes man in the world as he presents himself in a multitude of situations: at the restaurant, in the family, at war. In a general way, what interests psychology is *man in situation*. In itself it is, as we have seen, subordinate to phenomenology, since a truly positive study of man in situation would have first to have

elucidated the notions of man, of the world, of being-in-the-world, and of situation. But, after all, phenomenology is hardly born as yet, and all these notions are very far from a definitive elucidation. Ought psychology to wait until phenomenology comes to maturity? We do not think so. But even if it does not wait for the definitive constitution of an anthropology, it should not forget that this anthropology is realizable, and that if one day it is realized, all the psychological disciplines will have to draw upon its resources. For the time being, psychology should endeavour not so much to collect the facts as to interrogate the *phenomena*—that is, the actual psychic events in so far as there are significations, not in so far as they are pure facts. (Sartre 1962, 28–29)

My method also seeks meanings, and they are correlated with the facts. The tentativeness of the forged synthesis grounding the method may be a liability in the long run, but perhaps not as deleterious as an approach that is reductionistic and psychologically impoverished.

Modifications of the Philosophical Method to Meet Scientific Psychological Criteria

My strategy for delineating this method will be to follow the procedures for conducting sound scientific research on psychological phenomena, with digressions whenever necessary. The first thing to be appreciated is that the order of the steps differs with the implementation of the scientific psychological method. That is because the new data to be analyzed has to be obtained from others and not from the researcher. Those using scientific conventions or strategies in the present era are skeptical of situations in which the data are obtained and analyzed by the same person. The fear is that an uncheckable bias could enter into the process. Philosophical practices accept personal reflections and the descriptions produced are measured against the logic of the analysis, the carefulness of the description, or else the critic's own reflections. Thus, Husserl could start simply by describing the shift of attitude required in order to get into the attitude of the phenomenological reduction and then begin to describe some concrete experience. But if I were to try that in the current scientific climate, I know that there is one question that I could not satisfactorily answer in the mind of the critic: How does one know that your description of your experience is not unconsciously in the service of your theoretical perspective, thus demonstrating the validity of your theory? There are, of course, theoretical responses to this query that should satisfy the critic, but the response involves long arguments and repeated demonstrations that turn out to be distractions. It is easier to avoid the issue and get the original descriptions from others who know nothing about phenomenology. Besides, turning to others can be an extension of the application of phenomenology in the social and human sciences.

Descriptions from Others

The researcher begins by obtaining concrete descriptions of experiences from others who have lived through situations in which the phenomenon that the researcher is interested in have taken place. Usually, the descriptions are obtained by interviews and then transcribed, but written descriptions are also possible. This step fulfills partially the descriptive requirement of the phenomenological method. (Another phase of the descriptive demand, that performed by the researcher, will be described below.)

These descriptions are given by ordinary persons within the natural attitude. The situations to be described are selected by the participants themselves and what is sought is simply a description that is as faithful as possible to the actual lived-through event. This description is referred to as the raw data, and all of it has to be accounted for. The researcher, of course, analyzes the data from within the phenomenological reduction, with a psychological attitude and with special sensitivity to the phenomenon being researched.

The fact that the descriptions come from others could be challenged from a phenomenological perspective because one is to analyze only that which presents itself to the consciousness of the analyzer, whereas these experiences happen to others. This possible objection has to be considered, but the descriptions provided by the experiencers are an opening into the world of the other that is shareable. I (Giorgi 2000a, 2000b) have written on this issue before, so I will refer to it now only briefly. Even if the original description belongs to others, much of the situation in which the experience happened is on the side of the world and thus shareable with others. Of course, the very assumption behind writing is that others can read and understand what is written, that is, that access to what the writer or speaker is saying can take place. In addition, while the descriptions come from others, the analyses, the meaning discriminations, and intuitions into eidetic data take place in the consciousness of the analyzer. Thus, the results, in the form of structures of experiencing, come from the researcher, and in that sense satisfy phenomenological criteria.

However, support for my position is also provided by Spiegelberg (1964, 1986), who speaks of a special act of self-transposal when one tries to take the place of the other:

> Imaginative self-transposal requires a peculiar style of occupying the place of the other by our transformed self, not a complete fusion for good, but one which allows us to shuttle back and forth between our own understanding self and that of the other who is to be understood.... At this point begins the actual work of constructing the other and his world on the basis of the clues which we find in the situation into which we have put ourselves imaginatively.... At the same time we shall have to mobilize our critical faculties in order to avoid the pitfalls of imaginative license. (Spiegelberg 1995, 49–50)

Thus, Spiegelberg is specifying a type of attitude that will fulfill the phenomenological requirements for examining the experiences of others. Just as Husserl has written that one uses noematic clues to work back to noetic analyses, so Spiegelberg notes that in descriptions from others there are also noematic clues that one can use in order to access the noetic factors insofar as one is able to do so with the help of imaginative presencing. Thus, the researcher's consciousness is involved with both the presence to the experience and with the analyses. Hence, the grounds for consistent phenomenological modes of operating are there, and the fact that the descriptions initially came from others is not an obstacle to the claim that the analyses respect phenomenological criteria. I should note that Spiegelberg's specific strategy relates to therapeutic situations so I do not follow his strategy literally but merely offer it as a demonstration that phenomenologists are interested in studying the experience of others.

Assumption of the Phenomenological Reduction

No claim that an analysis is phenomenological can be made without the assumption of the attitude of the phenomenological reduction. However, there are different levels of the reduction. In philosophy, a follower of Husserl would use the transcendental phenomenological reduction. As we saw above, this attitude necessitates that one assumes an attitude of "consciousness as such," which means that one transcends the perspective of human consciousness. That attitude is not sensitive enough for psychological clarification. Rather, at the level of psychological science what is required is what Husserl (1977) calls the psychological phenomenological reduction.[1] With this reduction, the objects of experience are reduced (that is, reduced to phenomena as presented), but the acts of consciousness correlated with such objects belong to a human mode of consciousness. Philosophically speaking, this reduction is not as radical as the transcendental reduction, but is more appropriate for psychological analyses of human beings since the purpose of psychology as a human science is precisely the clarification of the meanings of phenomena experienced by human persons.[2] Since in the scientific phenomenological reduction one does not retreat to the highest perspective on consciousness, one is closer to the level of lived reality at which psychologically lived experiences dwell. Husserl (1977) concedes that operating with this reduction is a legitimate use of the term "phenomenological."

Another difference with the philosophical method springs from the fact that the provider of the data and the analyzer of the data are not the same person. I argue above that this procedure can be properly phenomenological, so I will not repeat the arguments here. Rather, the question is, do the participants of the research also have to assume the phenomenological reduction? Recall that training was required for the participants of Titchenerian introspective studies as well as with the Würzburg school. Consequently, in those introspective studies researchers alternated between being researchers and participants. However, primarily we use everyday persons in our studies (except for specialized purposes), and they describe their experiences from the perspective of the lifeworld, from within the natural attitude. However, the researcher does have to enter into the scientific (psychological) phenomenological reduction in order to do the analysis. Since the researcher operates from within the reduction, we still claim that the research procedure satisfies phenomenological criteria. The practical problem with trying to get the participant into the phenomenological reduction raises the whole question of adequate training for the participants. Goodness knows, it is difficult enough to train psychologists to practice the reduction correctly. This type of research would practically be halted at the starting gate if all participants also had to be trained in phenomenology.

However, it is theoretically desirable to have participants remain naïve with respect to phenomenological concepts and theories. For psychological analyses one does not need the raw data to be purified a priori but it needs to be complex and mixed precisely as it is lived, thick with its ambiguities and relationships. The method of analysis will distill the properly psychological but with the support of all of the intentional objects precisely as they were lived. After all, as Merleau-Ponty (1962, 26) says, "The phenomenological attitude is assumed because it tries to understand the natural attitude better than the natural attitude can understand itself." The naïveté of the participant also helps to prevent bias because he or she normally does not know what the researcher is seeking and so is usually at a loss as to how to "please" the researcher and as a consequence relates the experience being described rather straightforwardly. The subjects we use are phenomenologically naïve.

The researcher does, of course, assume the human scientific (psychological) phenomenological reduction. Everything in the raw data is taken to be how the objects were experienced by the describer, and no claim is made that the events described really happened as they were described. The personal past experiences of the researcher and all his or her past knowledge about the phenomenon are also bracketed. This bracketing results in a fresh approach to the raw data and the refusal to posit the existential claim allows the noetic-noematic relation to come to the fore so that the substratum of the psychologist's reality can be focused upon. That is, the particular way in which the describer's personal acts of consciousness were enacted to allow the phenomenal intentional objects to appear form the basis of the sense determination that the psychologist is interested in uncovering.

The Search for an Invariant Psychological Meaning

We saw that the philosophical method sought essences via the method of free imaginative variation. Even if the idea of essences is sometimes denied within philosophy, its use is common enough within that context not to cause serious difficulties. However, it is more problematic within scientific contexts. The word often triggers Platonic connotations (although such implications are not intended by Husserl), and most scientists react negatively to these connotations. So, instead of searching for essences through the method of free imaginative variation, I seek the structure of the concrete experiences being analyzed through the determination of higher-level eidetic invariant meanings that belong to that structure. While the process is not so different from what the philosopher does (except for the goal, the discussion of which will follow immediately), the terminology is more easily appropriated by scientists because of their familiarity with statistical variations and the idea of a measure of central tendency. The structure provides the analogue of a measure of central tendency that is provided by the mean, median, or mode in statistics. After all, each concrete description is chock full of specific, varied meanings, and the question arises as how to communicate in the best possible way what is the common meaning of the phenomenon being researched given all of the variations in the raw data. The structure of the experience is the answer to that question, and in order to appropriate the majority of variations, it has to be expressed at a higher level.

However, there is also a fundamental difference between the essence obtained by philosophers and the structures described by psychologists.

When seeking essences, philosophers always seek the most universal essence, that is, those characteristics without which the object would not be what it is. Universalizing in such a way transcends psychological interests. It represents a philosophical understanding of a psychological phenomenon but without the pertinent psychological dynamics or precise uncovering of the psychological nature of the phenomenon. For example, one could say that learning always involves doing or understanding something new. That statement is essentially true, but completely nonrevelatory about the psychology of learning. To understand the living of a learning experience one has to relate correct performances to errors as well as the emotional reactions to the errors. He must understand the motivation to initiate the learning and whether that motivation was self-posited or not, the consequences of failing to learn (if that happens), and the satisfactions involved in succeeding to learn and their consequences, if that takes place. For such reasons, the universal essence is not the best way of presenting psychological results. Rather, the claim that the researchers make for the structures obtained is that they are general in the sense that the findings transcend the situation in which they were obtained. The structures, even though they are the result of the use of imaginative variation, are too dependent upon context and specific horizonal factors and are too determined by psychological interests to ever arrive at universal epistemological claims. In brief, with this method, a researcher seeks psychological essences, not philosophical ones, although, as stated, we prefer not to call them essences. Husserl (1983) allows for different types of essences; I do not believe that I violate the spirit of his work by positing first the psychological perspective and then seeking the essence of the phenomenon.

Another relevant factor also comes into play here. Mohanty (1985) shows that while Husserl began with the description of essences as one of the goals of phenomenology, in later works he began to speak about clarifications of meanings as an equally important goal. Mohanty makes clear that Husserl never gave up his quest for essences, but he notes that "the specifically phenomenological enterprise of *clarification of meanings*...slowly moves to the forefront" and "the concern with meanings brings it (phenomenology) closer to the empiricistic tradition" (191). Following this reasoning, one could assert that the structures of experience obtained by the scientific phenomenological method are clarifications of the particular lived meanings discerned in concrete descriptions from a psychological perspective eidetically raised to a level of general invariance. The psychological perspective, the context of the lived situation, and the type of the generic phenomenon being studied (for example, learning a motor skill as opposed to learning a new language) all place constraints on the generalization. Nevertheless, the structures clarify the lifeworld situations in a psychological way and contribute to a deeper psychological understanding of the everyday situations.

Another difference between the philosophical method and the psychological phenomenological method is that the data will have come from multiple persons rather than a single individual. However, the unity of the consciousness of each person has to be respected, and so if a single structure is to emerge from the data it would have to be accomplished holistically and relationally. That is, each lifeworld meaning that gets expressed psychologically by the researcher still has to be related to the noetic dimension of consciousness and cannot be extracted from its spontaneous context. To try to abstract commonalities across participants would be to treat the parts as elements rather than as constituents. Gurwitsch (1964) makes the valuable distinction between elements and constituents clearly and directly: an element is a part that is independent of the whole in which it resides, whereas a constituent is a part that is mindful of its role in the whole. This means that if one makes a triangle consisting of three black dots, calling the top dot a "black dot" would be considering it as an element, but calling it the "apex of the triangle" would be considering it as a constituent because its position in the whole is taken into account. In creating structures one delineates constituents, but one has to be mindful that the constituents are interrelated. Or better, the structure is the relationship among the constituents.

Another way to state the above point is to say that the noetic-noematic correlation has to be respected while trying to describe the general structure of the experience. This also means that key noetic-noematic relationships have to be understood in their role in the structure as well as what they signify in themselves. A higher-order structural description is required if individual constituents are to be integrated within one structure. Examples will be provided below.

The idea of coming up with one structure to comprehend all of the data, even though supplied by different individuals, is more a matter of efficiency or convenience than theoretical necessity. If the data turn out to be completely disparate, then a structure could be written for every participant. There would still be interesting findings, beginning with the simple fact that all of the data could not be integrated into a single structure. It would mean that even if the phenomenon had a single label (such as learning), the living of that phenomenon would be highly diversified. It could also mean that the label is disguising different phenomena. If such were the case, that, too, would be an interesting fact to pursue further.

The notions that help to determine whether all of the data fit into a single structure or not are the concepts of "intrastructural variability" and "interstructural variability." As stated, because of its efficiency, one first tries to integrate all of the data from all of the individuals into a single structure. If that takes place, then one can speak of "intrastructural variability" because each variant belongs to the same structure. If two or more structures have to be written, then variants belonging to different structures would be considered as "interstructural." Thus, the guiding concept here is that all of the different transformed meaning units are assumed to come from the same population, and one tries to describe the general invariant meaning (structure) that would, at least implicitly, comprehend all of the lower-level variations of meaning.

One has to remember here that the structure is meant to be a psychological one that reveals the psychological aspects of the experience in a heightened way. Structures concerning psychological reality will never be the most general conceivable. Rather, they occur at the middle range of discourse. There will always be particular meanings expressed below the structural level, and the psychological structures could always be subsumed by more universal structures. Staying merely at the particular level reveals more about the individual undergoing the experience than about the phenomenon as such, and going to a more general level displays the most revelatory aspects of psychological reality. At this stage of the process, it is most difficult to specify the criteria for the proper level of description for such structures. The goal, however, is to make as explicit as possible the psychological aspects of the phenomenon being investigated in an invariant way for the context employed.

If one discovers that the description of the structure requires the use of terminology that is too abstract, then the data is telling the researcher that the variations are too large to be incorporated within a single structure. The differences are large enough to be "interstructural," and more than one structure will have to be written to do justice to the data. This is basically a judgment call on the part of the researcher and, again, the criteria are hard to specify. It takes a special psychological sensitivity to distinguish between intrastructural and interstructural differences. Obviously, more experience in these areas could help determine adequate criteria.

Consequently, even though the application of the phenomenological method in scientific psychology requires certain modifications, my claim is that the modifications do not vitiate phenomenological criteria. Getting descriptions from others in the natural attitude is simply extending the data base for analysis. The second-order descriptions (the structures) produced by the researcher do follow strict phenomenological criteria even if not transcendental ones. That is, the researcher must enter into the scientific phenomenological reduction in order to do the analysis. Finally, certain invariants using the method of free imaginative variation are obtained even though I do not call them essences, but as noted, part of Husserlian phenomenology involves the clarification of meanings as well as the discovery of essences. These differences respect the goals and practices of contemporary psychological science while operating within the framework of phenomenological philosophy.

To help understand how descriptions can be accomplished within the reduction, one has to keep in mind Husserl's (1983) noetic-noematic correlation. We know that phenomenology approaches consciousness from a relational perspective. There is a large group of acts that Husserl describes as "intentional" because they are directed toward objects of one type or another. To use a grammatical analogy, these acts are transitive, that is, they take objects. The term "act" in this context is better understood in the sense of "actualization" rather than activity. Consciousness makes objects become present. It actualizes presences. When speaking of the act side of the "act-object" correlation, Husserl uses the term "noesis." When he speaks of the object side of the correlation, he uses the term "noema."

The articulation of this relationship within the framework of consciousness or experience is what raises the possibility that the task of description could be rigorous. Whenever a description is concrete and sufficiently rich, the noetic-noematic correlation can be applied to it. One can then discern the act of the describer and the object that is correlated with it, hold the relationship apart temporarily, and then it can be analyzed and described from the perspective of the researcher. The noetic-noematic relation is a way of entering into the consciousness of the other and accurately exhibiting precisely the parts of the experience that contain the lived meanings that are the focus of the descriptive task. Because these parts are so clearly delineated, the critical other can more easily oversee the analysis that the primary researcher performed. That is why the meaning units are delineated and made explicit and a track record of the transformations of sense are also provided.

It should be noted that none of the other qualitative researchers whose work I covered above did anything like this. From James through Coles, basically, the raw data were presented and then the researcher provided the interpretation of the text that was exhibited. But what the researcher did to provide the interpretation is not revealed. What is understood is that the researcher read the raw data and then applied either the disciplinary perspective (for example, psychological) in the analysis, or else the more specialized theoretical psychological perspective (such as Titchenerian structuralism). But in the method I am articulating, the very process of the transformation of sense can be tracked as well as the move from sense transformations to structure (although the latter is harder to track). This is possible because of Husserl's claim that what can be intuitively presented can also be carefully described. But one has to be sure that one operates from within the phenomenological reduction and that what is presented is described precisely as presented. Of course, one can err, and so checks and balances are required, but it is also possible to be accurate.

A Human Science Interpretation of the General Research Schema

In order to show how the phenomenological approach influences all phases of the research process, I will be following the procedures one would have to follow in order to conduct sound scientific research on psychological phenomena. In the previous chapter I provided a schema for psychological research, and I will basically follow that schema now with digressions whenever necessary.

A Researchable Problem

One first has to realize that an entire interest cannot be researched within a single study but would have to be broken down into parts or aspects. Conducting empirically based research imposes more limits than one initially realizes. I would even venture to say that the better the limits of a study are articulated, the stronger the research. One also has to appreciate that the process of deciding upon the specifics of a research situation is holistic. That is, each decision or each commitment has a ripple effect upon all of the other decisions to be made. Sometimes the effects are major and sometimes they are subtle, but they are always there in one way or another. For example, if I decide that I want to obtain qualitative data, then a host of possible methods are no longer available to me. If I decide that I want to publish in a mainstream American Psychological Association (APA) journal, then I have to think through carefully how I might want to treat the qualitative data, for very few studies with qualitative data are published by APA journals. If I decide that I want to research some type of pathological phenomenon, then I have to worry about where I might find human subjects who have experienced that phenomenon as well as all the issues involved in clearing ethical hurdles.

I mention these several examples so that the reader knows that the early phase of designing a research strategy and selecting a problem is very critical. Many aspects of the research process that come to the designer's awareness have to be considered, thought through, weighed, and related to one another. The interlocking aspects are especially important. Consequently, firm decisions should be held off until the researcher knows that no insurmountable difficulty is implied in making such decisions.

Of course, many other cautionary comments about the research process could be made, but these can often be found in regular research textbooks. What I want to concentrate on here are the special concerns and decisions flowing from the synthesized perspective I forged from my knowledge of science, phenomenology, and psychology. The philosophical phenomenological perspective is most foundational, so I will consider that perspective first when it comes to the question of a researchable problem.

Basically, from a phenomenological perspective, what is being sought in psychological research is the phenomenal world or the experiential world of the participant. Unfortunately, there is no direct access to this world so it has to be accessed indirectly through some form of expression. There are many forms of expression, from concrete behavior to artistic, and each has its own set of peculiar difficulties with respect to the assessment of the participant's experiential world. Of course, one of the major forms of expression is language, and it holds a privileged, but not exclusive, place with respect to the determination of the world of the other. We often listen to the stories people tell us when they have had experiences that we have not. We often read travelogues or other accounts of travel in order to get a sense of places to which we have not been. These narratives extend our own experience by giving us insight into what others have experienced or, in other words, we learn something about the experiential world of the other as well as something about the world that was experienced by the other. These descriptive expressions also have vulnerabilities, and I will come back to them. For now I want to establish that the phenomenological goal of understanding the phenomenal world of the other is dependent upon some form of expressiveness.

It is generally acknowledged that a precise and undisputed definition of psychology is not yet a historical achievement. Indeed, there are even those who claim that it is theoretically impossible (Koch 1969). That is not my judgment. I believe that the precise determination of the meaning of psychology is a scholarly necessity if psychology is to become a sound and stable science (as opposed to a well-established sociocultural academic institution or even a profession). However, as stated above, this definition has not emerged as yet and we cannot stand still and do nothing until it arrives.

Historically, psychology has been defined as the study of consciousness, the unconscious, experience, or behavior. However, these terms merely circumscribe an area, but not the precise sense within each area that needs to be uncovered, nor how the four areas can be integrated. Up until now they have been competing definitions, with the possible exception of the expression "cognitive-behavioral," but then the term "cognitive" hardly exhausts the range of conscious phenomena. From a phenomenological perspective, the unconscious is a dimension of consciousness, so there is no tension there. Also, experience is a modality of consciousness as well and it straddles the conscious-unconscious dichotomy. Finally, behavior may seem to be difficult to integrate, but if the term "expressiveness" is used, then behavior is easily integrated. Indeed, using "behavior" instead of "expressiveness" is already a reduction because in spontaneous, everyday life we do perceive the expressions of the other. They are difficult to know precisely, and that may be why the term "behavior" is preferred by psychologists, especially when it is used in contrast to consciousness understood only internally.

While the phenomenological perspective may take a step toward the integration of the four classical definitions, it is still far removed from a definitive solution to the problem of the definition of psychology. The problem is not with the area designated (consciousness, experience, or behavior), but with the very term "psychological." After all, there is political behavior, aesthetic consciousness, and economic experience, plus many more variations. Precisely what does the adjective "psychological" communicate when it is added to each of the three nouns specified above? That question has not yet received a satisfactory answer.

I do not pretend to have *the* answer to this question, but my point of departure is as follows. Following phenomenological guidelines, I would say that the psychological is given in the phenomenal world of individual experience. This phenomenal world is not an absolutely true, objective, and valid world (Merleau-Ponty 1962, 50–57). It is a world where the pararational dominates; it is the "world-for-me" or the "world-for-one." It is the world where the meanings correlated with how things present themselves to one are dominant and such meanings do not guarantee harmony with objective reality. The phenomenal is also the place where subjective interests dominate and present objects, places, and persons with definitive valuations. Normally, these desires and interests are mediated by rational processes or encounters with a resistant reality so that objective understandings can ensue. But, then, the psychological is transcended but not entirely missing. The interactions with others and the world take place within the context of contingent norms, and when the expectations of these norms are not met it is usually because psychological factors dominate. The achievements of truth and objectivity require the cooperation and involvement of rational processes, but the psychological represents the level of functioning of life processes and its interests. It presents us with physiognomic objects and places and its spontaneous expressions are normally guided by self-interest.

Consequently, my reflections on the meaning of psychology also indicate that the phenomenal world of the individual person has to be interrogated. The point of departure has to be the concrete expressions produced by individual persons in response to the situations they are living through, or that they have initiated by their own activities. Descriptions of these activities are called for and the psychological aspect would be to tease out the subjective meanings lived by the persons on the basis of the rich, everyday descriptions provided by the participants. Other ways of getting the raw data are possible, but I will discuss variations later. Hence, the phenomenological and psychological requirements converge: details about the phenomenal world of an individual person are the raw material from which analyses can be conducted.

The most simple and direct statement that one can make about science is that it endeavors to establish the most stable knowledge possible about the phenomena of the world. However, since the phenomena of the world are so varied, science has to use different methods and strategies in order to come up with its hierarchically arranged knowledge. For many scholars, the understanding of science that is entertained comes largely from the practices and development of the natural sciences. Obviously that is because they have been genuinely successful and have contributed vastly to our knowledge of nature. But the contextual limitation of that development is often forgotten. The theories, practices, and norms of the natural sciences developed in dialogue with nature. The symbolic phenomenon that characterizes the object of the natural sciences is the "thing" and the processes that constitute it and interact with it. If the object of study changes radically, then one has to be cautious about how to extrapolate from natural science practices to practices with other types of objects. Such a radical shift occurs when humans and their relationships replace things and processes. One can still learn from the natural sciences but one has to be sure that the criteria are not tainted with characteristics of things. In addition, humans introduce certain qualitative differences that bring new problems.

Consequently, we do posit that the idea of science is applicable with respect to human phenomena, but also that significant differences have to be introduced to the practice of science when dealing with humans with which one did not have to be concerned when dealing with the phenomena of nature. At a high level of abstraction (because I want to be sure that the criteria are not tainted), I would say that scientific knowledge is knowledge that is: (1) general, (2) systematic, (3) critical, and (4) methodical.

To say that the knowledge gained is general means that it has applicability to situations other than the one in which the knowledge was obtained. Of course, universality would be desirable, but in the human world the role of context is too dominant. To obtain universality, one would have to abstract to a level so high that the psychological value of the experiences would be transcended. Generality would apply to context-similar situations. The specifying characteristics of contexts are the presuppositions brought into play by the individuals, the horizonal characteristics of their experiences, as well as the sociocultural factors accepted by the individuals. The inclusion of these factors is too vital to be ignored for psychological purposes, so the price paid has to be the level of generality of the knowledge. The only other solution would be to go across all known contexts, but that would be impractical. Here the communitarian aspect of science must play its role. That is, many scientists doing limited contextual studies need to interact with one another.

To say that scientific knowledge is systematic is to claim that, over time, the different kinds of knowledge gained would have to relate to one another in a harmonious way. This means that if we gain some knowledge about perception, then there should be implications for motivation, imagination, emotional life, and so on. The knowledge does not just stand alone. Of course, at any given moment in the history of a science there may be disharmony, but the demand for systematization calls for an eventual straightening out of the sources of disharmony.

Scientific knowledge also has to pass through a stage of critical inquiry, both by oneself and by others. This means that the knowledge gained has to withstand specific kinds of challenges, even by the researcher who is formulating the knowledge. Then, of course, when the research results are published, the members of the relevant scientific community also have the opportunity to challenge the findings.

Finally, the knowledge gained scientifically should have a recognizable method capable of being used by many researchers. A method is a regulated procedure by which a researcher can come up with findings that can be checked by others precisely because the procedure by which the findings were obtained was delineated. There are no results that are independent of methods within science. Moreover, a method has to be a procedure that can be implemented by many. A procedure that only one person can utilize is not a method. The use of methods clarifies the means by which knowledge can be gained and helps make knowledge more reliable.

The above brief exposition gives my view on the three enterprises guiding the task. They converge to form the following general question: How can we get stable knowledge of the meaning of an aspect of the phenomenal world of the other regarding a psychological phenomenon in a limited situation? This question then has to be made specific enough so that phenomenological, psychological, and scientific criteria can be met.

If one raises the question of why we choose to concentrate on the other rather than oneself, it is because of the tradition of scientific research. Philosophical tradition allows the use of self-knowledge, and it is rarely questioned as a methodology by other philosophers. Since phenomenology began as a philosophy, its literature contains many examples of reflective analyses done by solitary philosophers and so sometimes the expectation exists that phenomenological analyses should be done on oneself. However, this is a limited understanding of the phenomenological method. In fact, phenomenological analyses are not dependent upon the self-report, regardless of how frequently it is used. One can apply the phenomenological method to the behavior and actions of others. What is true is that the phenomenon must present itself to the experience of the phenomenologist, but the mode can be indirect as well as direct. A rich, concrete description of an experience by another can be the basis of my phenomenological analysis of that experience because the meanings being awakened by my analysis are being given directly to my consciousness and even being constituted by it. By means of the description, the phenomenologist is vicariously present to the experience as expressed by the experiencer, not to just words on a page. Thus, to work on the basis of the other is a concession to the tradition of scientific research.

If we return to the general question, the phenomenological perspective directs us toward the phenomenal world of the other, which simply requires some form of expressiveness. The psychological perspective demands that the subjective orientation of the other be highlighted, and that, too, can be captured with expressiveness. The scientific requirement demands that the knowledge gained from the expressions be as stable as possible while at the same time reveal maximally that toward which the phenomenological psychological theoretical interest is directed. The scientific perspective also requires that the critical other have as available as possible to him or her the method, procedures, and strategies of the analysis performed by the researcher.

The next step is to specify all of these considerations, and this process is obviously complex. Let us suppose that I have an interest in recurrent memories. As a person in the everyday world I hear about certain persistent and recurrent memories that people experience as intrusive. That is, they do not particularly choose to have them, but they find themselves experiencing them repeatedly without actively choosing to call them up. So this is a phenomenon that announces itself to me from my everyday life. I do not experience such memories myself, but others talk about them. As a phenomenological psychologist I begin to reflect upon the issue and I can see that such memories certainly have phenomenal characteristics. They appear to certain individuals and they can report them. Such memories also meet the psychological criteria since memories have subjective characteristics and individuated meanings, and these too can be obtained through expressions.

What about the scientific criterion? How do we get stable knowledge? First of all, we must obtain expressions from research participants who experience recurrent memories. What we need to obtain from them are concrete, detailed descriptions of such experiences. We do not seek explanations, interpretations, conjectures, or anything else, although such material will undoubtedly slip into naïve descriptions and the method of analysis can deal with the nondescriptive data. The method of analysis will have to be described sufficiently well so that any critical other who is knowledgeable in phenomenological psychology can follow the steps and either confirm or challenge the findings. More will be said about qualitative and descriptive research as we proceed, but we will now assume that a specific researchable problem has been delineated. We want to get several descriptions of instances of recurrent memories from several persons who experience them. We acknowledge that the phenomenon of involuntary recurrent memories is relevant and accessible to both phenomenological and psychological perspectives.

But we still have to make the research situation specific. How do we do that? It is here where the second step of our schema comes into play. The second step shows that there is a relationship between the lifeworld situation where the phenomenon usually takes place spontaneously, or perhaps intentionally in the course of a life, and how the research situation has to respect the key aspects of the lifeworld situation. In addition, the main features of the "researchable problem" have to be in line with that dialogue.

Research Situation as Analogue of the Lifeworld Situation

This is one place where differences in scientific strategies come to the fore. One key assumption guiding practices in the natural sciences is that one tries to capture relationships among variables in a pure state with a minimum of interference from context or other extraneous factors. The experimental tradition in psychology follows the same strategy. If one can imagine a way of disentangling complex phenomena and studying their variables in an isolated way, or of diminishing the role of context, then one does it. That is why laboratories were created. Phenomena in natural settings are complicated and it is difficult to know the role of the separate variables. The laboratory is a site that is wholly different from situations in the everyday world. It is a place where the ability to control dominates. Contexts are controlled by all sorts of artificial means—for example, soundproof rooms, dark rooms, size and intensities of stimuli, exposure of stimuli for set times, quality and nature of stimuli, and so on. It is a place where abstractions can become incarnated. If one needs an extremely small intensity of light, one that nature itself might never produce, well then, one builds a machine that can produce it. Does one need a wavelength of light to produce a color that can never be found in nature? It's okay, one builds a machine to produce one. Does one need to understand the effect of hunger on performance? One will then have animals that have not been fed for 24, 36, and 48 hours and one can observe the effect of hunger for food on behavior. The lab is a place where events take place that do not happen as they do in the everyday world.

However, when it comes to human experiences I believe that a different strategy has to be followed. Since contexts matter so much in human affairs it is important to try to approximate as much as possible the situations in everyday life where the phenomena we seek to understand actually take place more or less as a matter of course. One reason contexts matter is that we know that the stream-of-consciousness or experience consists of parts that are interconnected with one another and that they cannot stand alone. Husserl calls such parts "dependent parts" or moments. Since the parts cannot stand alone the context in which they occur becomes important for determining meaning. The implication is that we have to seek those situations in the lifeworld in which the phenomena stand out in a pronounced way and either try to reproduce them or else access them in their spontaneous settings. The most essential point of departure for a phenomenologically based psychology is the actual experiential living that takes place in a situation. Even if spontaneous happenings cannot be reproduced at will, one can have analogues of such situations or access to the spontaneous situations by means of retrospective descriptions.

Since the above strategy departs somewhat from the strategies of the natural sciences where manipulative control is more feasible, certain theoretical points will have to be introduced to justify the strategy I am recommending here.

Control as Concomitant Recording of Spontaneous Activity or Expressions

As mentioned above, in the natural sciences control is generally implemented by means of active intervention with the phenomenon or with the environment within which the phenomenon unfolds. Moreover, since the natural sciences deal more frequently with inanimate things, theorizing can be highly analytic. One can manipulate parts because relationships among parts are often external and so relative independence among them can be assumed. Obviously, this is not always true, as the principle of indeterminacy demonstrates, but the assumption does often hold for macrophenomena. One consequence is that control can be established by manipulation within the phenomenon or with the environment. One can change the nature of filings in order to see how well magnetism works with different kinds of materials, or one can create necessary environments such as dark rooms, soundproof rooms, or artificially control temperature to create freezing or tropical conditions. Such strategies work with inanimate objects because proper decomposition of an entity into parts does not harm the entity, and the differentiated effect of extreme conditions on the parts can be observed.

The human sciences can follow this strategy to a certain extent in limited situations. For example, whenever there is an experiment that has a treatment group and a control group, a direct comparison concerning performances can be relatively meaningful. But such a strategy only works with externally imposed factors. If a researcher is interested in spontaneous living, then other strategies will reveal more because with spontaneous living subjective factors usually dominate.

When psychologists seek to understand experiential phenomena that happen more or less regularly in everyday life they are far better off attempting to grasp the phenomena as actually lived than in trying to induce them in the lab. This can easily be done by having the experiencer recount one of the last times that he or she experienced the phenomenon of interest. So, if a person is experiencing recurrent memories in her life, then as a phenomenological psychological researcher I would ask her to describe for me, in concrete detail, exactly what the experience was like the last time it was experienced. I seek not an explanation, nor an interpretation (although either can slip into the account given by naïve persons in the natural attitude), but precisely a description. These retrospective descriptions would become the raw data for the research. Such a point of departure will undoubtedly raise many questions on the part of mainstream empirical researchers, so allow me to respond to some of them.

The first vulnerability one tends to encounter is that a retrospective account may be forgetful, or distorting in other ways, regarding what actually happened. This is undoubtedly true at a factual level, and it is a limitation of the approach of which one always has to be mindful, but it does not vitiate the approach as such. There is no research without some type of vulnerability. It is a question of choosing the least limiting condition given the purpose of the research. For example, an attempt to induce recurrent memories in the laboratory may result in memories that are detached from the vital concerns of the person reporting them and thus not have the impact that spontaneously generated memories would have. In addition, there would still be the concern over whether the reporting was accurate vis-à-vis the actual experiencing. There is always a possibility of slippage between the reporting of an experience and the actual experience, whether ongoing or retrospective. In my view, all human research will have limitations of this sort and they cannot be wholly eliminated. The implication of such limitations is that one has to be cautious in interpreting the findings.

A second point is that the role of retrospection has to be properly understood. Time's division into present, past, and future is understood in such a way phenomenologically that accessibility to the nonpresent is possible to be had accurately, although obviously it is not guaranteed. For Husserl (1991), the present is not limited to a conceptual "now" but is thicker because of retentional and protentional references to immediate past and future instances that actually belong to the present. The further one moves from the present, the greater is the recession of the instances from awareness until it would be necessary to perform a separate act to bring the instances to awareness again. These separate acts would be recollection for the past and expectation for the future. But proximate retention and protention belong to the experience of the present and help to account for the fact that we experience duration and objective reality. In other words, the temporal dimension of consciousness plays a role in all of our experiences, and without retention and recollection (and protention and expectation) there would be very little to describe. The temporal factor in the structure of experiences, however, does not negate the fact that over long periods of time our access to experienced events can diminish and become distorted. Forgetting, too, is a phenomenon, but retentive and recollective phenomena contribute to our experiences more pervasively than we realize and so cannot be used as sole factors for objecting to the use of retrospective description.

As mentioned above, even ongoing descriptions are not likely to do justice to the flow of experiencing (Aanstoos 1985). However, perfection is not a criterion, that is, it is not the case that each description of an experience, whether ongoing or retrospective, has to capture the prereflective flow perfectly. Rather, the criterion is one of adequacy, defined as a description that is sufficiently articulate so that new, insightful knowledge about the phenomenon being studied can be obtained.

Another factor that has to be kept in mind is the fact that all of the analyses take place within the perspective of the scientific reduction. This means that past knowledge about the phenomenon under study has to be bracketed by the researcher and also that what is presented in the description is taken to be a phenomenon, that is, is something that was experienced by the describer, but no claim is made that the object of the description really existed the way that it presented itself to the describer. Consequently, the actual reality of the object of the description is not an issue. What matters for phenomenologists is how the object presented itself to the describer. In that sense, the actual veridicality of the description vis-à-vis the object is not as critical in phenomenology as the sense that is revealed in the describer's mode of description. In my classes I used to give descriptive exercises to students and included describing a person from within the phenomenological reduction. After the semester was over and grades were given out, a student came to me and told me that he had not described a real person as he was instructed to do, but that he had made up the description without observing anyone. His purpose seemed to be that he had fooled me. But I reminded him that at the phenomenal level, even though the person he was describing was imaginary or fictive, he nevertheless created a certain physiognomy of a person and that physiognomy held even if the person was imaginary rather than real. The imaginary is a certain way that consciousness is related to an object and the manner of being related imaginatively can be studied and understood. The same is true of other descriptions. Even if a retrospective description is incomplete, it still reveals how experience was organizing or attempting to objectivate certain events or objects of the world. Thus, the veridicality of descriptions is not as critical as their richness and articulation, so long as they are honest.

Indeed, psychologically speaking, false memories can be more revealing than accurate ones because they reveal more about the psychological life of the individual. Even distorted memories are psychologically more interesting because the distortions reveal the workings of subjectivity. Knowing the objective facts or the objective situation is helpful as a contrast to the subjective distortion, but it is the latter that reveals the psychological reality. Thus it is how an object or event is taken up by an experiencer that is the theme of phenomenological psychological investigations. Knowledge of veridical experiences is obviously helpful in order to understand better the psychologically motivated distortions, but the psychological dimension of an experience can be accessed and understood to some degree even if the objective facts are not known.

Since consciousness and experience are presented as a constant flow even if certain substantial parts (James 1950) are contained within the flow, they obviously present themselves quite differently from the things of the world that are transcendent to consciousness. The reason that stable things external to consciousness can be solidly present is due to the synthetic activity of consciousness. When one perceives a cup, for example, and turns it about in one's hand, what is perceived is a single object with many sides, and the reason that each aspect is not seen as a separate object is because of the bestowal of identity and the synthetic activity of consciousness. Consequently, when investigating experience itself, because of its synthetic character, it would be wrong to try to isolate each aspect that can be mentally isolated and try to control for it in isolation. Aspects of the experiential realm are intrinsically related; what needs to be captured are the synthetic nodal points of the experience, and a key guide for this task is the discovery of the meanings contained within the experience via its report. What has to be kept in mind here is Husserl's (1970a) point that parts that cannot stand on their own are nonindependent parts (moments), and while they can be discriminated they also have to be related to other moments of the experiential stream in order to be properly understood.

A way of capturing both of the above points is to acknowledge that acts of consciousness bestow sense on their objects as well as present them. This is true even though the acts are directed to the objects themselves and a reflection on the intentional object is necessary to reveal the sense with which the object is being presented. Since phenomenological analyses wish to reveal the sense of the presentation, inaccurate factual understanding of presented objects is not so critical. And since an identity guides the synthetic activity of consciousness, it helps to understand the implicating relationships among the aspects, that is, the fact that there is no true independence among them. Of course, as psychologists (or human scientists in general) it is not the philosophical meaning that is being sought here but the psychological meaning (or the specific human science meaning), and I still have to delineate that. But the point is that the essential nature of consciousness or experience dictates a different approach in order to gain stable knowledge about their phenomena.

The Steps of the Method

The efforts I made with respect to trying to clarify the criteria of a human science approach to psychology were the results of my reflections concerning whether or not "method" was the chief difficulty that was holding back psychology's advances. My reflections led me to the belief that the major problem was not the method as such but the philosophy behind the method (Giorgi 1970). If one could articulate a different philosophy of science necessitated by the encounter with a different type of subject matter, then a different method could emerge. The debate had to take place at the level of what I called "approach" and not at the level of method itself, since a method is only as good as the criteria it tries to meet. While far from being the last word, I am satisfied that the analysis presented above is sufficiently sound to serve as a point of departure. Presumably, modifications, changes, and corrections would ensue as one gained more experience with the method.

Before detailing the steps of the method, one more critical point needs to be mentioned. As I reflected upon the problem of whether a qualitative method could be workable, it seemed to me that the crux of the problem was whether, and to what extent, a qualitative analysis seeking the psychological meaning of experiences via descriptions could be objective, or at least offer the promise of approximating objectivity. So the heart of the question for me was: How does one analyze a description of a concrete experience in a psychologically meaningful way and achieve at least the same degree of objectivity that quantitative analyses reach? With the help of Husserlian phenomenology and its theory of meaning, I was satisfied that the criterion I had posited could be reached.

One of the chief contributions of Husserlian phenomenology is that it provides an eidetic science to support empirical findings of a qualitative nature. Mainstream approaches have statistics and probability theory or the rules of logic. Husserl added morphological essences, which help give stability to the contents of experience. Some qualitative researchers boast that their research is empirical in nature whereas the genuine contribution would be how to shore up the intrinsic corrigibility of qualitative empirical data with eidetic support. None of the qualitative researchers I covered earlier struggled with this issue. After presenting the qualitative data the empirical researchers mentioned above came up with interpretations or theories, but not with eidetic findings that deepened the understanding of the raw data.

Data Collection Phase

All research has to begin with the specification of the research situation and the determination of the data to be obtained. Qualitative research is heavily dependent upon linguistic ability, both that of the participants and that of the research analyst. One simply has to take the prevailing language as it exists and try to make it specific to the discipline and more precise. The only way to achieve this aim is to make the meanings of the expressions more precise, which is basically what the descriptive phenomenological method aims to do.

Basically one has to get concrete and detailed descriptions of experiences by those who undergo the experiences in which the researcher is interested. There are several ways of doing this. One could ask each participant to write a description of the experience being sought. This is possible, but one drawback is that most persons do not write as extensively as they talk. Thus, the descriptions tend to be brief and the researcher does not get as many details as he or she would hope. Highly specialized and specific instructions can correct that limitation, but since the invention of the tape recorder, more often than not, the participant is interviewed about the experience and the interview is recorded and later transcribed.

There are many books (for example, Mishler 1986; Kvale 1996) with advice on how to conduct an interview, but none happens to be written with explicitly phenomenological criteria in mind. The basic problem is that there is a certain spontaneous quality to a good interview that cannot be completely prescribed. The criterion for a phenomenological research interview can be easily stated: What one seeks from a research interview in phenomenological research is as complete a description as possible of the experience that a participant has lived through. But achieving this aim is not as easy as it sounds. Many difficulties may emerge between the initial question and the end of the interview, from a certain reticence to speak to an unrestrained loquaciousness directed to everything but the topic of interest. It is very difficult to attempt to enumerate all of the contingencies that one might encounter, so I will not try, but the phenomenological researcher should try to use common sense and keep the criterion in mind. In their account, is the participant revealing an aspect of how he or she was present in the situation? If so, let the participant speak. If not, it is perfectly legitimate to try to steer the subject back to describing himself or herself in the situation that is being focused upon.

In the matter of interviews, one has to distinguish between "directing the participant" and "leading the participant." The latter refers to the attempt to get the participant to say certain specific things that the researcher is seeking in the data. Such an attempt would be an example of biasing the data. The former phrase, "directing the participant," refers to the fact that the researcher must have the participant speak to the researcher's phenomenon of interest. After all, one cannot simply say to a participant, "Speak!" A researcher has a specific interest and wants to be sure that the data collected are relevant to that interest. So, to direct a participant to a specific zone of experience is not prejudicial because, in the discovery approach used by phenomenological researchers (as opposed to an hypothesis-testing approach), the researcher does not care what the specific details or contents are, only that they are genuinely revelatory of the experience being researched.

Certainly, establishing rapport with the participant is critical, and perhaps too little time is invested in doing that in contemporary qualitative research. There is still too much concern about being "neutral" as was the practice in natural scientific psychology, which usually translated into being distant or uncaring. Of course, the opposite extreme, having only intimates as participants, would be equally erroneous. Rather, it seems that the ordinary sociocultural practices of society ought to be observed. If a researcher wants a deeply self-revealing experience to be articulated, then perhaps an intimate friend ought to be the participant (obviously, with anonymity guaranteed), or else the researcher ought to establish a relationship greater than that of passing acquaintanceship. If one is seeking a rather ordinary experience (for example, a learning situation), then strangers could be participants, but still, a certain degree of rapport should be established. The reason for this is that one never knows when certain boundaries of intimacy might be encountered in the telling of an experiential episode. Clearly, a certain degree of psychological sensitivity is required of the research interviewer, and if a researcher encounters an unanticipated difficulty that brings up ethical issues, then, always, in a conflict between ethics and science, ethics triumphs.

The difficulties that one might encounter become paramount when dealing with pathological or potentially embarrassing phenomena. In such cases, in addition to general psychological sensitivity, clinical skills will also be required. Much more time in establishing rapport will also be necessary. The interviewer who is simply a "friendly stranger" may not have established the best relationship for obtaining relevant data in depth. Again, the contingencies that one might encounter here are too vast to cover, but general awareness of these issues is necessary before embarking on a research project.

One should bear in mind what length of interview is adequate for the phenomenon being studied. A tendency of inexperienced interviewers is to go too long because they fear that they may not have sufficient data. But everything that is collected has to be analyzed. (Phenomenology's holistic perspective demands that all of the data that are collected be analyzed.) In addition to leading to a lot of work, data collected under such circumstances are usually not very revelatory since they are driven more by anxiety on the part of the interviewer rather than being directed awarefully to the content of what the participant is saying. Obviously, interviews can also be too short and thus equally nonrevelatory. A sense of proportion relative to the phenomenon being studied is required.

Interview data may also be too abstract, too general, or made up of opinions or attitudes rather than concrete and detailed descriptions, which is why the question the researcher poses should invite the interviewee to focus upon a specific situation that he or she actually experienced. The basic question usually takes the following form: "Please describe for me a situation in which you experienced learning" (or anything else). If the interviewee responds properly, then the focus on the situation keeps the narrator on the details of what was actually lived through to the extent that they can be recalled. The situation being described sets up the limits that are necessary in order for descriptions to be focused and manageable. But, of course, situations have to be understood experientially, which means that objective space-time features do not define it. There are horizontal factors, both retrospective and prospective, that belong to the situation that only the interviewee can reveal. Nevertheless, the concept of situation determines important limits and ensures that most of the descriptive material is relevant to the research question.

There is no perfect description in the sense that every aspect of a lived-through event is portrayed accurately. I am not supporting a "copy theory" of description whereby a description is meant to reveal all aspects of a lived-through experience that is completed. The relationship between experience and expression is far more complicated. As Merleau-Ponty states, "In already acquired expressions there is a direct meaning which corresponds point for point to figures, forms and established words. . . . But the meaning of expressions which are in the process of being accomplished cannot be of this sort; it is a lateral or oblique meaning which runs between words" (1964a, 46). Thus, a description portrays figural aspects of an experience, but there will always be embedded parts of the lived-through experience that do not get portrayed. The relationship is more like "figure-ground" and, in principle, not all of the ground can ever be expressed.

However, there can be adequate descriptions, which are those containing sufficient depth and detail so that some new psychological knowledge about the phenomenon can be obtained. They can also be described as those that allow the phenomenal world of the subject to reveal itself sufficiently enough so that the subject's manner of being present to a situation while experiencing a specific phenomenon can be discerned and the structure of that phenomenon described. Such descriptions are not that difficult to obtain and so a research program can be sustained with this approach.

Analysis of Descriptions

Once an interview has been conducted and its contents recorded and transcribed, it is ready for analysis. Obviously, some type of fixity of the raw data is necessary. One could possibly work with the taped interview, replaying parts of it over and over until an analysis is completed, but that becomes tedious and it is not easy to share with critical others. Visual stabilization through transcription serves the task of analysis and the sharing of the results with others much better. But it is helpful if the researcher is able to evoke imaginatively some of the liveliness of the original dialogue.

From a Husserlian perspective, the description, even though transcribed and possibly printed, still remains a description. I say this because some qualitative researchers call anything that is written a "text" and therefore argue that interpretive strategies must be used. But this is too simplistic. Not everything that is written down should be called a text in the strict sense of the term because there are many modes of reifying and communicating language nonverbally.

Basically, writing or printing is a way of reifying speech or linguistic communication. There are tremendous advantages to this capability, of course, but due to technological advances, writing is no longer the only way of reifying or preserving speech. Today there are audiotapes and videotapes as well. The virtual modes of presentation of the computer may also introduce new dimensions. However, the use of these latter techniques has not yet been integrated into scientific results, at least not in any standardized ways. Writing and print are still the standard ways of communicating scientific findings.

I do not want to go into all of the issues surrounding description and interpretation here, but a text that has to be interpreted has to have special features. If by "text" one simply means a visual reification of audible expressions, then I have no objection to the use of the term, but such a usage does not demand interpretive strategies. It simply refers to the fact of visual reification. A text that demands interpretation has to have some ambiguous features and often the ambiguities refer to the horizons of the text rather than the text itself. One can read what the author has written, but one can also question his or her intent. Is the author expressing that intent clearly? What perspective is implicitly assumed by the author such that his or her argument is not clear? Who is the audience that the author is speaking to? All of these can be legitimate questions that require interpretation. In addition, the further the author is from the times of the reader, the greater the need for interpretation. But this is still a horizonal factor. Would a novel written in the nineteenth century be interpreted the way I am doing so now in the early twenty-first century? Again, this can be a legitimate concern and it would demand interpretation.

However, a description obtained for research purposes is frequently acquired under very different conditions. It is usually obtained freshly and explicitly for the purpose of the research. The participants who generate the descriptions do so under the direction of a specific question formulated by the researcher. The basic demographic information about the participants is known by the researcher, and indeed, the participants are often selected because of the demographic information. Consequently, a lot of the horizonal factors that would motivate an interpretive strategy are missing. One focuses not on the horizonal features, but on the description itself.

There is also, obviously, an attitudinal difference between the task of interpretation and a descriptive analysis. An interpretive strategy tries to clarify ambiguities and some of the horizonal issues mentioned above. It seeks to come up with the best possible interpretation of ambiguous issues and this often makes necessary the introduction of assumptions, theories, or other nongiven factors in order to give a reasonable, "good" interpretation. A descriptive analysis, however, in principle, does not try to go beyond the given. The point to be established now is that a descriptive analysis attempts to understand the meaning of the description based solely upon what is presented in the data. It does not try to resolve ambiguities unless there is direct evidence for the resolution in the description itself. Otherwise, one simply tries to describe the ambiguity such as it presents itself. Thus, the attitude of description is one that only responds to what can be accounted for in the description itself. The descriptive researcher obviously sees the same ambiguities that an interpretive analyst would see but is not motivated to clarify them by bringing in nongiven or speculative factors. An interpretive analysis, from a scientific perspective, usually strives for an interpretation that is theoretically elegant or synthetically and relatively complete. A descriptive result is more inchoate; it dares not go beyond what is present. Gaps in the results are filled by obtaining more data, not by theoretical speculation. The result of a descriptive analysis is a second-order description. The scientific attitude behind such a procedure is that descriptive findings are more secure because they articulate what is given and can be directly checked by the critical other. They do not require the taking up of a nongiven factor that may be arbitrary, such as an assumption, hypothesis, or theory.

The Concrete Steps of the Method

(1) *Read for sense of the whole.* At this point, the researcher is faced with a transcribed description of a specific phenomenon. In order to begin the analysis the researcher must assume the attitude of the scientific phenomenological reduction, a psychological perspective, and be sensitive to the implications of the data for the phenomenon being researched. Since the person who analyzes the description need not have been the interviewer (and even if he or she was), the first obvious step is reading the whole description to get a sense of the entire description. The phenomenological approach is holistic since it realizes that meanings within a description can have forward and backward references and so analyses of the first part of a description without awareness of the last part are too incomplete. However, at this stage of the analysis one does not try to clarify or make more explicit the global sense of the description. The subsequent steps of the method achieve that task. One merely operates with a general sense of what the description is about.

I might add that the steps that I will be delineating are those that any qualitative researcher, regardless of perspective or theory, would have to follow, except that I implement them with phenomenological guidelines. Thus, qualitative researchers from any perspective would have to read the entire description, even if they began the analysis prior to reading the entire description. So the task in the first step is not so different with respect to the goal, but rather with respect to how the goal is implemented. This will be true with each of the steps. Another difference with the first step between phenomenology and other qualitative approaches is that the phenomenologist reads the description from within the phenomenological scientific reduction. This means that the focus of the reading changes. One gets the sense of the whole while sensitively discriminating the intentional objects of the lifeworld description provided by the participant, or as Cairns (1973) put it, while trying to discern the "intended-to's" contained in the description. Again, these are not noted or made explicit as yet but are simply observed and allowed to become part of the overall sense.

(2) *Determination of meaning units.* Since most of the descriptions obtained from interviews are too long to be dealt with holistically, one has to break them into parts in order to do them justice. Again, every qualitative procedure will require this step; the differences emerge with respect to how the partializing is done and how the parts are understood.

Since the ultimate goal of the phenomenological analysis is the meaning of the experience, the parts to be established should be sensitive to that goal. Consequently, the aim of this step is to establish some "units of meaning" that are contained within the description. Since the analysis is also meant to be psychological, then meaning units sensitive to that perspective are also required. Finally, since one is also within the phenomenological scientific reduction, phenomenological criteria are also being observed. Hence, the parts, or meaning units, are determined from a phenomenological psychological perspective, which makes them immediately relevant for the task at hand. As a contrast, for example, one could say that the parts of the description could be every sentence. But a sentence is a unit of grammar and not necessarily sensitive to psychological reality. In fact, sentences are psychologically neutral in the sense that they could be psychologically loaded or empty. Sentences are not the primary way that psychological reality reveals itself in expressions. Of course, grammar of some type is necessary, but it is another dimension of expressiveness and not well suited to reveal psychological meanings. Thus, the constitution of parts in the method are based upon the dimension that is most sensitive to the ultimate goal of the task.

Operationally, the meaning units are established in the following way. One goes back to the beginning of the description and one begins to reread it. Again, the attitude that has to be assumed is that one is in the phenomenological scientific reduction, within an overall psychologically sensitive perspective, and, finally, one is mindful of the specific phenomenon being investigated (for example, learning, anxiety, and so on). As one begins to reread the description, one makes an appropriate mark in the data every time one experiences a significant shift in meaning. The end of this step is that the description is broken down into a series of meaning units. Again, one does not yet interrogate the meaning units, nor does one establish a priori criteria for their determination. It is a spontaneous activity that is more experientially determined rather than intellectually so. The lived experience of the researcher plays a role here because the discriminations taking place are directed toward the lived experience of the other. Cognitive processes assume a greater role in the next steps.

The process of establishing these meaning units has a degree of arbitrariness to it. The meaning units that are constituted are strictly correlated with the attitude of the researcher. Different researchers could easily have different meaning units because there are genuinely different places where transitions in meaning can occur. But the meaning units in and of themselves carry no theoretical weight. They simply represent practical outcomes of making the description manageable and help the critical other locate places in the original description that motivate the transformations that the researcher makes. In other words, there are no "objective" meaning units in the description as such. They are constituted as a result of the psychological sensitivity that the researcher brings to the task. What ultimately matters is how the meaning units are transformed (which is the next step) and how, and to what extent, they are reintegrated into the structure of the experienced phenomenon, if at all.

(3) *Transformation of participant's natural attitude expressions into phenomenologically psychologically sensitive expressions.* The heart of the method is this third step, and it is perhaps the most intensively laborious. The task of carefully describing the transformations of the participants' raw data is not an easy one.

The descriptive analysis being recommended here is probably easier to justify, but more difficult to implement. It is easier to justify because the epistemological claim is that the results reflect a careful description of precisely the features of the experienced phenomenon as they presented themselves to the consciousness of the researcher. The claim implies that no speculative or nongiven factor influenced the findings. Such a claim immediately invites a checking of the findings by the critical other and this is welcomed. Scientific findings can only become stronger by such a give-and-take. The results of the descriptive approach imply strong knowledge claims because the results include descriptions of findings rather than theories or hypotheses. The second-order descriptions that constitute structures have the strength of facts, even though they are not pure facts. They are invariant meanings that should be repeated in subsequent research, even if the data upon which the structures are based are quite different. However, a limitation is that any given phenomenon analyzed at the psychological level may be organized as to type, and this fact could prevent perfect replication. Research experience shows that most phenomena can be typically described even though they appear to be univocally lived.

In this third step, one once again goes back to the beginning of the description that is now delineated into meaning units. Then the researcher starts interrogating each meaning unit to discover how to express in a more satisfactory way the psychological implications of the lifeworld description. In other words, for a psychological analysis to be fruitful, the psychological dimension of experience has to be highlighted. In a certain sense, what is to be expressed is constituted by the phenomenological psychological attitude of the researcher. The psychological dimension is not just lying there fully blown, ready to be picked out. It has to be detected, drawn out, and elaborated. The raw materials are individuated, concrete experiences with halos, margins, and interconnections that offer potentialities for development. A psychological attitude is required to develop these potentialities for psychology just as a physicist's attitude is necessary to develop the perspective of physics or a mathematical attitude to develop mathematics.

In addition, the many contingent expressions that make up the raw data have to be expressed in a more secure way. Consequently, a certain level of invariance of the variable meanings has to be achieved and in this process the phenomenological procedure of free imaginative variation is used. What this means is that the actually given data are imagined to be different from what they are in order to ascertain higher-level categories that retain the same psychological meaning but are not embedded within the same contingent facts. However, unlike in philosophy, this procedure is not pushed to the level of universality, but only to a level of generality that is appropriate for revealing psychological characteristics. In these analyses, one begins with a richer, more complex lifeworld perspective, and the psychological meanings that are embedded in the concrete description are teased out from it. In this process claims can only be made for psychological generality because of the heavy role of context and due to the fact that categories that are too abstract bypass the zone where psychological reality dwells.

In addition to highlighting the psychological, the transformation also tries to generalize the data to a certain degree so that it becomes easier to integrate the data from various participants into one structure. It is granted beforehand that every single description is going to be different from every other, even if the same phenomenon is being researched. However, even if facts differ, the psychological meaning can be identical. Psychological meanings achieve a level of invariance that can comprehend multiple facts. Thus, even though sensitive to the context in which they appear, psychological meanings can be expressed in such a way that the data of several participants can be integrated with them. Consequently, one is not limited to an individual, or idiographic, finding, but general structures for the phenomenon being researched can be achieved based upon the data of several individuals.

One has to appreciate that step 3 is a process that will take some time. It is not accomplished quickly. One has to dwell with the data, change and vary it imaginatively, which includes imagining the opposite of what one might desire to express, until one finds an expression that is suitable. The researcher may have to write several versions before achieving the desired expression.

I shall now use a phenomenological understanding of an aspect of the conscious processes that take place while performing this task. Part of Husserl's theory of meaning is based on the following schema:

consciousness enacts a signifying act, which establishes a meaning that seeks to be fulfilled, that is, is directed toward an object that will completely satisfy its specific but empty meaning. There can be many objects that might come close to satisfying the meaning, but unless the object satisfies it precisely, consciousness will continue to seek the precise solution. These would be known as fulfillments, but unsatisfactory ones. When an object satisfies the meaning completely, then an act of identification ensues, and the seeking on that particular issue ceases. So, the schema is: signifying acts → precise fulfilling act → act of identification. This is the process that takes place when transforming the lifeworld meaning units into psychological expression, and the process is aided by the method of free imaginative variation. Free imaginative variation is helpful in settling the difference between partial objects of fulfillment and those objects that fulfill the empty meaning precisely.

Now, what the signifying act emptily posits is the most invariant sense from the phenomenological psychological perspective that the meaning unit offers as contributing to the total structure of the phenomenon being researched. One has a vague sense of what one is looking for, but one cannot specify it exactly. The discovery of the correct invariant sense is an achievement of the process, and it is immediately recognized as correct when it presents itself. However, this immediate sense is not taken for granted—it is tested. One goes back to the data contained in the meaning unit and makes sure that the invariant sense truly comprehends all of the critical senses contained therein. This process is repeated until all of the meaning units have been transformed.

The key to this process from the phenomenological perspective is the ability to discern with accuracy the intentional object of the researcher's experience. The researcher is reading the participant's description, but within the reduction he or she awakens the phenomenal characteristics of the description, which in turn make the senses of the described experience more available. This is not as individualistic as it sounds. First of all, the researcher is in a research attitude, which means that an intersubjective attitude is adopted. The researcher is not responding as an individual but as a member of a community whose criticism he or she is well aware will pursue the analysis. That is why one can say that in all of these solitary analyses, the critical other is sitting on the shoulder of the analyzer. One makes sure that the invariant sense to be described is accessible to the critical other as well. Since no one can enter another's stream of experience, it is incumbent upon the researcher to make as explicit as possible the processes he or she is living through. That is why the process of determining the invariant senses is as protracted as it is. The critical other has the right to pursue the analysis as closely as he or she can.

While the procedure adopted has been to unfold the sense of the meaning units in columns, one should be aware that there is not a strict one-to-one relationship between the columns. Since context matters, it always has to be taken into account even as one is in the process of transforming specific meaning units. In other words, the meaning unit under consideration is the dominant factor, but it is not the only factor to be considered. Sometimes an important implicit psychological meaning is not stated anywhere, but it has a strong background presence, so one has to make it explicit somewhere and a relevant meaning unit can be chosen to do that. At other times there may be a repetitive theme, the psychological significance of which is critical, and so that particular sense is made explicit in one of the meaning units where a repetition occurs, but it could have been made explicit at any one of the repetitions. The meaning units should be conceived as figures against a contextual ground that spreads laterally across all of the other meaning units. It is not only legitimate but also necessary to draw from that ground in order to come up with transformations that accurately highlight the psychological dimensions of experience.

There is one piece of unfinished business that makes this labor especially difficult, and that is that the meaning of psychology in a comprehensive and accurate sense acceptable to most of the members of the discipline is not yet a historical achievement. As I mentioned before, there are even those who claim that psychology can never become a unified science (for example, Koch 1969), but that is not my position. I do believe it will be theoretically unified one day, but

I cannot wait until that day comes before starting my work. Practices within science often precede their clarified understanding.

Consequently, when I say that a psychological perspective has to be assumed, what I mean is a generic, atheoretical psychological attitude such as is often assumed by practicing clinicians and therapists every day—at least by those who do not adopt an explicitly theoretical perspective such as psychoanalysis, nondirective therapy, and so on. Sometimes such therapists describe themselves as eclectic, but I do not mean such an attitude if it means freely borrowing terms and ideas from different theories or systems. Rather, I mean it in a more naïve, pretheoretical way. It refers more to the way that the term is used in the lifeworld. Of course, when psychology is authentically established, it will be able to delineate specifically the aspect of expressive experience toward which the attitude should be directed as well as how to assume the correct attitude. At the moment, I can say that it is the total expression in its most concrete form that is analyzed from the perspective of individual subjectivity. The phenomenological attitude sets this up by reducing all things that are intentionally related to consciousness to phenomena and the psychological attitude focuses on the role of the individual subjectivity in constituting the specific presences and thereby making available the psychological meanings that play a role in the way that the phenomenal presences appear.

Basically, the focus of psychology is on how individual human subjects present the world to themselves and how they act on the basis of that presentation. The entire world of the subject is difficult to grasp and is accessible only over time and across many situations. Thus, concrete studies focus on situations, which are understood to be the smallest units of worlds that are lived through by individuals. It should also be borne in mind that the scientific phenomenological reduction is a partial reduction. While the objects are reduced, the acts are not, so they refer to a worldly subjectivity that is influenced by society, culture, others, and the world at large. To overlook these factors is to miss the psychological realm that is based upon the intentional activities of individual subjectivity, even if the origins of the intentional activities transcend the individual.

Now, an important phenomenological criterion is that epistemological claims should be based upon the direct consciousness of the researcher. Even though the original experience comes from an other, the phenomenological claim is met because all of the analyses are given to the consciousness of the researcher. Moreover, these analyses are conducted with an intersubjective attitude, which means that the critical other should also be able to access the transformations lived through by the primary researcher based upon the evidentiary traces that are left by him or her.

Certain features of this method are in common with a method invented by Dennett (2003), which he calls "heterophenomenology," but the theoretical bases for the method being described here and Dennett's method are radically different. Dennett calls his method heterophenomenological because he is dealing with descriptions from others (as I do), but he considers the verbal report itself, as it is, to be the data. For him, there are no implications beyond what is written. For my method, however, the written (or transcribed data) are expressions depicting the phenomenal world of the describer, and when I analyze the data, the written reports are understood to be a means by which we are imaginatively present to the same situation that the participant described. By only speaking of the report of the other Dennett seems to forget that the report is analyzed by means of his own consciousness. I have pointed out several times that in my analyses the intuitions described by the phenomenological researcher are given to the researcher's consciousness, thus meeting phenomenological criteria. I cannot pursue this issue further here, but I thought that these differences should at least be mentioned in order to avoid possible confusion.

Allow me to unpack as best as I can the analytic process lived through by the primary researcher when following descriptive criteria. The researcher rereads the description with the attitude described above and slowly moves from the everyday facts described by the experiencer and probes the immediate horizon surrounding the phenomenal presentation of the fact as it appears to the experiencer along with its co-present horizons in order to see what it means for the subject to have expressed himself or herself in this way. With the help of imaginative variation, one is able to discriminate and clarify the psychological meaning for the particular meaning unit and then one tries to express it as accurately as possible. What is expressed is dependent upon what is given to the researcher—that is, the intentional object as seen from a psychological perspective, and it is described precisely as it fulfills the signifying act that initiated the search. The claim is that the critical other within the same attitude and following the same rules is capable of seeing what the primary researcher sees. Of course, it is possible that the critical other will not see the identical intentional object, but then it is incumbent upon the other to describe what he or she does see, and this description can be compared with the former one in order to ascertain which description might be better. In other words, the situation, overall, is comparable to the situation when a replication study fails to confirm the original research. It becomes a special problem within the context of science that should be resolved in regular scientific ways. The most important criterion for the descriptive approach is that one neither adds to nor subtracts from the invariant intentional object arrived at, but describes it precisely as it presents itself. One continues to do this until the whole description has been transformed and the end result of the third step is a series of transformed meaning units.

In this chapter, I have detailed the basic steps required by the scientific phenomenological psychological method. It begins by having the researcher assume the attitude of the phenomenological reduction, with a psychological perspective and with a sensitivity toward the phenomenon being researched. When the researcher obtains a description of a phenomenon, she first reads it through entirely to get a sense of the whole. Afterwards, she breaks the lengthy descriptions into parts that are called meaning units. Finally, each meaning unit, originally expressed in the participant's own words, is transformed by the researcher by means of a careful descriptive process into psychologically pertinent expressions but without using the jargon of mainstream psychology. These transformed meaning units form the basis for the writing of the general structure of the experience.

Six

The Application of the Method

This book would appear to me to be deficient without some examples of the application of the method. I know that had I not tried to apply the method I would have written a very different version of the application of the phenomenological method as applied to psychology. A whole different set of issues comes to light when the method is actually used, and a purely theoretical or abstract description of the method would miss many significant issues. I learned as much in attempting to apply the method to psychological phenomena as I did in reading philosophical phenomenology. The actual practice in using the method contributed as much to the theory as did philosophical phenomenology. I will use as examples the type of description that I use in workshops and demonstrations. They are shorter and more manageable than the typical dissertation or research descriptions that are longer and more complex. However, the primary purpose of this book is to demonstrate how the method is applied in the analysis of qualitative data, and shorter descriptions can work just as well even if the outcomes are not as powerful and special problems presented by complexities are usually not encountered. I use shorter descriptions for such occasions because the method is holistic and one cannot write a structure based upon a partial analysis. The analysis of meaning units could be done, but even there, the proper context is lacking in a partial analysis in order to be able to transform each meaning unit properly. The method is strongly context dependent. I will present two brief descriptions of jealousy, and they will be analyzed by two experienced phenomenological researchers, myself (AG) and Barbro Giorgi (BG). Having two descriptions will allow me to show how a single structure can be achieved (if possible), and having another researcher will give me an opportunity to discuss whatever differences might emerge as a result of different persons analyzing the same data. These data were not seen by either of us before this task and I did not know how the analyses would turn out. I will now proceed to the application of the method in step-by-step fashion.

Because these descriptions were obtained in a workshop, they were written to begin with, so no transcription was necessary. I will label the participants of the two descriptions P_1 and P_2. The first analysis was done by AG and the second by BG.

Again, the purpose of these exercises is to reveal how the method is actually practiced and not so much for the outcome that is produced. After all, there are only four pages of data, hardly an amount to produce in-depth insights. Nevertheless, I will go through all four steps of the method so that the reader can see some sense of process, and I will present actual research results after the description of the process is complete.

The two descriptions follow below.

The Experience of Jealousy (P_1)

> Some years ago, I was with a group of people in a three-day training. I had a casual friendship with some of them, and one of them I had just formed a very close friendship with. We are each happily married to our spouses, then and today. I do not feel attracted to my friend in a romantic way, but care deeply for him, as if he were my brother, as he does for me, then and today.
>
> On the first full day of training, there was a lunch break. I had a cold and felt tired that morning. I knew I would not feel like walking to a nearby restaurant, so brought a snack. When it came time to break for lunch, my close friend turned to me to see what I was going to do. I told this person that the others were arranging a lunch together, but that I was going to stay in because I wasn't feeling well so brought some food. He decided to go out with the others, rather than stay in with me.

I understood why he decided to go with the others, because he didn't bring his lunch, but I really was secretly hoping he would stay in with me. It was perfectly reasonable that he would choose to go out but I felt hurt, and at the same time, silly at having that feeling. When he left with them I was amazed at myself because I actually felt abandoned. It stung, as if I were in a snowstorm with the driving wind turning my cheeks red. It was both an emotional and a physical stinging. My heart ached with sorrow and disappointment that was far beyond what seemed like I should be feeling; after all, it was a new friendship. I really wanted to be with him.

Later, it got worse. He didn't know any of the people in the lunch group that he went out with. I found out from other friends that were together with them, that one woman in the group was flirting with him over lunch. When they came back the same woman told me [that] she had an intense attraction to this man, and told him so at lunch. When we all were back in the group together, she continued to flirt with him. He looked at her in amazement, as did everyone.

I had images flash in my mind of pushing her out of the room and telling her to "stop it." It was a very strange feeling, something I don't experience often, and more aggressive than I remember ever feeling. I hoped that no one could see this was going on in me, but when I looked at her, then looked at him; looking at her as she flirted with him, I felt almost like standing up in a raging loss of self-control. It felt like I had energy pulsations coming up from my stomach into my chest, bursting with fire. Luckily, I managed to keep my composure and finished the day, amazed at myself for having such a negative and intense reaction to this woman.

THE EXPERIENCE OF JEALOUSY (P_2)

Pam is perfect and I hate feeling this way. She doesn't really even know I exist except for the fact she can probably identify my picture if pressed to do so. Yet her every movement, thought and pursuit is the standard by which I judge all my own.

We are both in the fifth grade in a little country school with six grades and only 62 students. We are not friends or enemies. She is part Cherokee, and it is the Native American blood in her that colors her straight, shiny hair black, skin light brown, and eyes as black as her hair. She looks different than all of us in our largely German-Scandinavian community. I admire her differences, but it really bugs me that everyone else does too, to the degree that no one else seems to be special when she is around.

She doesn't even need to try to get attention. All she has to do is stand there and her appearance does it for her. I know it doesn't have anything to do with the fact that she is a good student, especially pretty, remarkably kind and naturally thoughtful. Even if she were a witch everyone would prefer her over others anyway, because they do even before she opens her mouth.

The worst moment in this secret jealousy is right now—at school pet day. Among the assortment of yapping dogs, cats, tadpoles and hamsters, Pam's gleaming brown quarter horse literally and figuratively stand[s] head and shoulders above the rest. Being a country school, there are fields on all sides of us as well as a large pasture attached to the school for field days.

Pam stands in one of these fields in front of her horse holding its reins while it is being saddled. I am stunned. The entire school, with the exception of me, runs to stand near her, gazing at her without making any sound, "It just figures" I whisper to myself. As if she didn't already have it all, she has to show up with a horse. My parent had said no to one, even though we own barns, pastures, and our own grain supply. I take my little dog to a bench and stay away from the "fan club" that surrounds her. How could life be so unfair?

I try not to look, but I am just like the rest. I can't help but watch. The scene is beautiful, with a turquoise blue sky curving overhead, wild flowers quivering in a cool breeze, and two beautiful spirits—each equally shiny black hair—standing quietly and patiently before us all.

As soon as the horse is ready to ride, Pam slips into the saddle with a practiced lightness. She turns the horse with gentleness and skill and canters it in a wide circle around the field. Her hair and the horse's mane flutter in the rushing air. The throng of schoolmates that stood to watch her earlier now runs behind her waving wildflowers. I can't stand it. Why can't that be me? It is all I can do not to cry.

I will start with the first description and follow the steps outlined in the previous chapter. After reading the description over in order to get the overall sense of what the description is about, one breaks the description into parts by establishing what are called "meaning units" (MU). As I noted before, this procedure is completed in the following way: The researcher goes back to the beginning of the description and begins to reread it, more slowly this time, and the attitude adopted is a synthesis of the phenomenological reduction, a psychological perspective, and mindfulness of the fact that the description purports to be an experience of jealousy. Every time the researcher, from that perspective, experiences a shift of meaning in the description as he or she rereads it, a mark is made at that place in the description. The end product of this process is the full description broken down into meaning units. The same descriptions with the meaning units demarcated for P_1 and P_2 by AG are presented next.

THE EXPERIENCE OF JEALOUSY (P_1): AG'S MEANING UNITS

Some years ago, I was with a group of people in a three-day training. I had a casual friendship with some of them, and one of them I had just formed a very close friendship with. / We are each happily married to our spouses, then and today. I do not feel attracted to my friend in a romantic way, but care deeply for him, as if he were my brother, as he does for me, then and today. /

On the first full day of training, there was a lunch break. I had a cold and felt tired that morning. I knew I would not feel like walking to a nearby restaurant, so brought a snack. / When it came time to break for lunch, my close friend turned to me to see what I was going to do. I told this person that the others were arranging a lunch together, but that I was going to stay in because I wasn't feeling well so brought some food. He decided to go out with the others, rather than stay in with me. /

I understood why he decided to go with the others, because he didn't bring his lunch, but I really was secretly hoping he would stay in with me. It was perfectly reasonable that he would choose to go out but I felt hurt, and at the same time, silly at having that feeling. / When he left with them I was amazed at myself because I actually felt abandoned. It stung, as if I were in a snow storm with the driving wind turning my cheeks red. It was both an emotional and a physical stinging. My heart ached with sorrow and disappointment that was far beyond what seemed like I should be feeling; after all, it was a new friendship. I really wanted to be with him. /

Later, it got worse. He didn't know any of the people in the lunch group that he went out with. I found out from other friends that were together with them, that one woman in the group was flirting with him over lunch. / When they came back the same woman told me [that] she had an intense attraction to this man, and told him so at lunch. When we all were back in the group together, she continued to flirt with him. He looked at her in amazement, as did everyone. /

I had images flash in my mind of pushing her out of the room and telling her to "stop it." It was a very strange feeling, something I don't experience often, and more aggressive than I remember ever feeling. / I hoped that no one could see this was going on in me, but when I looked at her, then looked at him; looking at her as she flirted with him, I felt almost like standing up in a raging loss of self-control. It felt like I had energy pulsations coming up from my stomach into my chest, bursting with fire. / Luckily, I managed to keep my composure and finished the day, amazed at myself for having such a negative and intense reaction to this woman. /

THE EXPERIENCE OF JEALOUSY (P₂): AG's MEANING UNITS

Pam is perfect and I hate feeling this way. She doesn't really even know I exist except for the fact she can probably identify my picture if pressed to do so. Yet her every movement, thought and pursuit is the standard by which I judge all my own. /

We are both in the fifth grade in a little country school with six grades and only 62 students. We are not friends or enemies. / She is part Cherokee, and it is the Native American blood in her that colors her straight, shiny hair black, skin light brown, and eyes as black as her hair. She looks different than all of us in our largely German-Scandinavian community. / I admire her differences, but it really bugs me that everyone else does too, to the degree that no one else seems to be special when she is around.

She doesn't even need to try to get attention. All she has to do is stand there and her appearance does it for her. I know it doesn't have anything to do with the fact that she is a good student, especially pretty, remarkably kind and naturally thoughtful. Even if she were a witch everyone would prefer her over others anyway, because they do even before she opens her mouth. /

The worst moment in this secret jealousy is right now—at school pet day. Among the assortment of yapping dogs, cats, tadpoles and hamsters, Pam's gleaming brown quarter horse literally and figuratively stand[s] head and shoulders above the rest. / Being a country school, there are fields on all sides of us as well as a large pasture attached to the school for field days.

Pam stands in one of these fields in front of her horse holding its reins while it is being saddled. / I am stunned. The entire school, with the exception of me, runs to stand near her, gazing at her without making any sound, / "It just figures" I whisper to myself. As if she didn't already have it all, she has to show up with a horse. / My parent had said no to one, even though we own barns, pastures, and our own grain supply. I take my little dog to a bench and stay away from the "fan club" that surrounds her. How could life be so unfair? /

I try not to look, but I am just like the rest. I can't help but watch. The scene is beautiful, with a turquoise blue sky curving overhead, wild flowers quivering in a cool breeze, and two beautiful spirits—each equally shiny black hair—standing quietly and patiently before us all. /

As soon as the horse is ready to ride, Pam slips into the saddle with a practiced lightness. She turns the horse with gentleness and skill and canters it in a wide circle around the field. Her hair and the horse's mane flutter in the rushing air. The throng of schoolmates that stood to watch her earlier now runs behind her waving wildflowers. / I can't stand it. Why can't that be me? It is all I can do not to cry. /

The third step of the method requires the researcher to express each meaning unit more explicitly in language revelatory of the psychological aspect of the lived-through experience with respect to the phenomenon being researched. Since the psychological understanding of jealousy is the goal here, each meaning unit is interrogated for the insight or implications that it has for the experience of jealousy. The analysis of P_1 by AG follows. It should be noted that no fixed amount of transformations is required. The criterion is that the best transformation is desired—one that reveals as explicitly as possible the psychological sense regarding jealousy—whether it can be done in a single transformation or in several. It is not necessary that each meaning unit have the same number of transformations since they are not at all equally rich, psychologically speaking.

AG's Third Step on P₁'s Data

1. Some years ago, P₁ was with a group of people in a three-day training. P₁ had a casual friendship with some of them, and one of them P₁ had just formed a very close friendship with.	P₁ states that some years ago she was with a group of people in a professional setting requiring a three-day commitment. She states that she had a casual relationship with some of the group members, but with one of them P₁ had just formed a very close relationship.	P₁, a woman, discovered that she had formed a new, close relationship with a male member of a training group that was to meet over three days. Relationships with other members of the group were casual.
2. P₁ and her friend are each happily married to their spouses, then and today. P₁ did not feel attracted to her friend in a romantic way, but cared deeply for him, as if he were P₁'s brother, as he cared for her, then and today.	P₁ states that she and her new close friend were both in happy marriages with their spouses at that time and at the time of the writing of the description. P₁ explicitly states that she did not feel attracted to her new close friend romantically, but she did have feelings of care for him, as though he were a brother, and he reciprocated the same feelings	P₁ states that the relationship, though close, was not a romantic one but more like a sibling relationship, where each cared for each other during the training workshop and at the time of the writing.

	toward her, at that time and at the time of the writing of the description.	
3. On the first full day of training, there was a lunch break. P_1 had a cold and felt tired that morning. P_1 knew that she would not feel like walking to a nearby restaurant, so she brought a snack.	P_1 states that at lunchtime of the first day of the sessions, because she was a bit under the weather and fatigued, she anticipated that she would not feel like walking to a nearby restaurant with other group members, so she provided herself with food and decided not to join the others for lunch.	
4. When it came time to break for lunch, P_1's close friend turned to P_1 to see what she was going to do. P_1 told her close friend that the others were arranging a lunch together, but that P_1 was going to stay in because she wasn't feeling well so she brought some food. He decided	At lunchtime, P_1 states that her new close friend asked P_1 about her luncheon plans. P_1 responded that other members of the group were planning a group lunch, but that P_1 would not be joining them because she didn't feel well and anticipating	

to go out with the others, rather than stay in with P_1.

that lunch would be taken elsewhere by the others, she brought food for herself so she wouldn't have to go out. P_1's new close friend decided to join the group rather than remain with her.

5. P_1 understood why the new close friend decided to go with the others, because he didn't bring his lunch, but P_1 really was secretly hoping he would stay in with her. It was perfectly reasonable that he would choose to go out but P_1 felt hurt, and at the same time, silly at having that feeling.

P_1 claims to have understood intellectually that it was reasonable for her new friend to have decided to go with the group because he would have had no food to consume had he remained with P_1. However, P_1 states that she was covertly wishing that her friend would behave somewhat unreasonably and stay with her during lunch. P_1 states that her friend's reasonable decision to go with the others left her with a feeling of a sense of loss and emotionally upset, simultaneously with accompanying feelings

P_1 states that she was secretly entertaining the unreasonable wish that her new close male friend would forego lunch with the others and remain with her, even if no food was available. P_1 could intellectually acknowledge the reasonableness of his decision to join the others, but she felt simultaneously emotionally hurt by his choice but she also was aware of bemused self-deprecating feelings toward herself for feeling emotionally hurt. She recognized that her desire was not really rational, but she did feel that way and felt awkward because of it.

of oddness or
strangeness with
respect to herself
for experiencing
the emotional
upsetness that she
felt.

6. When he left with
them P_1 was amazed
at herself because she
actually felt aban-
doned. It stung, as
if P_1 were in a snow
storm with the driv-
ing wind turning her
cheeks red. It was
both an emotional
and a physical sting-
ing. Her heart ached
with sorrow and
disappointment that
was far beyond what
seemed like P_1 should
be feeling; after all, it
was a new friendship.
P_1 really wanted to be
with him.

P_1 states that she
was shocked by her
own reaction to her
new friend's depar-
ture with the group
because she felt like
he deserted her.
Her feelings were
so intense that she
felt both physical
bodily changes
and strong emo-
tional reactions.
P_1 expresses that
her reaction, both
in terms of disap-
pointment about
his decision to join
the group rather
than stay with her
and her emotional
reaction to that
decision were felt
by her far more
intensely than she
believed the situa-
tion warranted. P_1
reflects that it was a
new friendship, but
she also expresses
that she really
wanted to be with
him.

When her new friend
departed to join the
group for lunch, P_1
reports feeling physi-
cally and emotion-
ally devastated. She
strongly desired that
he should remain
with her and her
disappointment was
felt physically as
well as emotionally.
But P_1 was aware
that her reaction to
the departure was
far more deep and
intense than a ratio-
nal perspective on the
situation would have
warranted. P1 longed
to be with her friend
and felt frustrated
because her feelings
were not fulfilled.

7. Later, it got worse. He didn't know any of the people in the lunch group that he went out with. P$_1$ found out from other friends that were together with them, that one woman in the group was flirting with him over lunch.	P$_1$ states that the situation got worse for her. While P$_1$'s new close friend was unfamiliar with the people with whom he went to lunch, P$_1$ found out from other friends that were present at lunch that a particular woman was demonstrating romantic interest in her new close friend.
8. When they came back the same woman told P$_1$ that she had an intense attraction to this man, and told him so at lunch. When they all were back in the group together, she continued to flirt with him. He looked at her in amazement, as did everyone.	P$_1$ states that when the group came back from lunch the very woman that P$_1$ had heard was displaying romantic feelings toward her new close friend stated to P$_1$ directly that she had intense romantic feelings regarding him and told P$_1$ that she even communicated to her close friend that such feelings existed. P$_1$ reports that when the group gathered again to do work,

this woman con-
tinued displaying
romantic behaviors
vis-à-vis the new
friend. P_1's percep-
tion was that both
the man who was
the target of such
attention, and the
rest of the group,
were astonished at
her performance.

9. P_1 had images flash
in her mind of push-
ing her out of the
room and telling her
to "stop it." It was a
very strange feeling,
something P_1 doesn't
experience often, and
more aggressive than
P_1 remembered ever
feeling.

P_1 states that she
was imagining
herself pushing the
"flirting woman"
out of her new
close friend's space
in order to prevent
her from continu-
ing to display her
romantic incli-
nations toward
him. It was as
though the "flirt-
ing woman" was
usurping P_1's posi-
tion vis-à-vis her
new close friend. P_1
acknowledges own-
ing exaggerated
aggressive feelings
toward the "flirt-
ing woman" and
she recognizes that
her feelings toward
the woman were
unusual for her and

more aggressive than she had ever remembered feeling. It is interesting to observe that P_1 has moved from feelings of hurt from not being favored by her new friend to feelings of aggression toward another who, however playfully or realistically, is acting out warm feelings toward P_1's center of interest. P_1's feelings are now focused on the one who could be seen to have taken her place even though her feelings remained hidden.

10. P_1 hoped that no one could see this was going on in her, but when P_1 looked at her, then looked at him looking at her as she flirted with him, P_1 felt almost like standing up in a raging loss of self-control. It felt like P_1 had energy pulsations coming up from

P_1 states that she trusted that no one could see her imagined aggressiveness, but when she perceived the interaction taking place between her new close friend and the "flirting woman," her bodily reactions were becoming so strong that actual

her stomach into her chest, bursting with fire.	behavioral intervention could have erupted from her along with a loss of a sense of restraint. P_1 felt as though her feelings were erupting from her but she did ultimately maintain control.	
11. Luckily, P_1 managed to keep her composure and finished the day, amazed at herself for having such a negative and intense reaction to this woman.	P_1 states that it was only with good luck that she had managed throughout the day to maintain her serenity and not reveal her intense, negative reactions to the "flirting woman" who apparently had or was attempting to displace P_1 as the object of attention (desire) of her new close friend.	

The first thing to be noted about the transformations is that the column on the left repeats the words of the participant exactly except for one minor change: everything is changed into third-person expressions instead of first-person expressions. This makes it clear that the researcher is doing an analysis of another's experience rather than one's own. When introducing this method I found that students had a strong tendency to identify with the experience of the describer if the descriptions were left in first-person expressions, and that is not the proper attitude to adopt. One has to be sensitive to the viewpoint of the other, but identity with the other is not the goal. The viewpoint of the other has to be discerned from the perspective of the researcher's consciousness.

Second, while the transformations presented in the second column look neat and tidy, they were not lived so neatly. It would have lengthened this section unduly to demonstrate how the transformations were worked out and such detailed work properly belongs in a workbook or practice manual. It is important for the reader to know that the analysis requires discipline and many attempts at getting the right expression.

Third, the intent of the transformations is to describe carefully the intuitive psychological senses that present themselves to the consciousness of the researcher. But this step is a process. The first meaning that comes to mind may not be the best one and, in fact, it usually is not. Moreover, imaginative variation has to be used in order to ensure the eidetic status of the meaning to be described. A certain type of generalization must occur because it is assumed that more than one description is being analyzed in each research project, and it is taken for granted that each description will be very different from every other one. Thus, the only possibility for integrating results across participants is by generalizing, although such an integration is not guaranteed because the concrete descriptions could be highly varied.

Along with generalization, a heightened articulation of the psychological aspect of each meaning unit with respect to the phenomenon being researched is required. This does not mean using the psychological jargon of the various schools of psychology but precisely the avoidance of such jargon. Nor should each meaning unit be condensed into a label. Rather, to articulate the psychological aspect of each meaning unit means that one should assume a generic psychological perspective to the concrete, everyday description provided by the participant and then exhibit, or bring forth, the psychological meaning of what was said and note its relevance for the phenomenon being researched. This is the most difficult, and the most creative, aspect of the method in the sense of intuiting precisely. But it is also where the contribution of the researcher to the development of psychological knowledge really comes to the fore.

Let us now turn to some of the specifics in AG's analysis of P_1's description of jealousy. In the first couple of meaning units there is no dramatic departure from, or intensification of, what P_1 said (MUs 1–4). Basically the transformations parallel what P_1 said. The one clear difference is that the transformations detached P_1 from a training session as such and placed her in a professional situation with peers. The beginnings of stirrings relevant for the phenomenon of jealousy begin to take place in the next few meaning units (MUs 5–7). For reasons of her own, P_1 did not want to walk to the nearest restaurant to have lunch with the group and when her friend asked her what her plans were, which certainly was an expression of care on the part of the friend, P_1 told him that she would simply have a snack where she was. This information put her friend in a dilemma because he apparently wanted to have lunch with her, but it seems that he could not fully satisfy his initial desire since he had nothing to eat for himself. Hence, he decided to join the group. While P_1 can acknowledge the rationality of her friend's choice, she admitted to feeling hurt by his decision to leave her and have lunch with the others, but she acknowledged feeling simultaneously silly about feeling hurt.

Now, the thought does occur to the researcher that P_1's decision to snack rather than to walk with the group to the nearest restaurant may in fact have been deliberate in order to get an opportunity to be alone with her friend. However, there is no evidence in the data indicating that this was a deliberate strategy, so it seemed too speculative, or interpretive, to have made such a statement. But what was duly noted was P_1's sense of hurt concerning the fact that the friend did not unreasonably choose to remain with her and then her own reactions to her feelings of hurt, whereby she felt that such feelings were silly and uncalled for and far more intense than they should have been, given the status of their newly formed friendship. There was a certain spiraling of hurt feelings and reactions to such feelings that seemed to arise covertly within P_1. However, P_1's feelings continued to evolve in intensity to such an extent that she herself became shocked at their magnitude and she acknowledged that she felt abandoned, as though an old friend who had made a commitment to be with her had changed his mind at the last minute and did not fulfill what he had promised.

Basically, what the above analysis did was explore and make more manifest P_1's perceptions and feelings about the whole situation. It rendered more visible her phenomenal world, the meanings that she was bestowing on the situation even though they may have been unnoticed by others. They became available to us as researchers because of her description. The transformations try to make as manifest and clear as possible one way in which what psychologists label "jealousy" is lived out. In the part of the description that has been analyzed so far, P_1 desired to be the center of attention of her new friend but circumstances prevented that from happening and P_1 is left with feelings of hurt because her friend chose a reasonable course of action, but it excluded the possibility of centering on her. But then she also feels "silly" for feeling hurt, that is, perhaps somewhat embarrassed before her more rational side for the fact that her feelings of hurt were so intense.

Then, with MU 7 through to the end, the situation became exacerbated because of the presence of the other woman who was freely expressing warmth and other positive feelings toward the new friend—feelings that P_1 was hiding—and, in P_1's eyes, the woman was usurping P_1 as the center of attention of the new friend. Thus, the living of the experience of jealousy is complicated in the sense that it includes both a lack of centering on the experiencer (P_1), which she desired, and P_1's strong negative feelings toward another, who is perceived by the experiencer (P_1) to be attempting to become the object of such attention by the very person P_1 desired to concentrate on her. Again, all of these dynamics are hidden from others and P_1 herself is amazed at the reactions she had toward herself as a consequence of her strong feelings toward the other woman. P_1 admits that she almost made a public expression of her emotional feelings, and if she had, she undoubtedly would have felt embarrassed before the others as she did before her more rational side.

On the surface, P_2's description seems to be very different from that of P_1. But we can notice an immediate common point. Both experiences of jealousy take place exclusively within the phenomenal world of the experiencer. In each case, there is no evidence that the other(s) knew the turbulent feelings taking place within the experiencer. Let us now turn to AG's analysis of P_2's experience.

AG's Third Step on P$_2$'s Data

1. Pam is perfect and P$_2$ hates feeling this way. She doesn't really even know that P$_2$ exists except for the fact she can probably identify her picture if pressed to do so. Yet her (Pam's) every movement, thought and pursuit is the standard by which P$_2$ judges all her own.	P$_2$ perceives the object of her attention (a fellow student) to be perfect which precipitates in her an intense dislike of her own feelings with respect to the fellow student. P$_2$ acknowledges that the object of her intense attention probably does not know that P$_2$ exists with the possible exception that her fellow student, if given a picture of P$_2$, might recognize her as a classmate. Despite this distance between them, P$_2$ acknowledges that every movement, thought or endeavor of her fellow student is the criterion by which P$_2$ judges herself.	P$_2$ perceives a classmate to be an ideal of what she herself would like to be and P$_2$ is conscious of every movement of the ideal person as a standard to be emulated by her. Yet P$_2$ is also aware that she (P$_2$) is barely perceived or acknowledged by her ideal person. A lack of reciprocity in the awareness of each other is disturbing to P$_2$, but equally disturbing is how P$_2$ feels toward herself because of her feelings concerning her ideal. The way that P$_2$ expresses herself here reveals a prior history in which such attitudes were formed.
2. P$_2$ and Pam are both in the fifth grade in a little country school with six grades and only	P$_2$ describes the circumstances of their acquaintanceship. She and the person who is the object	P$_2$ explains the nature of the acquaintanceship that exists between herself and her ideal, which is

62 students. They are not friends or enemies.	of her attention are in the same grade in a small, country school and P$_2$ states that she and her classmate are neither very close nor at odds with each other but merely acquaintances.	distant familiarity and not overtly antagonistic.
3. Pam is part Cherokee, and it is the Native American blood in her that colors her straight, shiny hair black, skin light brown, and eyes as black as her hair. She looks different than all of us in our largely German/Scandinavian community.	P$_2$ identifies the classmate she admires as a part–Native American and she admiringly describes her appearance emphasizing her darker color, apparently a desirable feature contrasted with the lighter appearances of herself and her other classmates, who come from northern European backgrounds.	P$_2$ describes how her ideal's very appearance, due to background, makes her stand out against her and her peers and enables her to be an object of desire.
4. P$_2$ admires her differences, but it really bugs her that everyone else does too, to the degree that no one else seems to be special when she is around.	P$_2$ acknowledges admiring the different characteristics that the classmate's appearance presents, but she is also upset that everyone else admires the	P$_2$ acknowledges that her ideal is special not only to her, but to all of her peers as well. P$_2$ notes that it is difficult for any other student to stand out when her ideal is

classmate as well, so much so that no other person can stand out when the admired classmate is present.

present. P_2's admiration reflects a longing to be in her ideal's place or at least to be the center of such attention and yet there is displeasure in P_2's recognition that no peer can stand out when her ideal is present.

5. Pam doesn't even need to try to get attention. All she has to do is stand there and her appearance does it for her. P_2 knows it doesn't have anything to do with the fact that she is a good student, especially pretty, remarkably kind and naturally thoughtful. Even if she were a witch everyone would prefer her over others anyway, because they do even before she opens her mouth.

P_2 observes that her admired classmate requires no effort on her part to attract attention. From P_2's perspective, all she has to do is stand there and her very appearance does everything for her. P_2 goes on to observe that, in addition to being physically attractive, her classmate has other positive attributes that depend upon some action on her part, and if others were to know them, they would admire her even more. P_2 notes that even if her classmate were

P_2 states that her ideal becomes the center of attention effortlessly and even prior to demonstrating other positive attributes that depend upon actions or personal knowledge of her. P_2's admiration is such that she declares that her ideal would be the center of attention even if she had negative personal characteristics. Implicit in the last statement is the sense that P_2 herself could never measure up to her ideal.

	to be an evil character (a witch), others would still prefer her because they do so now before she expresses anything about herself.	
6. The worst moment in this secret jealousy is right now—at school pet day. Among the assortment of yapping dogs, cats, tadpoles and hamsters, Pam's gleaming brown quarter horse literally and figuratively stands head and shoulders above the rest.	P₂ admits that the worst experience of her secret desire to be in the place of the admired one was during a special school day when the children were to bring in their pets. P₂ describes how among the ordinary pets that children of that age normally have, the person she admired stood tall and outstanding next to the extraordinarily large, atypical animal she brought with her.	P₂ admits that the worst moment of her secret love-hate relationship with her ideal occurred on a special school day when students were allowed to bring in their pets and how she and her peers brought in typical domestic pets whereas her ideal stood out by bringing with her a large, atypical pet. It seems that the more her ideal stands out, the more P₂ feels that all of the admired one's advantages should belong to her (P₂).
7. Being a country school, there are fields on all sides of us as well as a large pasture attached to the school for field days.	P₂ describes the environment in which the school is located and many wide open spaces prevail. The admired one is in one such open space	P₂ notes that her ideal has assistance in preparing the animal to be mounted by humans while she stands before the animal keeping it under control.

Pam stands in one of these fields in front of her horse holding its reins while it is being saddled.	in front of her large animal, holding its reins while others are adjusting accoutrements appropriate for the animal so that it can hold the admired one.	
8. P$_2$ is stunned. The entire school, with the exception of P$_2$, runs to stand near her, gazing at her without making any sound.	P$_2$ states that the scene shocks her. Everyone involved in the day's activities, except for P$_2$, runs to the place where the admired one is standing, and they silently stare at the admired one with her large animal. P$_2$'s making herself an exception to the general adulation of the other students seems not to diminish her admiration.	P$_2$ is astonished when all of her peers silently gather around her ideal and watch her as though she and her animal were a special pageant. P$_2$'s feelings do not allow her to join her peers in acknowledging the special status her ideal was commanding.
9. "It just figures" P$_2$ whispers to herself. As if she didn't already have it all, she has to show up with a horse.	P$_2$ thinks to herself that it would be just like the admired one, who already stands out in her peer group, to come to the special school day with a preferred animal that makes her stand out from the group even more.	P$_2$ acknowledges that it would be characteristic of her ideal, who already commanded such attention because of her perfection, to do the extraordinary thing that would make her stand out even more.

10. P₂'s parent had said no to one, even though they own barns, pastures, and our own grain supply. I take my little dog to a bench and stay away from the "fan club" that surrounds her. How could life be so unfair?

P₂ states that she had desired the same large animal that was now enhancing the admired one's status, but her parent did not grant her permission despite the fact that their country home had all the requirements necessary to own such an animal. P₂ then takes her small animal to a part of the field that is away from the admired one and all of her enthusiastic admirers and isolates herself. She wonders why life can be so unfair and seems to be smarting because of what is taking place.

P₂ reflects on the circumstances surrounding herself and her ideal and wonders why life can be so unfair. She is aware that her home has all of the physical necessities to accommodate a large animal such as her ideal has, but her parent refused her permission to have such an animal despite her desires. Again, her ideal person has what P₂ desires but lacks, and P₂ is not comfortable with the difference and is hurting.

11. P₂ tries not to look, but she is just like the rest. She can't help but watch. The scene is beautiful, with a turquoise blue sky curving overhead, wild flowers quivering in a

P₂ said that she tried not to observe the spectacle, but just like the others in her peer group, she cannot help but to watch the scene. The whole setting was beautiful, P₂

P₂ wished to avoid observing the spectacle but, like the others, she could not resist. She had to acknowledge its attractiveness — two outstanding figures in a beautiful setting.

cool breeze,
and two beauti-
ful spirits—each
equally shiny black
hair—standing qui-
etly and patiently
before us all.

stated, and pictur-
esque, and at the
center were two
wonderful figures,
each with attrac-
tive, shining black
hair—standing
quietly and patiently
before all the
observers.

Her observance of
the setting in a way
reduces her to the
status of her peers
who are fascinated by
the admired person.
P_2's remaining apart,
even if unnoticed,
expresses her hidden
hurt.

12. As soon as the
horse is ready to
ride, Pam slips into
the saddle with a
practiced lightness.
She turns the horse
with gentleness and
skill and canters it in
a wide circle around
the field. Her hair
and the horse's mane
flutter in the rush-
ing air. The throng
of schoolmates that
stood to watch her
earlier now runs
behind her waving
wildflowers.

P_2 states that as
soon as the large
animal is readied,
the admired one
mounts the saddle
with grace and
then with utmost
gentleness and skill
directs the animal
around the field
in an elegant trot.
Her hair and the
animal's hair are
equally brushed
by the breeze. The
peer group that pre-
viously simply stood
and watched the
admired one now
runs behind them
waving flowers.

P_2 then observes that
the admired person
gracefully and com-
petently mounts and
rides the animal and
her peers chase after
her waving flowers.

13. She can't stand it. Why can't that be her? It is all P₂ can do not to cry.	P₂ can barely watch the scene. She wonders why it cannot be she that could have the large animal and be the center of attention. It takes all of her power for P₂ not to cry.	P₂ is near despair at that moment and it takes all of her strength not to cry. She wishes with all her heart that she could be the center of such attention and she tends to empha- size the feeling of loss she feels vis-à-vis the admired one who has it all.

P₂'s jealousy description is concretely different from P₁'s but not so different psychologically. P₂ states that the person toward whom she expresses both resentful and admiring feelings is physically distinc- tive from her and her classmates, and this fact allows her to stand out naturally against the background of her (P₂'s) similar-looking peers. Moreover, according to P₂, if one gets to know the one about whom P₂ is jealous, one would find that she is a decent person and that it is easy to admire her. P₂ is aware that it is effortless for the envied one to be the center of attention and others can easily admire her demeanor and her considerateness (MUs 1–5). The intensity of P₂'s jealousy really increased on the school's pet day because, while she and her peers brought typical domestic pets to school, P₂'s ideal person brought a horse and rode it flawlessly and with style. Her boldness in bringing a horse, the way she carried it all off, and the adulation the ideal person received from all of her peers was more than P₂ could handle. Thus, we now have to go to the dark side of the experience of jealousy.

The most negative effect of the living of jealousy is actually with the relationship of the experiencer with herself. With P₁, the strong nega- tive feelings that erupted within her, to her own astonishment, were accompanied by feelings of silliness for having such strong emotional responses. The appreciation of the inappropriateness of the emotional response brings a sense of shame or embarrassment to P_1, which also contributes to a certain diminished sense of self (silliness). Her feelings get even more complex and entangled when she perceives that the flirtatious woman is acting out romantic feelings toward the person whom she wants to center on herself. P_1 is also aware that the flirtatious woman actually dares to express feelings that P_1 keeps hidden. Anger arises in her which she also dares not to express and barely manages to keep hidden.

The same is true of P_2, who sees perfection in her classmate, who is physically different from her, which implies that she herself lacks the characteristics that can make her perfect. Since her ideal has perfect characteristics, P_2 assumes that she cannot have them. It is as though two persons could not share desirable characteristics or be desirable despite different physical characteristics. This assumption is not rational, but the experience of jealousy seems to contain distorted subjective desires. P_2 believes that she could never have the attention and adulation that she perceives her ideal enjoys. Jealousy seems to produce a reduced sense of self in the jealous person. It is as though good things cannot be shared. In the eyes of the jealous one, the situation becomes competitive and only one person can enjoy good qualities. Alternatively, there is also a kind of entitlement whereby the jealous one believes that whatever good another is receiving, the jealous one is equally deserving of it.

It should be noted that P_2's description contains the same dynamics (that is, the same network of complicated relationships) that P_1's description disclosed. That is, P_2 perceived that Pam received as much attention from others as she did from P_2 herself and this observation disturbed P_2. The whole tone of the first 5 or 6 MUs is that P_2 desires, or indeed, deserves, the attention that Pam is receiving and that P_2 is secretly desiring that very attention. In the last MU (13), P_2 makes explicit that she desired to be the center of attention of others just as Pam was. Thus, both aspects of the jealousy experience are present here as well: P_2 desires to be the center of attention of others and at the same time is upset that someone else is receiving the attention she is lacking.

In addition, P$_2$'s feelings are secretly endured and not expressed, as with P$_1$, and finally, P$_2$ is aware of reactions to her pent-up feelings since she "hates" feeling the way that she does. There seems to be a more "objective" perspective toward herself whereby she dislikes the jealous feelings she entertains, as though she were perceiving herself from the perspective of others.

The next step is the writing of the structure, and it is presented below. The decision was made that the two descriptions could be incorporated within a single structure. This is achieved by scanning all of the last transformed meaning units and comparing and contrasting what appear to be the most diverse ones in order to ascertain if they could have come from the same type of experience. The point here is to determine if the differences are small enough to be designated intrastructural differences, or so large that they have to be designated as interstructural. The difference between the two types of structure is the type of unity that the researcher intuits as appropriate. Rarely, however, is the unity a single idea. Rather, the structure usually consists of several key constituent meanings and the relationship among the meanings is the structure. The key test of a structure is to see if the structure collapses if a key constituent is removed. Thus, in the structure of jealousy for these two descriptions, if the meaning that the experiencer wanted to be the center of attention of another, or others, were removed, then the structure would not be a faithful accounting of the two concrete descriptions of jealousy.

The structure is meant to depict the lived experience of a phenomenon, which may include aspects of the description of which the experiencer was unaware. The psychological structure is not a definition of the phenomenon. It is meant to depict how certain phenomena that get named are lived, which includes experiential and conscious moments seen from a psychological perspective. A psychological perspective implies that the lived meanings are based on an individual but get expressed eidetically, which means that they are general. And because they are general, it means that in principle the structures are applicable to more individuals than the persons upon which they were based. The psychological structures are not the same as philosophical structures that would be pure and transcendental. The psychological structures are based on empirical factors even though they get somewhat transcended because of the use of imaginative variation.

In the process of writing the structure, the researcher has to be careful not to be too bound up with the language of the transformations. Sometimes such languaging can be carried over to the structure, but often it cannot because it is based upon partial analyses rather than an overview of the whole description. Thus, the writing of the structure takes a much more holistic perspective than the transformations themselves required.

AG's Structure for P_1 and P_2

For P (an ideal), jealousy is experienced when she discovers a strong desire in herself to be the center of attention of a significant other, or others, that is not forthcoming even though such attention would require irrational conditions. Alternatively, jealousy is experienced when P perceives that another is receiving significant attention that she wishes were being directed to her and the attention the other is receiving is experienced as a lack in her. Even though P acknowledges that a rational consideration of the situation in which jealousy occurs is understandable, the emotional investment in the desire dominates P's experience and her subjective concerns become the primary determiner of the meaning of the experience. Whether P is focusing on the attention that the other(s) are experiencing, and she is not, or focusing on the lack of proper attention that she feels is her due, her genuine feelings are not expressed to others, and the awareness of the dynamics of the situation precipitate in P feelings of physical and emotional pain. The emotional pain that P suffers also induces in P feelings of a diminished sense of self either for demanding the attention she is lacking or because aggressive or negative feelings toward the other are arising.

Before commenting further on my analyses, I shall present BG's analyses. First, P_1's description of jealousy is given with BG's meaning units and then her analysis of P_1. These are immediately followed by

P_2's jealousy description with BG's meaning units and then her analyses. Finally, her structure for these data is presented.

EXPERIENCE OF JEALOUSY (P_1) WITH BG'S MEANING UNITS

Some years ago, I was with a group of people in a three-day training. I had a casual friendship with some of them and one of them I had just formed a very close friendship with. We are each happily married to our spouses, then and today. I do not feel attracted to my friend in a romantic way, but care deeply for him, as if he were my brother, as he does for me, then and today. /

On the first full day of training, there was a lunch break. I had a cold and felt tired that morning. I knew I would not feel like walking to a nearby restaurant, so I brought a snack. / When it came time to break for lunch, my close friend turned to me to see what I was going to do. I told this person that the others were arranging a lunch together, but that I was going to stay in because I wasn't feeling well so brought some food. / He decided to go out with the others, rather than stay in with me.

I understood why he decided to go with the others, because he didn't bring his lunch, but I really was secretly hoping he would stay in with me. It was perfectly reasonable that he would choose to go out but I felt hurt, and at the same time, silly at having that feeling. / When he left with them I was amazed at myself because I actually felt abandoned. It stung, as if I were in a snow storm with the driving wind turning my cheeks red. It was both an emotional and a physical stinging. My heart ached with sorrow and disappointment / that was far beyond what seemed like I should be feeling; after all, it was a new friendship. I really wanted to be with him. /

Later, it got worse. He didn't know any of the people in the lunch group that he went out with. I found out from other friends that were together with them, that one woman in the group was flirting with him over lunch. / When they came back the same woman told me [that] she had an intense attraction to this man, and told him so at lunch. / When we all were back in the group together, she continued to flirt with him. He looked at her in amazement, as did everyone. /

I had images flash in my mind of pushing her out of the room and telling her to "stop it." / It was a very strange feeling, something I don't experience often, and more aggressive than I remember ever feeling. / I hoped that no one could see this was going on in me, but when I looked at her, then looked at him; looking at her as she flirted with him, I felt almost like standing up in a raging loss of self-control.

It felt like I had energy pulsations coming up from my stomach into my chest, bursting with fire. / Luckily, I managed to keep my composure and finished the day, amazed at myself for having such a negative and intense reaction to this woman. /

BG's Third Step on P_1's Data

1. Some years ago, P_1 was with a group of people in a three-day training. P_1 had a casual friendship with some of them,	P_1 describes a situation where she was part of a group that was going to spend the next three days in a shared context (training). P_1 had some former relationships, casual friendships, with some of the group members.
2. And one of them P_1 had just formed a very close friendship with. Both are each happily married to their spouses, then and today. P_1 did not feel attracted to her friend in a romantic way, but cared deeply for him, as if he were her brother, as he does for her, then and today.	P_1 also had a relatively new but more intense close friendship with one group member. P_1 states that the friendship was a deep but platonic friendship and both P_1 and her friend were happily married to their own spouses.
3. On the first full day of training, there was a lunch break. P_1 had a cold and felt tired that morning. P_1 knew she would not feel like walking to a nearby restaurant, so brought a snack.	As part of the schedule for the group, a lunch break was arranged but as P_1 was not feeling physically well she had made plans and prepared in advance so she could stay behind and not join the other group members for lunch.

4. When it came time to break for lunch, her close friend turned to her to see what she was going to do. P_1 told this person that the others were arranging a lunch together, but that she was going to stay in because she wasn't feeling well so brought some food.

As the group started to gather and organize themselves for the lunch break, P_1's close friend inquired about P_1's plans for lunch. P_1 told him that other group members were planning to go together to attain their lunch but that P_1 had made arrangements and planned not to join the group.

5. He decided to go out with the others, rather than stay in with P_1. P_1 understood why he decided to go with the others, because he didn't bring his lunch, but P_1 really was secretly hoping he would stay in with her. It was perfectly reasonable that he would chose to go out but P_1 felt hurt, and at the same time, silly at having that feeling.

P_1's close friend decided to join the group rather than stay behind with P_1. P_1 understood his choice since he had made no prior arrangements and staying with P_1 would have had negative practical consequences for him (nothing to eat). However, P_1 was hoping that her close friend would choose to stay with her. P_1 felt disappointed and hurt but felt conflictual about having these feelings since she did not have legitimate grounds for having such feelings.

6. When he left with them P_1 was amazed at herself because she actually felt abandoned. It stung, as if she were in a snow

When P_1's close friend left, P_1 was surprised at her own reaction. P_1 experienced intense feelings of abandonment, sad-

storm with the driving wind turning her cheeks red. It was both an emotional and a physical stinging. Her heart ached with sorrow and disappointment

ness and disappointment along with physical aches and pains.

7. that was far beyond what seemed like P_1 should be feeling; after all, it was a new friendship. She really wanted to be with him.

P_1's intense negative emotions and physical response appeared out of proportion to P_1 in light of the circumstances but these rational reasons did not diminish P_1's desire to be with her close friend.

8. Later, it got worse. He didn't know any of the people in the lunch group that he went out with. P_1 found out from other friends that were together with them, that one woman in the group was flirting with him over lunch.

This, for P_1 a difficult situation, escalated when she found out from other friends upon the group's return that one woman in the group had made romantic advances toward P_1's close friend.

9. When they came back the same woman told P_1 that she had an intense attraction to this man, and told him so at lunch.

The woman who had made advances toward P_1's close friend then explicitly told P_1 that she had strong romantic feelings for P_1's close friend, and furthermore she told P_1 that she had told P_1's close friend directly about her feelings for him.

10. When they all were back in the group together, she continued to flirt with him. He looked at her in amazement, as did everyone.

As the group resumed their group activities, P_1 observed that the other woman continued overt expression of her romantic feelings for P_1's close friend. P_1 had the impression that the whole group as well as P_1's close friend found this behavior out of the ordinary.

11. P_1 had images flash in her mind of pushing her out of the room and telling her to "stop it."

P_1 found herself fantasizing about getting rid of the other woman from the room and directly confronting her with the demand to stop her behavior.

12. It was a very strange feeling, something P_1 didn't experience often, and more aggressive than P_1 remembers ever feeling.

These strong feelings seemed unfamiliar and strange to P_1. P_1 found herself feeling more aggressive than what P_1 had experienced in herself previously.

13. P_1 hoped that no one could see this was going on in her, but when P_1 looked at her, then looked at him; looking at her as she flirted with him, she felt almost like standing up in a raging loss of self-control. It felt like P_1 had energy pulsations

P_1 was concerned that her strong negative experience would be visible to the other group members. However, P_1's negative feelings were also intensified when she further observed the other woman overtly continuing to express

coming up from her stomach into her chest, bursting with fire.

her attraction and seeing how P_1's close friend was also noticing this. The intensity of this heightened P_1's desire to lash out against the other woman, an experience that was both intensely emotional as well as physical.

14. Luckily, P_1 managed to keep her composure and finished the day, amazed at herself for having such a negative and intense reaction to this woman.

P_1 expresses gratitude that she was able to suppress her desire to aggress against the other woman. She was able to remain outwardly calm while she was taken aback by the intensity of her own response to this woman.

EXPERIENCE OF JEALOUSY (P_2) WITH BG'S MEANING UNITS

Pam is perfect and I hate feeling this way. / She doesn't really even know I exist except for the fact she can probably identify my picture if pressed to do so. Yet her every movement, thought and pursuit is the standard by which I judge all my own. /

We are both in the fifth grade in a little country school with six grades and only 62 students. We are not friends or enemies. / She is part Cherokee, and it is the Native American blood in her that colors her straight, shiny hair black, skin light brown, and eyes as black as her hair. She looks different than all of us in our largely German-Scandinavian community. / I admire her differences, but it really bugs me that everyone else does too, to the degree that no one else seems to be special when she is around. /

She doesn't even need to try to get attention. All she has to do is stand there and her appearance does it for her. / I know it doesn't have anything to do with the fact that she is a good student, especially pretty, remarkably kind and naturally thoughtful. Even if she were a witch everyone would prefer her over others anyway, because they do even before she opens her mouth. /

The worst moment in this secret jealousy is right now — at school pet day. / Among the assortment of yapping dogs, cats, tadpoles and hamsters, Pam's gleaming brown quarter horse literally and figuratively stand[s] head and shoulders above the rest. / Being a country school, there are fields on all sides of us as well as a large pasture attached to the school for field days.

Pam stands in one of these fields in front of her horse holding its reins while it is being saddled. I am stunned. The entire school, with the exception of me, runs to stand near her, gazing at her without making any sound, / "It just figures" I whisper to myself. As if she didn't already have it all, she has to show up with a horse. / My parent had said no to one, even though we own barns, pastures, and our own grain supply. / I take my little dog to a bench and stay away from the "fan club" that surrounds her. How could life be so unfair? /

I try not to look, but I am just like the rest. I can't help but watch. / The scene is beautiful, with a turquoise blue sky curving overhead, wild flowers quivering in a cool breeze, and two beautiful spirits — each equally shiny black hair — standing quietly and patiently before us all.

As soon as the horse is ready to ride, Pam slips into the saddle with a practiced lightness. She turns the horse with gentleness and skill and canters it in a wide circle around the field. Her hair and the horse's mane flutter in the rushing air. The throng of schoolmates that stood to watch her earlier now runs behind her waving wildflowers. / I can't stand it. Why can't that be me? It is all I can do not to cry. /

BG's Third Step on P₂'s Data

1. P₂ states that Pam is perfect and P₂ hates feeling this way.	P₂ identifies another child in her school as flawless and acknowledges that this gives her feelings she does not like.

2. She (Pam) doesn't really even know P_2 exists except for the fact she can probably identify her picture if pressed to do so. Yet her every movement, thought and pursuit is the standard by which P_2 judges all her own.	P_2 does not think that she has any significance for the other schoolgirl while in contrast the other schoolgirl is of utmost significance and importance for P_2. P_2 uses the other schoolgirl as a measuring stick for judging her own worth and value.
3. They are both in the fifth grade in a little country school with six grades and only 62 students. They are not friends or enemies.	The context of the shared environment (school, grade 5) of the two girls is small but the actual relationship between them is neutral, neither friendly nor hostile.
4. She is part Cherokee, and it is the Native American blood in her that colors her straight, shiny hair black, skin light brown, and eyes as black as her hair. She looks different than all the others in the largely German-Scandinavian community.	P_2 describes the other schoolgirl as standing out in a positive way among all the other children because of her different ethnic background (Native American while the others are of Northern European heritage).
5. P_2 admires her differences, but it really bugs her that everyone else does too, to the degree that no one else seems to be special when she is around.	Although P_2 finds the way the other schoolgirl is different from all the others admirable, she is upset by the fact that everyone else feels the same way and this robs everyone else, including P_2, of the chance to be noticed and appreciated.

6. She doesn't even need to try to get attention. All she has to do is stand there and her appearance does it for her.	P₂ feels that the other schoolgirl's difference is an unfair advantage as it gives her a privileged position without any further requirements on the other schoolgirl's part.
7. P₂ knows it doesn't have anything to do with the fact that Pam is a good student, especially pretty, remarkably kind and naturally thoughtful. Even if she were a witch everyone would prefer her over others anyway, because they do even before she opens her mouth.	P₂ acknowledges that the other schoolgirl has a number of positive qualities both in her appearance and in her behavior, but P₂ feels that the other schoolgirl would still have this privileged position even if her behavior were negative and unpleasant. The other schoolgirl seems to be given this position simply based on her attractive and different appearance.
8. The worst moment in this secret jealousy is right now—at school pet day.	P₂'s unpleasant emotions in regard to the other schoolgirl are intensified when the school puts on a special event for all the children when they have a chance to bring something meaningful to them from home (pet) to show to all the others.
9. Among the assortment of yapping dogs, cats, tadpoles and hamsters, Pam's gleaming brown quarter horse literally and figuratively stands head and shoulders above the rest.	P₂ states that what most of the other children brought was normal, average, even unimpressive (cats, dogs, toads), but what the other schoolgirl brought stood out as very different and very impressive (a horse).

10. Being a country school, there are fields on all sides as well as a large pasture attached to the school for field days. Pam stands in one of these fields in front of her horse holding its reins while it is being saddled. P_2 is stunned. The entire school, with the exception of P_2, runs to stand near her, gazing at her without making any sound,

The shared environment easily accommodated what the other schoolgirl brought and the other schoolgirl occupies the space and the situation with ease. P_2 experiences disbelief as she witnesses everyone observing the other schoolgirl with awe and admiration.

11. "It just figures" P_2 whispers to herself. As if she didn't already have it all, she has to show up with a horse.

P_2 privately expresses resentment toward the other schoolgirl, feeling that the other schoolgirl is already in such a privileged position that her bringing something that stands out so far above what everyone else brought puts her intolerably above P_2 and the others.

12. P_2's parents had said no to one, even though P_2's parents owns barns, pastures, and her own grain supply.

P_2 reflects on the fact that she had wanted exactly what the other schoolgirl had brought but had been denied this by her parent although everything that was required to maintain it was ready at hand and available at her home.

13. P_2 takes her little dog to a bench and stays away from the "fan club" that surrounds her. How could life be so unfair?

P_2 states that she avoided the other schoolgirl and her display watched in admiration by all the others. P_2 moves away with her by comparison unimpressive showpiece and isolates

	herself from the others with the sense that the whole world is unfair.
14. P₂ tries not to look, but she is just like the rest. She can't help but watch.	Even though P₂ moved away to try to avoid the situation, she finds herself compelled, like the others, to watch it from her isolated position.
15. The scene is beautiful, with a turquoise blue sky curving overhead, wild flowers quivering in a cool breeze, and two beautiful spirits—each equally shiny black hair—standing quietly and patiently before us all. As soon as the horse is ready to ride, Pam slips into the saddle with a practiced lightness. She turns the horse with gentleness and skill and canters it in a wide circle around the field. Her hair and the horse's mane flutter in the rushing air. The throng of schoolmates that stood to watch her earlier now runs behind her waving wildflowers.	As P₂ watches, she sees a display of grace, skill and beauty and watches how all the others are following the other schoolgirl with eagerness and enthusiasm.
16. P₂ cannot stand it. Why can't that be her? It is all P₂ can do not to cry.	P₂ finds it intolerable and questions wishfully why she could not be in the place occupied by the otherschoolgirl. P₂ finds it difficult to contain her difficult feelings and has a difficult time suppressing an open display of her emotions.

BG's Structure for P_1 and P_2

Jealousy is experienced in a situation where P is not receiving sufficient attention and appreciation for herself and another person actively robs P of the already lacking attention and appreciation desired by P. Intense feelings of resentment and hostility toward the other is experienced when the other seems to take advantage of an unfair privileged position and uses this privilege to undermine P's position and P's possibility to attain the attention she seeks. P finds these negative strong emotions and physical responses uncomfortable and P intensely wishes to hide her responses from others.

Commentary on the Analyses

If we now compare the meaning units established by each researcher we can see that they are not all identical. There are some commonalities and some differences. This is to be expected, but the method is not judged on the basis of a partial step, but in terms of results. AG and BG differ with respect to the first meaning unit, but they come together in determining the second one. They agree again with the third one but disagree on the fourth. It is not necessary to make further comparisons because whether they are the same or different simply does not matter. Meaning unit comparisons are not a problem since this second step is a practical one and carries no theoretical weight. The meaning units simply help keep the focus on parts of the whole so that detailed analyses can take place. Ultimately what matters is how each meaning unit is transformed and contributes to the writing of the structure. The constitution of the meaning units simply makes the analysis more feasible because it is difficult to retain the whole description in mind while doing detailed analyses. This is not so apparent with the examples I have provided because they are short, but it becomes transparent when lengthy descriptions constitute the raw data. The reader will also note that AG used three columns in the analysis and BG only two, but that again is a practical difference and has no theoretical weight. It simply means that AG transformed more slowly than BG.

One should be aware that two possible errors could take place with respect to meaning units: Either they could be made too small or too large, but usually the process is self-correcting. If they are too small, the researcher usually finds that meaningful transformations cannot be written, so he or she begins combining two or three meaning units so that a meaningful transformation can be made. If the meaning units are too large, then the researcher finds that he or she might have to separate certain parts of the large meaning unit and make smaller ones because it is too rich or complex. Changing meaning units during the process of analysis is perfectly legitimate since the researcher is the one who made the original meaning units in the first place. We do not have to remain victims of our prior decisions.

In addition, certain syntheses can take place as one transforms meaning units several times, and that too is perfectly legitimate. If it takes several columns to achieve the optimal transformation the researcher may notice that several adjacent meaning units can be reduced to a single expression because a deeper partial unity is perceived. Then such a reduction should take place. This possibility usually happens with long descriptions and the brief descriptions provided above do not display an example of this move.

The second step requires the researcher to transform the original expressions by the participant into expressions that are more directly psychologically revealing as well as more generalized.

CIRCUMSCRIBING THE PSYCHOLOGICAL

It should be borne in mind that the method through the second step has not as yet changed anything the participant said except to put into third-person format any first-person expressions that the participant may have uttered. But we know that the description provided by the participant was given in the natural attitude and from an everyday perspective. The analysis, however, takes place from within a phenomenological psychological (scientific) reduction with a psychological perspective and with a special sensitivity to the phenomenon being researched — jealousy. Since I am applying a psychological perspective to a lifeworld description, one could say that I am making a psychological interpretation of a lifeworld event. That would be true, but I am doing so by means of a descriptive method.

With this procedure, what comes to intuitive givenness to the researcher is something quite other than what the participant was aware of while providing the description. The participant recounts the living of the situation as she experienced it, but the researcher focuses on *how* the participant lived in the situation by highlighting the relationship between the participant and the worldly circumstances. The focus of consciousness is different in the two cases. In other words, the participant focuses on the situation as lived from her perspective, the researcher focuses on what the participant was aware of and actually lived unawarefully to the extent that such factors reveal themselves. Descriptions reveal more than what the describer is aware of, and that is one reason the method works.

To say that the participant's description was in the natural attitude is to say that there is no critical reflection upon how the experience of the phenomenon is unfolding. It is taken for granted that a person can somehow reflectively describe what she is living through (or has recently lived through). What is being said is not thematically analyzed by the participant with respect to its mode; the focus is usually on what happened and what that was like. When the participant's attitude is described as "everyday," it means that the participant is speaking from a basic commonsense perspective. She is talking the way she might tell a friend what happened. The social and cultural norms are observed and the assumption is that everything that is uttered or described is being understood by the listener in an everyday way.

When the researcher assumes a researcher's attitude in order to analyze the data, the same material is viewed in a different light. To assume the phenomenological attitude means to enter into the scientific phenomenological reduction, which means that all of the objects, persons, and states of affairs that the participant describes are taken to be phenomenal givens, that is, they are seen as subjectively construed givens, fully embedded within the subjective desires and interpretations within which the subject perceived and understood them. It is not claimed that the givens existed in actuality the way that they presented themselves to the describer, but what is noted is how they appeared to be for the consciousness of the participant. The consciousness of the participant is considered to be an individuated, worldly consciousness, and the meanings bestowed on the presences are meant to reflect her personal, worldly subjectivity. Obviously, this means that the scientific phenomenological reduction is a mixed reduction wherein the objects that are presented to the subject are taken to be phenomena, that is, presences, but the consciousness to which the presences are given is taken to be a worldly, individuated, personal one. The psychological is transcended at the level of transcendental consciousness.

To assume a psychological perspective toward the data implies a certain kind of delimitation. The researcher is not interested equally in all of the data (although it is all reviewed and analyzed), but mostly in those aspects that have the potentiality of revealing the psychological meanings contained in the data. Thus, the researcher has to be especially sensitive to the meaning units where psychological richness exists. The method demands that this step be something "lived" rather than intellectualized. From within the psychological attitude one allows one's felt sensitivity to direct one to the aspects of the meaning units that seem to be especially revealing in a psychological sense. However, the revealing meaning units stand out against all of the other units, so that is why all of the meaning units have to be covered and all of them have to plumbed for their psychological sense. Obviously, the psychological sense then has to be articulated. It is not enough to merely point to the relevant meaning unit, or to express the sense vaguely, or even to leave it in the participant's own words. The most precise articulation of the psychological sense has to be made. Again, every meaning unit has to be interrogated but not all meaning units are equal, psychologically speaking. Some are very rich and may require several transformations to be done correctly. Some can be quite impoverished psychologically and the best that can be done is to note their role in the description. Consequently, the number of transformations per meaning unit can vary.

Now, a problematic issue announces itself here. What does it mean to assume a psychological perspective? It is well known that the precise meaning of psychology is not yet a historical achievement. Psychology is fragmented into several theoretical perspectives—behavioristic, cognitive, psychoanalytic, and so on—and as a consequence there is no unified perspective that is accepted by the majority of psychologists. So what is to be done?

I can only answer on the basis of a phenomenological perspective, but before I do, I would like to point out that, in general, this answer is lived in practice more frequently than it is theoretically. A good example of this common understanding is the practice of therapy. Except for the case of strict theoretical practitioners, such as Freudian psychoanalysts or strict behavior therapists, where theoretical perspectives dominate, most practitioners adopt an eclectic theoretical attitude with respect to their practice. They recognize common psychological characteristics or pathologies prior to any theoretical interpretation of them. This is the kind of lived response that we expect phenomenological psychological researchers to make, except of course, from a purely psychological perspective rather than a clinical psychological perspective. Also, I am not advocating eclecticism, which uses concepts from varied theories without worrying about consistency, but rather a generic understanding of the psychological independent of all theorizing. The clarification of the meaning of the psychological is subsequent to its discrimination. One has the felt sense that a certain meaning unit is pregnant with psychological possibilities, and as the analysis progresses one tries to articulate its precise sense. It is more a matter of clarifying the sense from a psychological perspective than of using established psychological concepts. But a possible outcome is that such an articulated sense might not be forthcoming, which means that the detected promise perceived to be present was perhaps a false one. So the analysis contains a type of critical self-correction, for ultimately it is the fully articulated sense that matters, not its promise.

It has to be emphasized that what is required for psychological clarification of sense is a careful description of the sense that presents itself to the researcher, not a mere labeling of it. In general, most established mainstream psychological terminology is to be avoided because most of it is theory-laden. The attitude assumed by the researcher helps to determine the sense that will emerge, and the attitude includes being in the scientific reduction, a descriptive perspective and the use of imaginative variation. The final description of the psychological sense usually consists of ordinary words conjoined in such a way that the psychological sense of the experience is heightened. A full, careful description is what enables the psychological sense to stand out.

Now, from a phenomenological perspective, psychological subject matter follows the path of the intentionality of subjectivity. Husserl discussed intentionality initially within the context of mental processes but later, when he discovered that the body also partook of consciousness, intentionality was extended to the body. Consequently, we can use the term "subjectivity" to encompass mind and body as the basic source of intentionality. Husserl states, "Under intentionality we understand the own peculiarity of mental processes to be consciousness of something" (1983, 200). In effect, intentionality refers to the fact that a large group of acts of human subjectivity are directed toward objects or situations in the world. This being directed to other than itself on the part of subjectivity is what intentionality means, although reflectively, subjectivity can make aspects of itself an object of such directed activity. However, what is constant is that the object of an intentional act always transcends the act in which it appears. The intentional relation is the basis of meaning and so phenomenological psychological analyses seek a type of meaning as the basis for understanding psychological reality. This is in contrast to natural scientific psychology, which interprets psychological reality in terms of cause-effect relations.

We say that psychological meaning is a "type of meaning" because for Husserl the bestowal of meaning by an intentional act produces a content that is irreal and so would transcend the naturalistic perspective of traditional psychology. For Husserl, meanings as ideal beings require a different perspective to be properly apprehended. In addition to the sensory stuff that every perception of a physical object provides, which Husserl calls "hyletic data," there is also an ideal component to every perception that Husserl calls the "noema," or the sense of the perceptual act, and "it is to be taken *precisely* as it inheres immanently in the mental process of perceiving" (1983, 214). The noema refers to the object as meant and intended; "*the perceived as perceived*" (214), and so it always refers to the "object-side" of the act-object relationship. Husserl calls the characteristic of the act that is correlated with the noema the "noesis." Natural scientific psychology tries to reconstruct the percept by tracing the energy emitted from the object through the appropriate sensory organ and through nervous connections to the brain, and then the stimulation of the brain somehow produces the percept. How this is done has not yet been fully explained. In this view, while the organism is surely understood to be alive and the nervous system active, overall the initiative comes from the energy emitted from the physical object and the organism is mostly passive. Sometimes it is acknowledged that the mind somehow intervenes and helps organize the data (see, for example, Rock 1984), but the explanation of how this is done is also lacking. The concept of meaning does not play a role in the natural scientific explanation of perception.

While I cannot here go into a full description of Husserl's phenomenological theory of perception, I do want to indicate how it is counter to the psychological approach briefly sketched above. First of all, Husserl (1983) considers perception strictly from the perspective of subjectivity. Moreover, as McKenna (1989) points out, the idea of perception in Husserl is much broader than what is found in psychology. For Husserl, perception is not limited to physical objects and entities with sensory inputs. Anything that is given originarily, according to its proper mode of being, is called perception. Thus, thoughts and ideas can be perceived even though they do not present themselves in a sensory way. The clarification of a perceptual experience comes by means of an analysis of its meaning.

From the subjective perspective, consciousness constitutes its perceived objects, and it is capable of constituting them objectively; the constitution of an object includes a perceptual sense. The perceptual sense is conceived to be ideal, and as such transcends the cause-effect relationship of the naturalistic perspective. The theory holds that the sense is constituted by the processes of consciousness. The sense, or noema, is that which is common to a series of different appearances of the same object. In phenomenology constitution is not creative, but it simply means allowing an object to be what it is. Constitution is the "bringing about of manifestation (of phenomena) *that we explore by way of the reduction*" (Overgaard 2004, 60).

The reason that this theory is problematic psychologically is because from a Husserlian perspective, which I adopt, the noema is an ideal, universal sense that transcends psychological reality. It is not the noema as universal sense that I am seeking, but the psychological meaning. Merleau-Ponty saw this problem in an acute way when he wrote,

> Is it not true that an eidetic psychology, reflectively determining the basic categories of psychic life by reflecting on my experience of myself and the other, reduces psychology, in the narrower sense, to a very restricted role? Is it not, then, limited to a mere study of details? ... If one clings to formulae of this kind, everything essential seems to be furnished by phenomenology, or philosophic insight. Nothing more is left to psychology than to study certain empirical curiosities within the frames furnished by phenomenology. (1964b, 65–66)

In other words, if all meanings transcend the psychological realm, does it not make the very expression "psychological meaning" an oxymoron? Can there be a place for the expression "psychological meaning"? I believe that there is and that Merleau-Ponty in raising this point wanted to make room for a psychology that could investigate meanings.

But before trying to resolve this issue, we have to acknowledge that there are some ambiguities in trying to circumscribe and understand the domain of psychology. For phenomenological philosophers, psychology refers to an individuated, worldly experience of a single person. The individual exists in space and time and is under the influence of causal interactions. However, phenomenological philosophy also sees consciousness as other than naturalistic and its intentional activity bestows meanings on the objects of the world. The meanings are considered to be ideal and they transcend naturalistic interactions.

Mainstream psychologists, in contrast, see consciousness, experience, and behavior as either extensions of the naturalistic view or as concomitants of the naturalistic process (isomorphism). The sense that consciousness is individuated is taken for granted. Psychology studies the behaving and experiencing individual in relation to the world. Since the human is related to the world and a natural science perspective is adopted, the naturalistic concepts developed by natural scientists are frequently used by psychologists to help explain human behavior and experience. In general, the cause is assumed to be on the side of the world and the effect shows itself in experience and/or behavior. However, not all psychologists deny causality to consciousness or experience but explanations in terms of causes still prevail.

There seems to be considerable tension, if not a complete break, between mainstream psychology and philosophical phenomenology when consciousness is considered. Mainstream psychology is naturalistic in its approach and it wants to explain all human action from that perspective. Phenomenological philosophy insists that there is a difference between consciousness and that which manifests itself to consciousness (Husserl 1983, 89–92) and it takes the side of consciousness in order to render phenomena intelligible. Yet, phenomenological philosophy admits that there can be a legitimate naturalistic psychology, only it does not believe that it could comprehend the full range of phenomena that psychology would be interested in understanding. Moreover, phenomenological philosophy acknowledges that there should be a phenomenological psychology that would have different assumptions about psychological phenomena and that would be practiced in a different way. Can these two approaches be integrated or must we admit that two distinct psychologies are necessary?

There are times when I believe that Husserl gives over too much of psychological reality to the naturalistic and objective perspective. However, there are also texts in which Husserl (1989) talks about other insights that I think can help us get a better sense of the realm of the psychological. For example, he speaks about the personal attitude and contrasts it with the naturalistic one, but he does not speak to the issue of whether the phenomena treated naturalistically by mainstream psychology can also be approached phenomenologically but prepersonally. One needs merely to acknowledge the idea of an anonymous subjectivity in order to achieve that goal. However, the discrimination and identification of psychological phenomena is a huge issue that cannot be taken on fully here, but a certain aspect of the problem needs to be discussed in order to understand what the method is trying to accomplish. Husserl makes two distinctions that I believe can help us understand the psychological realm in a better way: We must distinguish between naturalistic and world-related and between objectivating acts and acts that access subjectivity precisely as subjective.

For Husserl, the real is that which is in space-time and is regulated by causality. Perception of a physical object is an example of the perception of something real. However, from a holistic perspective, the causal influences involved in perception are exhausted before the perceptual act is fully lived out and completes itself in the perception of the object. That is, intentional activity is triggered before the perceptual act is completed. And since it is the transcendent object itself, in "person," that is reached in perception, then it is indeed the world that is reached. Thus, consciousness relates to worldliness and in such a way that purely naturalistic factors are transcended. Subjectivity is engaged in world-relatedness in nonnaturalistic ways even if triggered by natural causes at times, and some of those nonnaturalistic relations belong to the psychological realm. Worldliness has to be understood here as the ultimate horizon of experience, the context within which all entities and persons are met. In this sense, what stands out as relevant for consciousness psychologically speaking is subjectively determined and thus basically on the side of subjectivity's intentional acts. What stands out psychologically is a sense that is determined by the interests, motivations, and desires of the subject. In other words, psychological meanings are " individual subject dependent." Husserl's noema is ideal and entails rational involvement that transcends the dependency on individual subjectivity. The point here is that there are prepersonal, subjectively constituted meanings that are of interest to psychology and can be properly understood within the context of subject-world relations without being naturalistic.

With respect to nonobjective apprehensions, in philosophy there is a long debate concerning reflection and the status of the reflected-upon. Zahavi (2005) has covered this debate to some extent and we need not enter into it here. His conclusion, from a phenomenological perspective, is what interests us. In dealing with the question as to whether the "reflected-upon" must be an object, Zahavi, following Husserl's leads, writes:

> The obvious way to dismantle the dilemma is to concede that we are aware of our own experiences in an immediate, pre-reflective, and non-objectifying manner. If we are to avoid an infinite regress, this primitive, pre-reflective self-awareness cannot be a result of a secondary act or reflex, but must be a constitutive aspect of experience itself. Prior to reflection, experiential states do present themselves, but not as objects. Metaphorically speaking, experiential states are characterized by a certain self-luminosity; they are self-intimating or selfpresenting.... Thus, the first-personal givenness of experience should not be taken as the result of a higher-order representation, reflection, internal monitoring, or introspection, but rather should be treated as an *intrinsic feature* of experience. (61)

Objectivating acts relate to certain kinds of presences, but not necessarily to all of them. For example, in person perception, it is quite possible to be aware of the subjectivity of the other without necessarily reifying the other. Thus, one may perceive that the other is disturbed or upset, even if the reason for that emotional state is not present. To perceive the "disturbed state" of the other implies a certain sensitivity to the other's subjective disposition. This means that the other, as a person in the world, can allow his subjective disposition to be revealed without its being reified. From (1971) has researched these types of perceptions with a descriptive method and clearly demonstrates that in everyday life the subjectivity of the other is perceivable, although it does depend upon the assumption of the correct attitude.

With respect to one's own subjective acts, there are types of awareness that can capture such acts in their subjective activity so that they are understood in the manner in which they are lived. They do not have to be distorted and become objects of a reflective act, although that could occur too. But in such cases, the latter result is something to be avoided. In any case, that is the privileged type of act, but not the only one, required by the researcher who wishes to apply the method being described in this book. One assumes the attitude of the scientific reduction and the attitude of heightened psychological sensitivity. Neither the transcendental philosophical phenomenological perspective nor the naturalistic perspective of mainstream psychology is the correct perspective for understanding humans in the world in a psychological way when using this method. In developing this type of psychology we believe that we are more faithful to discovering what it is like to experience different aspects of the world. In order to develop it we have chosen to come down from the philosophical phenomenological perspective than to try to correct the approach of naturalistic psychology because of its limiting assumptions.

Consequently, to circumscribe psychological reality one has to access the subjective acts addressed to objects or situations in the world on the part of individual persons (we restrict ourselves here to human psychological reality) and to determine their psychological meanings. What differentiates psychological meanings from the universal, ideal meanings that phenomenological philosophy investigates is the fact that they are constituted by an individual subjectivity that is influenced by the world and others. Husserl has written that psychological subjectivity is the self-constitution of transcendental subjectivity. But even though constituted, psychological subjectivity is still capable of constituting phenomena but at a different level and in a more contingent way. Phenomenal meanings participate in an individual subjectivity's space, time, body, and world.

Specifically, psychological meanings can be differentiated from the ideal noematic meanings that Husserl articulates by beginning with the concrete details of a description and with the proper phenomenological psychological attitude, intuiting the role that the concrete details played in the constitution of the psychological meaning and then articulating that meaning as precisely as possible. The participant may not have lived the situation fully aware and precisely the way the research psychologist articulates it, but the meaning that the psychologist articulates is a way of understanding the participant's lived experience from a psychological perspective. Of course, the psychologist also has to transcend the concrete details, but not in the same way that the phenomenological philosopher does. The psychologist has to come up with the psychological meaning of the details, which is a type of invariance that is different from the philosophical essence. To do a psychological analysis means to understand the phenomenal organization that an individual lives through in a situation, especially when the subjectivity of the experiencer dominates the situation so that, as a result, certain contingent meanings begin to color a basic situation.

For example, in the first jealousy description the basic situation is whether to have lunch together or not. P_1's new friend decides to join the others and has no knowledge of P_1's hurt feelings and her strong desire to have him stay with her. These are contingent meanings added to the basic situation by P_1's subjective desires. They are not essential to the objective situation of having lunch together or alone but they are essential from a psychological perspective because her feelings change the very meaning of having lunch alone. Thus, to grasp a psychological meaning accurately one has to maintain a nonobjective presence to the living subjectivity that is bestowing contingent meanings on a situation. These meanings can only be properly understood as being dependent upon the subjective perspective of the experiencer, and that requires a different mode of being present.

Perhaps the difference between the psychological invariance and the philosophical noema can be demonstrated another way. The classic way in which phenomenological philosophers distinguish between the intentional object and its meaning is to cite "Napoleon, the victor at Jena" and "Napoleon, the vanquished at Waterloo." The object in both cases is the same, but the meaning is radically different. The psychological invariance does not cancel the philosophical meanings in any way but rather speaks about them in a more embedded or typical way because the particularities of the subjectivity have to be taken into account. For example, it might relate the victory to an ingenious strategy that Napoleon employed based upon his particular perception of the enemy's weakness. Similarly, the defeat at Waterloo may have been due to a certain assumption that Napoleon brought to the battle based upon certain past victories, but Napoleon did not perceive that the situation at Waterloo was not identical to the circumstances that produced his victory. Thus, certain details about *what* was perceived, given certain *motives* concerning *how* to proceed, become explicit and get generalized to produce the psychological invariant understanding.

Perhaps examples from my own data would be helpful. Examining the data from P_1, one might say that it certainly is at least a partial truth about a type of jealousy that a person desires for herself positive feelings that are going toward another or others. One could say that such an expression captures at least an essential constituent of jealousy, if not the very essence of it, because it expresses both the idea that one desires to be a center of attention that is not forthcoming as well as the idea that another is receiving the attention that one desires for oneself. This would be a philosophical level of understanding jealousy. There is nothing in that statement that is explicitly psychologically interesting, or at least the psychological implications would have to be worked out and elaborated. However, instead of elaborating the psychological implications speculatively, one could turn to the concrete data and intuit what is psychologically relevant because what needs to be said is contained therein.

Let's look at the examples. P_1 desired to have an exclusive lunch with her new friend, but since he had no food with him, he decided not to stay with P_1 and joined the others. P_1's friend followed a rational course of action, but P_1's expectation was that he should choose an irrational option and remain with her even though there was no food for lunch. (Perhaps P_1 did not think of sharing her food because she herself only had a snack, or perhaps she thought it might be too forward to make such a suggestion.) In any case, her friend took a perfectly rational option, yet P_1 felt a certain loss, a lack of something desired. In addition, she felt hurt, which is a certain intensification of the loss. Then P_1 acknowledges feeling silly about her hurt feeling. The silly feeling is a reaction to her hurt feelings, which perhaps reflects P_1's awareness that for her desire to be fulfilled her friend would have had to act somewhat unconventionally, if not irrationally. Or perhaps the silly feeling reflected her awareness that the other, after all, was only a newfound friend and not an intimate friend. The silliness was perhaps a glimpse of how she would appear before others if others were aware of her exaggerated desires. Psychologically speaking, it also seemed to be critical that the exaggerated desires remained a secret. Presumably, no one else was aware of the intense feelings taking place within P_1. Then, when the other woman thrust herself into the very position that P_1 desired, the situation was exacerbated and then feelings of aggressiveness and hostility emerged within P_1, even though she believed that she was able to disguise them.

Let us now turn to P_2. The description begins with an implied history that indicates that everyone is aware of and admires Pam, including P_2, but she is aware that the positive feelings are not reciprocated by Pam to P_2. P_2 is also aware, or at least it is her perception, that all of her classmates admire Pam, not just P_2. P_2 also acknowledges that her admiration for Pam, and her envy of her, are secret. Perhaps that is why she is standoffish and refuses to join the crowd of peers when they admire Pam. She seems to be caught in a conflict of feelings, genuinely admiring Pam and at the same time not wanting to show it in front of others and also not wanting to show any negativity before others. P_2 attributes a large part of the admiration for Pam to physical characteristics, and P_2 implies that she wished that she could stand out physically the way that Pam does. Of course, this too exhibits an irrational desire. One cannot radically, nor easily, change one's physical characteristics. One can perhaps enhance them, or modify them somewhat, but one cannot radically change skin color or height. Then the whole situation gets exacerbated when Pam brings a horse to pet day and handles the horse expertly. P_2 perceives that all of her classmates rally around Pam but P_2 remains aloof and is filled with intense feelings of loss and of diminishment. She then hates herself for feeling that way. Just as with P_1, a reaction to her feelings of loss breaks into P_2's awareness. She too desired to have a horse, but her parent denied her desire, so P_2 gazes longingly at Pam for all of her gifts and possessions. Yet, all of these turbulent feelings remain secret with Pam.

It takes some hard work to arrive at a typical psychological invariance of the experience of jealousy. The precise structure is given above, but I only want to contrast the philosophical essence with the psychological invariant. Philosophically, jealousy, based on the two descriptions given here, manifests itself when a person desires for herself positive feelings that are going toward another. However, psychologically, one has to be more longwinded and say, "When someone desires for herself positive feelings that are going to another, there is an experience of a lack or loss in oneself, and such an experience evokes in the person feelings that are self-critical and she entertains desires that are exaggerated or irrational, and yet all of these mixed feelings remain hidden within the person. The initial situation can be exacerbated in various ways and this fact intensifies and complicates the feelings that were initially present."

The description of the psychological invariance tries to articulate and render visible the peculiar quality of the relationships among the subject, others, and the situation that constitute experiential phenomena of a certain type. The invariance is not as specific as the details of the original description, but neither is it universal. It is a generalization of the middle range, an eidetic type. It is eidetic because imaginative variation is used, and certain possibilities are considered, but the psychological focus keeps it from being universal. Perhaps it can best be understood phenomenologically by referring to the noema-object structure, or perhaps better, using Merleau-Ponty's profile-object terminology. Merleau-Ponty (1963) argued that the profile-object structure was still opaque and needed to be clarified further. But it is at least clear enough to support the kind of analysis that we just conducted. The psychological invariance includes much more of the profile than the philosophical essence because one is tapping into the details of a worldly subjectivity. As noted above, Napoleon a "victor" and Napoleon as "vanquished" reduces the profile to its ultimate outcome. The psychological invariance has to include what is essential to the process as well as the outcome. This requires careful consideration of the concrete, detailed data. One has to go *through* the concrete details in order to arrive at what is general and not bypass the details by assuming an abstract attitude. The profile represents the subjective, phenomenal organization through which the object is apprehended and knowledge of that is essential for psychological understanding.

In addition, since the analysis takes place within the scientific phenomenological reduction, the concrete descriptions provided by the research participants contain many phenomenal clues that indicate the nature of the acts that the participants engaged in. Moreover, perceived as phenomena, the objects being described can be understood to be "para-objective." Psychological reality is not what is objectively true, but rather is a type of falling away from truth, objectivity, rationality, or even normative experiences. In order for truth or objectivity to be achieved, the constitutive activity has to be such that the interests of psychological subjectivity are effaced or transcended so that the object or situation can manifest itself as it is. But when psychological interests dominate, which is a type of phenomenal or subjectively dominated organization, the intentional experiences reflect the perspective of individual subjectivity rather than a high-level truth or the objective state of affairs. Individual intentions dominate rather than become effaced. Thus, the discovery of the noematic correlate with its concrete context as constituted by individual subjectivity becomes the goal of the researcher. This reveals the psychological world of an individuated, situated subjectivity because those subjective intentions dominate the transaction. It is, in some sense, the triumph of subjectivity, but a limited, world-centered subjectivity. Thus, psychology is the study of the individuated, subjectively construed meanings imposed on situations in the world.

Eidetic Generalization

The second type of transformation that is required of the meaning units is that they be expressed eidetically with the help of imaginative variation. Husserl states that we empirically encounter individual things all the time. That is how objects in the world are given to us. However, Husserl also affirms that by a mere shift of attitude we can intuit any number of categories that belong to the individual empirical object. For example, suppose that I perceive the chair that is in my room. It shows itself to be full of details. It has wooden arms and legs and a green colored leather seat and back. Husserl's point is that it has a horizon of possible categories that could be intuited to fulfill specific purposes. I might say that a chair is a piece of furniture if I am speaking to a man who moves furniture for a living. I could also say that it is a material object if I want to give an example of a material object in class. Both "furniture" and "material object" are categories that belong to "chairness" just as much as the physical characteristics of woodenness or the color green.

Thus, while an eidetic form of expression has to be formulated, for psychological purposes it cannot be at the highest level of abstraction (or universal) because such a high level of abstraction transcends psychological interests. Using the chair example above, to say that a chair is a material object loses all sense of its function for human experience. To say that a chair is a piece of furniture at least provides some sense of its human usefulness. Basically, what is called for here is a generalization that takes place in what sociologists have called the "middle range." In part this is necessary because psychological reality is spatio-temporally limited and is highly influenced by the specific sociocultural context within which the individual experiences his or her situation. Finally, the contents of experience are very important for understanding psychological reality, and the essentialization of contents (morphological essences) is much more limited than formal essences. Consequently, general claims are made for such psychological analyses because universal claims would require the analysis of too many varied contexts.

The achievement of such an eidetic typology is a bit tricky. We want to claim that imaginative variation is employed so that an eidos is obtained, but we also want to claim that the eidos is a type rather than a universal category. Its scope is much more limited, yet it is also not an empirical generalization. An empirical generalization refers to a category arrived at based upon the number of cases on hand, but an eidos is a generalization that sets the boundaries for possible instances of occurrences because possibilities are considered. However, unlike in philosophy, in psychology the boundaries are set by a type of the phenomenon and not its universal characteristics. The idea of a generalized type is further reinforced by the awareness that, since we are dealing with experiential contents, the essence is a morphological one. For Husserl (1983), morphological essences are in principle inexact. Formal essences, like squares, circles, rectangles, and the like, are exact *eide* because they are empty of content.

Having articulated to some extent the sense of the psychological that is guiding us and the type of generalization we are seeking, let me provide a few examples. If we look at AG's analysis of P_2 and select MU 11, we see that he described the scene that increased P_2's sense of jealousy as a "spectacle," especially since all of the other children were gathering around the ideal person. Thus, the specific details that it involved a pretty young girl with a horse are not required, but the fact that the girl and the horse comprised a "spectacle" and were phenomenally the center of attraction that did not include P_2 is both an eidetic generalization and a more psychological way of understanding the concrete situation that led to the experience of jealousy. Or if we look at MU 6 in AG's analysis of P_1, we no longer know the specific details, but we know that P_1 felt devastated because she was not the one her friend chose to be with, despite the fact that it made good sense for him not to choose to be with her, and we know that she experienced the disproportion between her strong emotional reaction and the objective circumstances to which she was reacting. Thus, eidetic generalizations do not distort the psychological relationships but they express the lived relationships in a more psychological way, which in turn heightens the researcher's grasp of what is taking place psychologically.

It should be noted that we are interested in the structure of the phenomenon as such, regardless of who the individuals are. This is a nomothetic result, not an idiographic one. Obviously, individual experiencers are required in order for the phenomenon to exist, but results that are idiosyncratic are not taken up as such but are generalized so that the general patterns of the phenomenon are understood. That is why I never recommend that only a single subject be used unless one is doing idiographic research. The research then centers only on how a particular individual experiences a phenomenon. One reason is that the distinction between what belongs to the individual and what belongs to the phenomenon as such is difficult to make with only one subject. It places too heavy a burden on the imagination. Hence, Edwards (1991) is wrong when he tries to categorize this method as a case study method because the goal is not the experience of a particular individual, which is how Edwards defines the case study method when he writes "in CSRM (case study research method) attention is focused on a single case which is examined in depth" (54). Even though Yin (2004, xv) allows for "multiple case studies," that is, the use of more than one case to count as examples of the case study method, the goals of the two methods are not the same because in the psychological phenomenological method the researcher abstracts from the individual and concentrates on the phenomenon. Also, multiple methods are never used in phenomenological studies and they are typical with case study methods. Edwards (1991) confuses depth research strategies with types of methods.[1]

In phenomenological research, depending upon the amount of raw data collected, at least three subjects are always required because it is important to have variations in the raw data. There is a trade-off between the amount of data collected per subject and the number of subjects required. The greater the amount of data obtained from each subject, the fewer the number of subjects required, but there should always be at least three. In any case, it is the structure of the phenomenon that we are seeking, not the individualized experience of the phenomenon.

In addition, it can be argued that what has to be counted is not the number of subjects but the number of instances of the phenomenon that are contained in the descriptions. Numerous varied aspects of the phenomenon are detailed in concrete descriptions. Research based upon depth strategies should not be confused with research based upon sampling strategies. The criteria in the two cases are different, but this is not the place to go into that discussion. But it should be realized that the method is very much a labor intensive one and so depth research strategies have to be adopted.

The Structure of the Experience

At the end of the third step one has a series of transformed meaning units. These form the basis for the writing of the structure. For this last step, the researcher once again has to use imaginative variation in order to try to determine the most invariant constituents of the experience. An important criterion in this process is whether the structure would collapse if a potential constituent were removed. If it does, the constituent is essential; if the structure does not collapse, then the constituent is not essential. Again, it must be remembered that this process requires the use of the imagination. The attainment of the structure is not based on facts alone, but also on eidetic intuitions.

It also has to be kept in mind that the constituents to be determined may be expressed in words quite different from the words used in expressing the separate meaning units as indeed the structure usually is. The context for formulating the transformation of the meaning units is narrower than that employed for the structure as a whole. In addition, the expression of the essential constituents requires a more global perspective because one has to take into account the other constituents since a structure is the relationship among the constituents. Consequently, another order of description is required here.

The description of the structure is also based upon a careful description of the intentional objects that are deemed to be essential for the structure. It is a second order description (the first description being the raw data provided by the participants) that highlights the psychological understanding of the lifeworld phenomenon. Every lifeworld description will be richer than the psychological structure derived from it, in part because the psychological structure is a consequence of a perspective more narrow than the lifeworld perspective that produced the raw data. A deeper appreciation of the psychological reality is gained, but the price paid is that anything that is not psychologically relevant is left out. An analysis such as this can never grasp the totality of the original experience and such limits have to be respected when it comes to interpreting the results of the study.

The description of the structure is not the final step of the research process. The structure should provide a deeper insight into the unified dynamics taking place across varied experiences, and it serves as the basis of essential communication. But with the insights provided by the structure one can return to the raw data and make better sense of the variations contained therein. One can also give examples of the essential insights and help flesh out the sometimes more abstract points contained within the structure.

The structure of the experience is a way of understanding the unity of the concrete data. It is a way of understanding why diverse facts and concrete details can belong to the same phenomenon. It is something like a measure of central tendency in statistics. The structure is the identification of the constituents that are essential for the phenomenon to manifest itself in this particular way as well as an understanding of how the constituents relate to each other. As Sokolowski (1974, 75) states, the essential structures are not metaphysical statements about things or real events but refer to phenomenal givens: how things appear.

Structures are obtained by examining the last column of transformed meaning units, and with the help of imaginative variation, determining which ones are truly essential for the phenomenon to present itself to a consciousness. One should be careful here not to be too empirical as one reviews the transformed meaning units. The transformations of meaning units were determined by examining parts of the description; the structure has to be mindful of the whole. Consequently, the description of the structure itself could be quite different from the way that the meaning units themselves were described. It is not a matter of simply listing the meaning units together but of bringing a holistic perspective to them and imaginatively trying to determine the key constituents of the structure as well as trying to remove the key ones in order to see if the phenomenon stands or collapses.

Two structures were given above when we presented the analyses of our examples of jealousy, one by AG and one by BG. We deliberately chose to present two findings because colleagues often wonder if it is possible to get agreement among different researchers. Both AG and BG are experienced users of the method and they worked independently in order to come up with appropriate structures. First, both agreed that both concrete descriptions of jealousy could be described by a single structure. That is, the concrete details and empirical variations that the original descriptions provided, from a psychological perspective, were not essentially different. In other words, both researchers agreed that from a psychological perspective the variations contained within the two descriptions could be considered intrastructural.

AG's and BG's structures (reproduced on pages 167 and 179) are essentially identical even though different words are used and different dimensions of the experience are emphasized. This leads us to the first point that we want to establish about descriptive phenomenological findings: there will always be a one-to-many relationship between the intuited meaning and the words used to articulate it. That is, an identical meaning can be expressed in multiple ways and cannot be reduced to only one expression except by convention or agreement. What matters is the meaning and not the words used to express it. Thus, the situation is very different from mathematics, where univocity is the norm. Of course, there are boundaries or limits to the expression selected because not any statement will convey the correct meaning, but it is more like an acceptable range of expressions will meet the requirement. So, saying "Don't shut the door" or "Leave the door open" are both correct if indeed one intends that the door should remain open, but saying, "The door has a window" would clearly not convey the same meaning.

So what are some of the linguistic differences between the two structures? AG stresses the fact that P discovers a strong desire to be the center of attention of another(s) and BG stresses that P is not receiving sufficient attention and appreciation for herself. Actually, these are opposite expressions referring to the same meaning: P is experiencing a lack of attention centering on her. Both add the important fact that another is receiving the very attention that P desires. This leads to the second point that I want to make about phenomenological structures: they are syntheses or "central tendencies," but they are not the last word regarding the findings of the research project. After the structure has been obtained, it is then applied to the empirical data in order to highlight the findings and draw out implications. The structure cannot present all of the data any more than a mean can present all of the numbers upon which it is based. It would no longer be an essential description. Rather, the structure is pregnant with implications that have to be spoken to just as a fact is surrounded by a horizon of possibilities, and in phenomenology both implications and possibilities contribute to the clarification of meaning.

One complicating factor is that P_1's description explicitly details two phases of jealousy. The first was when the man she was interested in chose to go to lunch with the other members of the group and not stay with her. It heightened when she heard that the other woman began to zero in on her friend, and when she observed some of that behavior herself. When that happened, P_1's description begins to resemble that of P_2. I believe that for P_2 there was also a first phase because P_2 does imply some of that history, but her description is focused on the second phase. But the very first meaning unit in P_2's description shows that P_2 was very much aware of Pam's existence and MU 3 details how Pam stands out in her group, and to stand out in such a way means psychologically that she is noticed. Rendering explicit the possibilities of the horizons of the experiences shows how both descriptions contain a phase of lack of centering, and then a phase where the attention turned onto another person exacerbates the first phase. Both researchers picked up both of these aspects of the experience.

Both structures also were in agreement concerning three other critical points: first, that negative, angry, and hostile feelings were aroused in the one who experienced jealousy (for P_1 the feelings were directed toward the woman who expressed romantic interest in her friend, and for P_2 they were aimed toward the person who was receiving the attention); second, for each P the negative feelings toward the other person aroused in each of them uncomfortable or negative feelings toward themselves; and third, the experiencers of jealousy hid their feelings from others. All three of these points are important constituents for the experience of jealousy as lived by these participants understood psychologically.

One apparent difference between AG and BG is that AG seems to emphasize the diminished sense of self that accompanies the experiencer of jealousy, whereas BG does not. However, BG does say in her structure that "P is not receiving sufficient attention and appreciation for herself" and this clearly implies that P feels that she is deserving of more attention than she is receiving and that feeling implies a certain sense of loss. Again, the same meaning is noticed but is expressed in different words.

The last apparent difference is that AG explicitly mentions the role of rationality and irrationality, whereas BG does not. Again, however, it is there by implication and implications are important for structures because their intent is to reduce data. If every empirical fact had to be mentioned the result would be a summary and not a structure. So, when BG writes that "another person actually robs P of the already lacking attention" and that "the other seems to take advantage of an unfair privileged position," both expressions contain elements of irrational perceptions or thinking. In whose eyes does the so-called privileged position exist, and who is the one who experiences "attention" being taken away from her? No, these are perceptions or thoughts infused with the subjective desires of the perceiver and express interpretations that are beyond what the facts would allow. It is imaginable that in jealousy perceptions could be in line with the objective facts, but in this case they are not. This experience belongs in the phenomenal realm.

The last few paragraphs represent the type of analyses that more properly belong in the discussion section of a research report, although the direct comparison between two researchers is really an example of a dialogue concerning the replication of a study. That particular discussion would not normally appear in the discussion section of a research report, but a similar discussion could take place if one of the two studies had already been published. It would then become an example of dialoguing with the literature.

While I believe that the two structures are essentially the same, it would not have been a disaster if they were not. It is frequently the case that an empirical replication experiment does not confirm the findings of the original study. One does not condemn the science or the approach because one realizes that phenomena of the world are complex and it requires time and careful work to win knowledge about the world's phenomena. If the two structures had differed one would follow the typical scientific procedures for resolving differences.

In the scholarly literature a sharp distinction is made between jealousy and envy. A philosopher, Cobb-Stevens, writes, "To be jealous is to be apprehensive about a potential loss of something: of one's time, of some privilege, or of a beloved's affection. To be envious is to desire what is possessed by another: fame, wealth, affection of a third party" (2003, 96). And Tellenbach, a phenomenological psychiatrist, writes, "Wherever jealousy arises, something is in danger of being lost which I regard as belonging to me. . . . Envy, on the other hand, is always directed toward something that is *primarily* someone *else's*. Jealousy is not a wanting-to-have, but rather a wanting-to-hold, an objection to loss" (1974, 462). While these distinctions make sense formally and in the abstract, the data show that the two emotions can be lived confusedly in one situation. I asked for descriptions of jealousy, and according to the above definitions, got envy as well. It is not necessary that the two should always appear together but it shows how data obtained from concrete lived situations reveal the complexity of life and can lead to more adequate theoretical formulations. This finding raises the question of why these two emotions can be confused in a concrete situation when certain feelings about others, and selves, are aroused.

ACTUAL RESEARCH RESULTS USING THE PHENOMENOLOGICAL PSYCHOLOGICAL METHOD

Because we used abbreviated descriptions to exemplify the method, the reader may not get an accurate picture of what research results are really like when employing this method. Consequently we will describe the findings that Barbro von Knorring-Giorgi (1998) produced in her doctoral dissertation.[2]

The topic of her research was "Pivotal Moments in Psychotherapy as Experienced by Clients." She interviewed three participants who were among the names given to her by a therapist who was one of her acquaintances. Two of the clients had terminated therapy years before participating in the research and one was just finishing up. After contacting the clients and receiving permission from them to participate in the research, von Knorring-Giorgi first determined whether they had actually experienced a pivotal moment—"a moment experienced by the client that dramatically changed something for the better for him or her" (von Knorring-Giorgi 1998, 38). If the clients stated that they did experience such an event she interviewed each client for about an hour. The interviews resulted in about 45 single-spaced pages of text and the analysis ended up with 247 meaning units for all three clients. Von Knorring-Giorgi also interviewed the therapist regarding each client and analyzed that data as well, but it is not necessary to display those results to make my key point. It is sufficient to simply consider the data of the clients.

Based upon all of that data, von Knorring-Giorgi came up with the following psychological structure for the experience of a pivotal moment in therapy as experienced by clients:

> One type of pivotal moment in therapy takes place in the context of a therapeutic process and occurs in a situation in which a client will finally allow emotions and perceptions of self as well of others and of the world associated with certain familiar, safety promoting but self-handicapping established living patterns to be confronted in a challenging way. The pivotal moment takes place within a therapeutic relationship felt as safe and supporting and is a consequence of a new type of relationship burgeoning within the life of the client. Process-long concomitant contextual constituents necessary for the support of the pivotal moment are: motivation for change; openness; trust and safety; emotional involvement. Proximate contextual constituents are: increased awareness; changed assumptions; increased tension; and challenge to old assumptions. (1998, 44)

Thus, 45 single-spaced pages have been reduced to a paragraph. Of course, it will take considerable discussion to unpack all of the implications contained in the structure. But the structure is intended to present only the essence of the experience, not all of the ramifications of the experience in a detailed way. The discussion section of the research report serves that purpose.

However, the verbal presentation of the results hides certain other important features of the findings. So von Knorring-Giorgi (1998, 54–55) also presented the findings in a diagrammatic form because not all of the constituents of the experience play the same role and it is equally important to understand the role they play as well as discover what the constituents are (see fig. 2). Figure 2 shows the relationships among the constituents. At the lowest level of the figure, we see the experiential state with which the client enters therapy. They are suffering negative emotions and they have a low evaluation of themselves. Then within the therapeutic process itself, the client must be *open* to becoming *emotionally engaged,* but the client must also experience the process *trustfully* and *as safe.* Equally important is that the client is *motivated to change.* Now, all of these factors can be in a successful therapeutic process without a pivotal moment occurring. Also, these were labeled "process-long constituents" of therapy, which means that they have to be present throughout the therapy. Obviously, they are present dynamically: one may recede while another constituent gets stronger or one may be challenged while others are neglected, and so on. That is, they do not all have to be figural all the time. But they all have to be called upon when needed if a pivotal moment is to take place. I am not speaking about cause-effect relationships here. The process-long factors may be present without a pivotal moment taking place. Rather, the relationships have to be understood more along the lines of a founding-founded relationship as described by Husserl (1970b, 435–48). The process-long factors have to be present if a pivotal moment is to take place, but they do not guarantee it. When they are present, the possibility of a pivotal moment is awakened, but more is required. The four constituents have to be understood as nonindependent parts of a whole that need other moments in order for the phenomenon to be experienced. Husserl calls such nonindependent parts "moments," so the idea of moment is not so much temporal as one referring to a part of a whole that needs other moments to be completed.

What is also required is listed on the next level in von Knorring-Giorgi's figure 2. Once "motivation to change" is awakened in the client, other necessary constituents become possible. These were discovered to be: *increased awareness, challenge to old assumptions, changed assumptions,* and *increased tension.* At some point in the course of therapy clients have to become more aware of exactly how they are living their lives. Perhaps it is the monotony of her existence that she has to confront, or perhaps he becomes aware of how he is consistently repressing his anger, or perhaps just how he participates in making his life more miserable than it has to be. This increased awareness becomes a challenge to the assumptions by which the client is living and it motivates him or her to change the taken-for-granted assumptions. Change of habitual ways of doing things is always challenging and the idea of change introduces increased tension into the client's life. This is a vulnerable moment for the client. He or she can either change for the better or fall back into old ways of self-handicapping. The role of the therapist is critical here. If the tension is too much, the client could easily cease trying to change and hence remain in the old ways of living; if there is no tension the client is not motivated to reach the state of "readiness to change." But if she does reach the level of readiness to change, then the pivotal moment has a good chance of being actualized. Again, this step is not automatic. It still requires some initiative on the part of the client to actualize the good possibilities that are offered by the readiness to change. If the good possibilities have been accepted and fully lived through, then we could say that the pivotal moment has occurred. Or we could say that the therapy was successful. When it is successful, the client has a healthier openness to the world and the quality of her emotional engagement is positive. In any case, there is a second order of interrelated moments that also have to be satisfied for the pivotal moment to take place. Again, all of these moments have to be present in order for a pivotal moment to

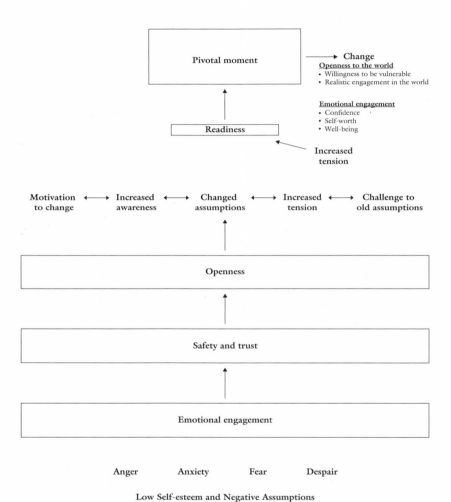

Fig. 2. Interrelated phases and constituents in the overall process of
therapy containing the pivotal moment.

take place, but they do not cause it. Rather, they change the client's experiential flow sufficiently so that the possibility of significant change announces itself in a potentially effective way. But it is more of an invitation than a cause.

In addition to figure 2, von Knorring-Giorgi also produced table 2 (1998, 46–47), which indicates how each subject lived through each of the essential constituents of the structure. Table 2 is a summary of the findings with respect to each constituent by each of the subjects. The constituents in the table were, of course, derived from the structure, and the empirical summaries or quotations in the table were derived from the raw data.

Table 2. The constituents of the structure and their empirical basis for each subject

CONSTITUENTS	S#1	S#2	S#3
MOTIVATION & OPENNESS	High due to general and therapist specific positive expectations	High due to therapist specific circumstances	Low due to past experience and to involuntary entry into therapy
TRUST & SAFETY	Straightforward, clear, emotionally engaged communication leaving S in charge of own decisions	Warmth and understanding, nurturing support	Respectfulness, genuine care, explicit and concrete show of concern
EMOTIONAL INVOLVEMENT	Allowing herself to express herself with emotional intensity	New acknowledgment of both resentment and desire	Dealing with difficult affective material from childhood previously avoided
INCREASED AWARENESS & NEW INSIGHT	Moderate increase in awareness; critical working through fears linked to projections about future consequences	Initial awareness level low because of active avoidance and denial. Gradual increase in awareness; allowing negative emotions to surface	Initial awareness level high, therefore increase less critical; acknowledging and working through pain from traumatizing experiences

Table 2 (*cont.*)

CONSTITUENTS	S#1	S#2	S#3
CHANGED ASSUMPTIONS & NEW RELATIONSHIP UNDERSTANDING	**From**: "I'm no good; I can't do what it takes to make my life work."	**From**: "I have to sacrifice myself because I don't deserve."	**From**: "I am condemned to be no good because I have problems."
	Through: New type of relationship speaking to idiosyncratic meanings of affect and perceptions.	**Through**: New type of relationship speaking to idiosyncratic meanings of affect and perceptions.	**Through**: New type of relationship speaking to idiosyncratic meanings of affect and perceptions.
	To: "I am worthy; I am strong and I can do this."	**To**: "I am not so bad that I have to sacrifice myself, I do deserve."	**To**: "I am worthy, my problems are not all my fault, and I can solve my problems."
INCREASED TENSION & READINESS	Frustration over goals, needs, and desires not met, increased belief in own capacity.	Tension from conflict between own desires and initially perceived impossibility, then acceptance of possibility.	Fear of future implications if change not achieved.
CHALLENGE TO OLD ASSUMPTIONS	Confrontation and demand for concrete action challenging old assumptions about self and old response patterns.	Demand for concrete action challenging old assumptions about self and a recontextualization of old bad experience.	Confrontation of future likely serious problems and challenge to old patterns of responding to future problems.

To summarize: when the data are extensive and rich some significant and complex findings can emerge when the descriptive phenomenological psychological method is employed. The use of the jealousy examples was exclusively for purpose of demonstrating the process of the analysis and the emphasis was not intended to be on the outcome because the data base was too small. However, in principle, any phenomenon that can be experienced and described can be analyzed by the use of this method. That makes its application very broad.

■ ■ ■

In this work I have tried to correct an imbalance that I have seen in the development of psychology as a science. Understandably, since by the time psychology got started toward the end of the nineteenth century, the natural sciences were basically 200 years old with a history of successes behind them. Consequently, it seemed only natural that psychology should imitate what they were doing and hope for the same success. Thus, psychology moved from a philosophical style of scholarship to a natural scientific style, so psychology established labs, brought in instruments, designed strict experiments, and emphasized quantitative approaches. The fact that human beings replaced, as Morawski (1988, vii) states, "gases, minerals, cells, molecules and drosophila," produced no radical change in research strategies, with only certain obvious modifications (for example, one could provide linguistic instructions to the participants). Psychology as a natural science may have gotten a slow start, but eventually it took off and became the dominant paradigm in the field.

However, there were also some prominent dissenters to this approach, or at least some psychologists who thought differently about how to conduct research on psychological phenomena in order to understand them. These psychologists believed that quantification was not the only path to secure kowledge. They held, and I tried to demonstrate, that the qualitative dimension of reality is an irreducible category that needs to be respected and treated in its own right. Fortunately, there was available in my lifetime a new philosophy, phenomenology, which began in the year 1900, and which thematized as its focus the relationship between acts of consciousness and the objects that presented themselves to consciousness. Phenomenology also developed a method for probing consciousness' relation to its objects. From my perspective, the two advantages that phenomenology brings to the study of psychological phenomena over empiricism, the primary philosophy that has guided the development of science in the West since its beginning, are: (1) its understanding of consciousness is deeper and more nuanced, and (2) its method is descriptive, which means that it can accommodate qualitative phenomena in a far more useful way. It also advocates the study of human phenomena in a strict nonreductionistic way.

In this book I discussed the principles of phenomenology that are important for guiding the understanding of consciousness. The proper understanding of consciousness is critical since without consciousness there is no knowledge. In these pages I articulated the philosophical method as Husserl developed it, modified it to make it appropriate for psychological phenomena at a scientific level of understanding, and then provided examples of its application. The sense of science from which I write is a human science perspective and not a natural scientific one. The human science perspective also supports a nonreductionistic appproach, sees value in seeking the meaning of qualitative aspects of phenomena, and acknowledges the nonnaturalistic status of consciousness.

I am aware that the biggest stumbling blocks to the acceptance of this method is the lack of knowledge concerning continental phenomenology among contemporary scientists and the fact that the human science approach has not yet received its "classical" presentation. If the method is judged by empirical criteria, it does not come off well because it did not try to meet those criteria. In the conflict between a theoretical exposition and a practical one, I have chosen the latter, so that perhaps, since the steps are clearly delineated, the theoretical justification for the steps of the method will be more easily understood.

NOTES

Notes to Chapter One

1. While the term "given" is often used to account for whatever is not consciousness in a particular experience, it is usually placed within quotation marks because, strictly speaking, there is no purely given object because within phenomenology all objects are considered to be constituted by consciousness. This means that consciousness plays a role in how an object appears, but the constitutive process of consciousness is neither creative nor causal with respect to the "given."

2. One hardly has to argue for the fact that psychology desired to become a natural science since such an approach is what we today call "mainstream psychology." Nevertheless, this idea had to be justified in the early days of psychology's independence from philosophy. Titchener (1898), for example, expressed the view that the best hope for psychology was structural analyses of the type he advocated, and the use of the experimental method. Scripture contrasted introspective approaches with physiological ones, and states, "The new psychology gives both what they wish: a purely mental science founded on careful experiment and exact measurement" (1914, 14); Ebbinghaus states, "In the realm of mental phenomena, experiment and measurement have hitherto been chiefly limited in application to sense perception and to the time relations of mental processes. By means of the following investigations we have tried to go a step farther into the workings of the mind and to submit to an experimental and quantitative treatment the manifestation of memory" (1964, xiii). As late as 1929 Boring states: "The author believes that the application of the experimental method to the problem of mind is the great outstanding event in the history of the study of mind, an event to which no other is comparable" (1929, 859). The thought that the experimental method might not be the most appropriate method for the advancement of psychology never crossed the mind of its proponents in the era of the founding of psychology, or of its most famous American historian of psychology. However, that sentence was removed in the 1950 edition of Boring's book.

Notes to Chapter Two

1. Spiegelberg (1972) clarifies how Snygg came to use the term. According to him, Snygg was expressing his interest in the perceptual field and its importance for

understanding behavior to his professor in Toronto, William Line, and he told Snygg that "he was using a phenomenological approach" (147). Snygg then adopted the term.

2. I would like to thank Fred Wertz for alerting me to the implications for qualitative research of this book. While I had been aware of the book for quite some time, I was not motivated to consult it because I thought that it dealt with clinical implications of the personal documents, somewhat like Allport's (1965) *Letters from Jenny*. However, *The Use of Personal Documents in Psychological Science* is quite systematic in raising basic questions concerning qualitative analyses in psychological research.

3. I cannot cover all of Piaget's contributions to psychology here, but I do want to concentrate on his manner of empirical research. Because of my own narrow aim in this book, many of his conceptual and theoretical contributions will also have to be ignored.

Notes to Chapter Three

1. All researchers may not follow the steps of the process exactly as they are presented here, but each step will have to be considered at some time if a research design is to be completed.

Notes to Chapter Four

1. I am aware that meanings are looked upon suspiciously by researchers with strong objectivistic leanings. I will discuss the issue of objective and subjective phenomena below, but here I want to elaborate briefly on the phenomenological understanding of meaning in order to indicate why it is serviceable in scientific contexts.

2. A possible criticism of this method is that the human science approach that emerges from such a dialectic is still under the sway of the natural sciences in terms of criteria met despite the use of analogical thinking. There could be some truth to this criticism. But when I began practicing I had no other guide except my training and the amount of general phenomenological philosophy I had acquired at that time, which was little. Today, with a clearer understanding of Husserlian phenomenology and a better understanding of the philosophy of science contained within that mode of thought, I would start differently. I would posit the richest philosophical anthropology that I could describe and then logically work through how a phenomenological theory of science would deal with it. I do not know how that would affect what I have written, but I am confident that the above presentation would not be completely undermined. I suspect that it would be improved.

Notes to Chapter Five

1. Husserl calls this version of the reduction the phenomenological psychological reduction, and that is correct from his perspective. While that meaning fits comfortably with a psychological perspective, the method being described can easily be used by other human sciences as well—for example, sociology, education, nursing, anthropology, and so on—so to call it a psychological reduction seems to limit it to psychology, but that is not the case. Of course, the disciplinary attitude will differ with each science, but the type of reduction and the steps of the method will not. That is why I label it the scientific phenomenological reduction, meaning by that term a human science perspective.

2. The strategy being suggested here is not the only conceivable way to practice phenomenological psychology. It is conceivable that one could enter the transcendental phenomenological reduction and clarify the key concepts necessary to understand a specific experience in a psychological way and then return to the experience understood psychologically, that is, more narrowly than the transcendental attitude, and apply the clarifications achieved transcendentally to the experience understood psychologically. However, such transcendental analyses are a purely philosophical labor, are difficult to carry out, and only few examples exist in the literature. When psychologists attempt such analyses, there is always the difficulty that a truly transcendental level is not reached. For example, Davidson and Cosgrove (2002) attempted such an analysis and while they theoretically seem to understand quite well what Husserl intended, the bulk of their energy seems focused on the clarification of what the return from the transcendental could mean. Their effort is commendable and while the intersubjective aspect of the transcendental is duly noted, it also seemed to be limited to human modes and perhaps not truly philosophically transcendental. I prefer to work out pretranscendental psychological analyses at this stage of development of transcendental philosophy and, while these pretranscendental phenomenological analyses, in my view, are better than the naturalistic mainstream psychological analyses that are currently prevalent, they too lack adequate grounding, and that lack would call for a transcendental perspective. I expect the need for transcendental grounding will become apparent as pretranscendental phenomenological psychology is employed. That is one reason that I returned to Husserl from Merleau-Ponty.

Notes to Chapter Six

1. Actually, one could in principle use the psychological phenomenological method on a single case, but if one does, the researcher is picking the most difficult situation for using the method because the method is more productive when there are multiple variations. If one were interested in how a single individual experiences a particular phenomenon—for example, anxiety—I would still try to get several descriptions from such an individual about how he or she experienced

anxious situations and then apply the method to those situations. This strategy would reveal the individual's style of living anxious situations far more readily than a single situation would. This strategy would still not fall under case study research methods as it is currently defined. Thus, the phenomenological psychological strategy is to get several individuals in order to focus on the phenomenon or several instances of the phenomenon to focus on the individual. For a more complete critique of Edwards 1991, see Giorgi (2008).

2. While Barbro was actually my wife at the time she completed her doctoral dissertation, the Province of Quebec insists that a woman's maiden name be attached to any work produced by a woman, so the name von Knorring-Giorgi is used on her dissertation.

Aanstoos, C. 1985. The structure of thinking in chess. In *Phenomenology and psychological research*, ed. A. Giorgi, 86–117. Pittsburgh: Duquesne University Press.

Adler, H. 1994. The European influence on American psychology. In *Aspects of the history of psychology in America: 1892/1992*, ed. H. Adler and R. W. Rieber, 113–22. New York: New York Academy of Sciences.

Allport, F. 1955. *Theories of perception and the concept of structure*. New York: Wiley & Sons.

Allport, G. 1942. *The use of personal documents in psychological science*. New York: Social Science Research Council.

————. 1943. The productive paradoxes of William James. *Psychological Review* 50:95–120.

————. 1965. *Letters from Jenny*. New York: Harcourt, Brace & World.

————. 1968. An autobiography. In *The person in psychology: Selected essays*, 376–409. Boston: Beacon Press. (Orig. pub. 1967).

Allport, G. W., and P. E. Vernon. 1931. *A study of values*. Boston: Houghton Mifflin.

Asch, S. E. 1956. Studies of independence and conformity: A minority of one against a unanimous majority. *Psychological Monographs* 70 (9, Whole No. 416).

Ash, M. G. 1985. Gestalt psychology: Origins in Germany and reception in the United States. In *Points of view in the modern history of psychology*, ed. C. E. Buxton, 295–344. New York: Academic Press.

Bartlett, F. C. 1958. *Thinking: An experimental and social study*. New York: Basic Books.

————. 1995. Preface to *Remembering: A study in experimental and social psychology*, xvii–xix. Cambridge: Cambridge University Press. (Orig. pub. 1932).

Beams, H. L., and G. V. Thompson. 1952. Affectivity as a factor with perception of the magnitude of food objects. *American Psychologist* 7:323.

Bettelheim, B. 1984. *Freud and men's soul.* New York: Vintage Books.

Binet, A. 1903. La pensée sans images. *Revue Philosophique* 55:138–52.

Blumenthal, A. L. 1975. A reappraisal of Wilhelm Wundt. *American Psychologist* 30:1081–87.

———. 1980. Wilhelm Wundt and early American psychology: A clash of cultures. In *Psychology: Theoretical-historical perspectives,* ed. R. W. Rieber and K. Salzinger, 25–42. New York: Academic Press.

———. 1985. Wilhelm Wundt: Psychology as the propaedeutic science. In *Points of view in the modern history of psychology,* ed. C. E. Buxton, 19–50. New York: Academic Press.

Boring, E. G. 1929. *A history of experimental psychology.* New York: Century.

———. 1950. *A history of experimental psychology.* 2nd ed. New York: Appleton-Century-Crofts.

———. 1953. A history of introspection. *Psychological Bulletin* 50: 169–86.

Brentano, F. 1973. *Psychology from an empirical standpoint.* New York: Humanities Press. (Orig. pub. German, 1874).

Brower, D. 1949. The problem of quantification in psychological science. *Psychological Review* 56:325–33.

Bruner, J. S., and C. C. Goodman. 1947. Value and need as organizing factors in perception. *Journal of Abnormal and Social Psychology* 42:33–44.

Cairns, D. 1973. An approach to Husserlian phenomenology. In *Phenomenology: Continuation and criticism,* ed. F. Kersten and R. Zaner, 223–38. The Hague: Martinus Nijhoff.

Callaway, W. R. 2001. *Jean Piaget: A most outrageous deception.* Huntington, NY: Nova Science Publications.

Camic, P. M., J. E. Rhodes, and L. Yardley, eds. 2003. *Qualitative research in psychology.* Washington, DC: American Psychological Association.

Carr, D. 1987. World, world-view, lifeworld: Husserl and the conceptual relativists. *Interpreting Husserl,* 213–25. Dordrecht: Martinus Nijhoff.

Cloonan, T. 1995. The early history of phenomenological psychological research in America. *Journal of Phenomenological Psychology* 26:46–126.

Cobb-Stevens, R. 2003. Husserl's fifth logical investigation. In *Husserl's logical investigations,* ed. D. O. Dahlstrom, 95–107. Dordrecht: Kluwer Academic.

Coles, R. 1967. *Children of crisis: A study of courage and fear.* New York: Dell Publishing. (Orig. pub. 1964).

———. 1971. *Migrants, sharecroppers and mountaineers,* vol. 2, *Children of crisis.* Boston: Little, Brown.

———. 1977. *Privileged ones,* vol. 5, *Children of crisis.* Boston: Little, Brown.

———. 1989. *The call of stories.* Boston: Houghton Mifflin.

Combs, A. W., and D. Snygg. 1959. *Individual behavior.* New York: Harper & Row.

Combs, A. W., A. Richards, and F. Richards. 1988. *Perceptual psychology: A humanistic approach to the study of persons.* Lanham, MD: University Press of America. (Orig. pub. 1976).

Cowen, E. L., and E. G. Beier. 1950. Influence of threat expectancy on perceptual threshold. *Journal of Personality* 19:85–94.

Craik, F. I. M. 1979. Human memory. *Annual Review of Psychology* 30:63–102.

Danziger, K. 1990. *Constructing the subject: Historical origins of psychological research.* Cambridge: Cambridge University Press.

Davidson, L., and L. Cosgrove. 2002. Psychologism and phenomenological psychology revisited II: The return to positivity. *Journal of Phenomenological Psychology* 33:141–77.

Dennett, D. 2003. Who's on first? Heterophenomenology explained. *Journal of Consciousness Studies* 10:10–30.

Dewsbury, D. A. 1994. John B. Watson: Profile of a comparative psychologist and proto-ethologist. In *Modern perspectives on J. B. Watson and classical behaviorism,* ed. J. T. Todd and E. K. Morris, 141–44. Westport, CT: Greenwood.

Dilthey, W. 1977. Ideas concerning a descriptive and analytic psychology. *Descriptive psychology and historical understanding,* trans. R. M. Zaner and K. L. Hughes. The Hague: Martinus Nijhoff. (Orig. pub. German, 1894).

Ebbinghaus, H. 1964. *Memory* Translated by H. A. Ruger and C. E. Bussenius. New York: Dover. (Orig. pub. German, 1885; first English ed., 1913).

Edwards, D. 1991. Duquesne phenomenological research method as a special class of case study research method. In *Dialogue beyond polemics,* ed. R. van Vuuren, 53–70. Pretoria: Human Science Research Council.

Ericsson, K. A., and H. A. Simon. 1984. *Protocol analysis: Verbal reports as data.* Cambridge, MA: MIT Press.

Evans, R. I. 1970. *Gordon Allport: The man and his ideas.* New York: E. P. Dutton.

Fay, J. W. 1939. *American psychology before William James.* New Brunswick, NJ: Rutgers University Press.

Flavell, J. 1962. *The developmental psychology of Jean Piaget.* Princeton, NJ: D. van Nostrand.

Frenkel-Brunswik, E. 1950. Intolerance of ambiguity as an emotional and perceptual personality variable. In *Perception and Personality,* ed. J. S. Bruner and D. Krech, 108–43. Durham: Duke University Press.

Freud, S. 1938. The interpretation of dreams. In *The Basic writings of Sigmund Freud,* ed. A. A. Brill, 183–549. New York: Random House. (Orig. pub. German, 1900).

———. 1966. Project for a scientific psychology. In *Standard Edition,* vol. 2, ed. J. Strachey. London: Hogarth. (Orig. pub. German, 1895).

From, F. 1971. *Perception of other people.* Translated by B. Maher and E. Kvan. New York: Columbia University Press. (Orig. pub. Danish, 1953).

Gifford, G. 1978. Psychoanalysis in Boston: Innocence and experience. Introduction to the panel discussion, April 14, 1973. In *Psychoanalysis, psychotherapy and the New England medical scene, 1894–1944,* ed. G. E. Gifford, 325–44. New York: Science History Publications.

Ginsburg, H., and S. Opper. 1969. *Piaget's theory of intellectual development: An introduction.* Englewood Cliffs, N.J.: Prentice-Hall.

Giorgi, A. 1970. *Psychology as a human science.* New York: Harper & Row.

———. 1976. Phenomenology and the foundations of psychology. In *Nebraska symposium on motivation 1975: Conceptual foundations of psychology,* ed. J. K. Cole and W. J. Arnold, 23:281–348. Lincoln: University of Nebraska Press.

———. 1977a. The implications of Merleau-Ponty's thesis of the "Primacy of Perception" for perceptual research in psychology. *Journal of Phenomenological Psychology* 8:81–102.

———. 1977b. Phenomenological psychology. In *International encyclopedia of psychiatry, psychology, psychoanalysis and neurology,* ed. B. B. Wolman, 8:64–67. New York: Aesculapius Publishing.

———. 1983a. Concerning the possibility of phenomenological psychological research. *Journal of Phenomenological Psychology* 14:129–69.

———. 1983b. The importance of the phenomenological attitude for access to the psychological realm. In *Duquesne Studies in Phenomenological Psychology IV,* ed. A. Giorgi, A. Barton, and C. Maes, 209–21. Pittsburgh: Duquesne University Press.

———. 1985. The phenomenological psychology of learning and the verbal learning tradition. In *Phenomenology and psychological research,* ed. A. Giorgi, 23–85. Pittsburgh: Duquesne University Press.

———. 1987. The crisis of humanistic psychology. *The Humanistic Psychologist* 15:5–20.

———. 1992. A phenomenological reinterpretation of the Jamesian schema for psychology. In *Reinterpreting the legacy of William James,* ed. M. E. Donnelly, 119–36. Washington, DC: American Psychological Association.

———. 2000a. Concerning the application of phenomenology to caring research. *Scandinavian Journal of Caring Science* 14:11–15.

———. 2000b. The status of Husserlian phenomenology in caring research. *Scandinavian Journal of Caring Science* 14:3–10.

———. 2008. Concerning a serious misunderstanding of the essence of the phenomenological method in psychology. *Journal of Phenomenological Psychology* 39:33–58.

Graumann, C. F. 1980. Experiment, statistics, history: Wundt's first program of psychology. In *Wundt studies,* ed. W. G. Bringmann and R. D. Tweney, 22–41. Toronto: C. J. Hofgrefe.

Greenwood, J. D. 2003. Wundt, *Volkerpsychologie* and experimental social psychology. *History of Psychology* 6:70–88.

Gurwitsch, A. 1964. *The field of consciousness.* Pittsburgh: Duquesne University Press. (Orig. pub. French, 1957).

———. 1974. *Phenomenology and the theory of science.* Edited by L. Embree. Evanston, IL: Northwestern University Press.

Hardy, L. 1992. The idea of science in Husserl and the tradition. In *The phenomenology of natural science,* ed. L. Hardy and L. Embree, 1–34. Dordrecht: Kluwer Academic.

Harvey, C. W. 1989. *Husserl's phenomenology and the foundations of natural science.* Athens: Ohio University Press.

Henle, M. 1990. Some neo-gestalt psychologies and their relation to Gestalt psychology. In *The legacy of Solomon Asch: Essays in cognition and social psychology,* ed. I. Rock, 279–91. Hillsdale, NJ: Lawrence Erlbaum Associates.

Hevern, V. W. 1999. *Allport's (1942) use of personal documents:* A contemporary reappraisal. Paper presented at annual American Psychological Association meeting, Boston, August 1999.

Hilgard, E. 1987. *Psychology in America: A historical survey.* New York: Harcourt Brace Jovanovich.

Hull, C. L. 1943. *Principles of behavior: An introduction to behavior theory.* New York: Appleton-Century.

Humphrey, G. 1963. *Thinking: An introduction to its experimental psychology.* New York: Wiley & Sons.

Husserl, E. 1962. *Ideas. General introduction to pure phenomenology,* book 1, trans. W. R. B. Gibson. New York: Collier Books. (Orig. pub. German, 1913).

———. 1965. Philosophy as rigorous science. In *Edmund Husserl: Phenomenology and the crisis of philosophy,* trans. Q. Lauer, 71–147. New York: Harper Torchbooks. (Orig. pub. German, 1911).

———. 1970a. *The crisis of European sciences and transcendental phenomenology.* Translated by D. Carr. Evanston, IL: Northwestern University Press. (Orig. pub. German, 1954).

———. 1970b. *Logical investigations,* Vols. 1 & 2. Translated by J. N. Findlay. New York: Humanities Press. (Orig. pub. German, 1900).

———. 1977. *Phenomenological psychology.* Translated by J. Scanlon. The Hague: Martinus Nijhoff. (Orig. pub. German, 1962).

———. 1980. *Ideas pertaining to a pure phenomenology and to a phenomenological philosophy.* Book 3. Translated by T. E. Klein and W. E. Pohl. The Hague: Martinus Nijhoff. (Orig. pub. German, 1971).

————. 1983. Ideas pertaining to a pure phenomenology and to a phenomenological philosophy. Book 1. Translated by F. Kersten. The Hague: Martinus Nijhoff. (Orig. pub. German, 1913).

————. 1989. *Ideas pertaining to a pure phenomenology and to a phenomenological philosophy.* Book 2. Translated by R. Rojcewicsz and A. Schuwer. Dordrecht: Kluwer Academic. (Orig. pub. German, 1952).

————. 1991. *On the phenomenology of the consciousness of internal time (1893–1917)* (Tr. J. B. Brough). Dordrecht: Kluwer Academic. (Orig. pub. German, 1928).

James, W. 1902. *The varieties of religious experience* N.Y. The Modern Library.

————. 1950. *Principles of psychology* N.Y. Dover. (Orig. pub. 1890).

Kintsch, W. 1995. Introduction to *Remembering: A study in experimental and social psychology,* ed. F. C. Bartlett, xi–xv. Cambridge: Cambridge University Press. (Orig. pub. 1932).

Klein, G. S. 1951. Personal world through perception. In *Perception: An approach to personality,* ed. R. R. Blake and G. V. Ramsey, 328–55. New York: Ronald Press.

Koch, S. 1969. Psychology cannot be a coherent science. *Psychology Today* (March): 14, 64, 66–68.

Kockelmans, J., and J. Kisiel, eds. 1970. *Phenomenology and the natural sciences: Essays and translations.* Evanston, IL: Northwestern University Press.

Koffka, K. 1928. *The growth of mind.* 2nd ed. Translated by R. M. Ogden. London: Routledge and Kegan Paul. (Orig. pub. 1924).

Kuenzli, A. E., ed. 1959. *The phenomenological problem.* New York: Harper.

Kvale, S. 1996. *InterViews: An introduction to qualitative research interviewing.* Thousand Oaks, CA: Sage.

Leary, D. 1978. The philosophical development of the conception of psychology in Germany, 1780–1850. *Journal of the History of the Behavioral Sciences* 14:113–21.

Linschoten, H. 1968. *On the way toward a phenomenological psychology: The psychology of William James.* Pittsburgh: Duquesne University Press. (Orig. pub. Dutch, 1959).

Luchins, A. 1951. An evaluation of some current criticisms of Gestalt psychological work on perception. *Psychological Review* 58:69–95.

MacLeod, R. B. 1947. The phenomenological approach to social psychology. *Psychological Review* 54:193–210.

———. 1951. The place of phenomenological analysis in social psychological theory. In *Social Psychology at the Crossroads*, ed. J. H. Rohrer and M. Sherif, 180–240. New York: Harper.

———. 1964. Phenomenology: A challenge to experimental psychology. In *Behaviorism and phenomenology*, ed. T. W. Wann, 47–48. Chicago: University of Chicago Press.

———. 1970. Psychological phenomenology: A propaedeutic to a scientific psychology. In *Toward unification in psychology: The first Banff conference on theoretical psychology*, ed. J. R. Royce, 246–66. Toronto: University of Toronto Press.

Maslow, A. 1966. *The psychology of science: A reconnaissance*. New York: Harper & Row.

Matson, F. 1964. *The broken image*. New York: Braziller.

Mauran, M. 1998. Measurement as a normative practice: Implications of Wittgenstein's philosophy for measurement in psychology. *Theory and Psychology* 8 (4): 435–61.

May, R., E. Angel, and H. F. Ellenberger, eds. 1958. *Existence: A new dimension in psychiatry and psychology*. New York: Basic Books.

Mayer, S. J. 2005. The early evolution of Jean Piaget's clinical method. *History of Psychology* 8:362–82.

McKenna, W. R. 1989. Husserl's theory of perception. In *Husserl's phenomenology: A textbook*, ed. J. N. Mohanty and W. R. McKenna, 181–212. Washington, DC: University Press of America.

Merleau-Ponty, M. 1962. *The phenomenology of perception*. Translated by C. Smith. New York: Humanities Press. (Orig. pub. French, 1945).

———. 1963. *The structure of behavior*. Trans. A. Fisher. Boston: Beacon Press. (Orig. pub. French, 1942).

———. 1964a. Indirect language and the voices of silence. In *Signs*, ed. M. Merleau-Ponty, trans. R. C. McCleary, 39–83. Evanston, IL: Northwestern University Press. (Orig. pub. French, 1960).

———. 1964b. Phenomenology and the sciences of man. Translated by J. Wild. *The primacy of perception*, ed. and trans. J. Edie, 43–95. Evanston, IL: Northwestern University Press.

Michell, J. 2000. Normal science, pathological science and psychometrics. *Theory and psychology* 10:639–67.

Mishler, C. G. 1986. *Research interviewing—Context and narrative.* Cambridge, MA: Harvard University Press.

Mohanty, J. N. 1985. *The possibility of transcendental philosophy.* Dordrecht: Martinus Nijhoff.

Morawski, J. 1988. Introduction to *The rise of experimentation in American psychology,* ed. J. Morawski, vii–xvii. New Haven, CT: Yale University Press.

Orne, M. T. 1962. On the social psychology of the psychological experiment: With particular reference to demand characteristics and their implications. *American Psychologist* 17:776–83.

Overgaard, S. 2004. *Husserl and Heidegger on being in the world.* Dordrecht: Kluwer Academic.

Pettigrew, T. F. 1970. Introduction to *Gordon Allport: The man and his ideas,* by R. I. Evans, xv–xxv. New York: E. P. Dutton.

Piaget, J. 1926. *The language and thought of the child.* New York: Harcourt, Brace.

———. 1928. *Judgment and reasoning in the child.* New York: Harcourt, Brace.

———. 1929. *The child's conception of the world.* New York: Harcourt, Brace.

———. 1930. *The child's conception of physical causality.* London: Kegan Paul.

———. 1932. *The moral judgment of the child.* London: Kegan Paul.

———. 1974. *The place of the sciences of man in the system of sciences.* New York: Harper Torchbooks. (Orig. pub. 1970).

Piaget, J., and B. Inhelder. 1941. *Le développement des quantités chez l'enfant.* Paris: Nenchotee Delachaux et Niestle.

Politzer, G. 1968. *Critique des fondements de la psychologie.* Paris: Presses Universitaires de France. (Orig. pub. French, 1928). Translated by M. Apprey as *Critique of the foundations of psychology: The psychology of psychoanalysis.* Pittsburgh: Duquesne University Press, 1994.

———. 1973. *Ecrits 2: Les fondements de la psychologie.* Edited by J. Debouzy. Paris: Editions Sociales. (Orig. pub. 1924–39).

Reeder, H. 1997. Husserl's phenomenology and contemporary science. In *Husserl in contemporary context,* ed. B. C. Hopkins, 211–34. Dordrecht: Kluwer Academic.

Rock, I. 1984. *Perception.* New York: Scientific American.

Ronda, B. 1989. *Intellect and spirit: The life and work of Robert Coles.* New York: Continuum.

Ross, B. 1978. William James: A prime mover of the psychoanalytic movement in America. In *Psychoanalysis, psychotherapy and the New England medical scene, 1894–1944,* ed. G. E. Gifford, 10–23. New York: Science History Publications.

Salzinger, K. 1994. On Watson. In *Modern perspectives on John B. Watson and classical behaviorism,* ed. J. T. Todd and E. K. Morris, 151–58. Westport, CT: Greenwood Press.

Sartre, J.-P. 1962. *A sketch for a theory of the emotions.* Translated by P. Mairet. London: Methuen. (Orig. pub. French, 1939).

Scripture, E. 1914. *The new psychology.* New York: Charles Scribner's Sons.

Skinner, B. F. 1938. *The behavior of organisms: An experimental analysis.* New York: Appleton-Century.

———. 1950. Are theories of learning necessary? *Psychological Review* 57:193–216.

Smith, J. A., ed. 2003. *Qualitative psychology: A practical guide to research methods.* Thousand Oaks, CA: Sage.

Smith, L. D. 1995. Inquiry nearer the source: Bacon, Mach and the behavior of organisms. In *Modern perspectives on B. F. Skinner and contemporary behaviorism,* ed. J. T. Todd and E. K. Morris, 39–50. Westport, CT: Greenwood.

Snygg, D. 1941. The need for a phenomenological system of psychology. *Psychological Review* 48:404–24.

Sokolowski, R. 1974. *Husserlian meditations: How words present things.* Evanston, IL: Northwestern University Press.

Spiegelberg, H. 1964. Phenomenology through vicarious experience. In *Phenomenology: Pure and applied,* ed. E. Straus, 105–26. Pittsburgh: Duquesne University Press.

———. 1972. *Phenomenology in psychology and psychiatry: An historical introduction.* Evanston, IL: Northwestern University Press.

———. 1981. *The context of the phenomenological movement.* The Hague: Martinus Nijhoff.

———. 1986. Putting ourselves into the place of others: Toward a phenomenology of imagining self-transposal. In *Steppingstones toward an ethics for fellow-existers: Essays 1944–1983,* ed. H. Spiegelberg, 99–104. Dordrecht: Martinus Nijhoff.

———. 1995. Phenomenology through vicarious experience. In *Doing phenomenology,* ed. H. Spiegelberg, 35–53. The Hague: Martinus Nijhoff.

Spiegelberg, H., with K. Schuhmann. 1982. *The phenomenological movement: An historical introduction.* 3rd ed. The Hague: Martinus Nijhoff.

Spranger, E. 1928. *Types of men: The psychology and ethics of personality.* 5th ed. Translated by P. J. W. Pigors. Halle: Niemeyer. (Orig. pub. German, 1913).

Stapleton, T. J. 1994. Heidegger and categorial intuition. In *The question of hermeneutics,* ed. T. J. Stapleton, 209–36. Dordrecht: Kluwer Academic.

Stout, J. 1903. *The groundwork of psychology.* New York: Hinds and Noble.

Ströker, E. 1997. *Husserlian foundations of science.* Dordrecht: Kluwer Academic.

Sully, J. 1884. *Outlines of psychology.* London: Longmans, Green.

Taylor, E. 1982. *William James on exceptional mental states: The 1896 Lowell Lectures.* New York: Charles Scribner's Sons.

Tellenbach, H. 1974. On the nature of jealousy. *Journal of Phenomenological Psychology* 4:461–68.

Titchener, E. B. 1898. The postulates of a structural psychology. *Philosophical Review,* 7:449–465.

———. 1901a. *Experimental psychology: A manual of laboratory practice.* Vol. 1, *Qualitative experiments,* part 1, *Student's manual.* New York: Macmillan.

———. 1901b. *Experimental psychology: A manual of laboratory practice.* Vol. 1, *Qualitative experiments,* part 2, *Instructor's manual.* New York: Macmillan.

———. 1905a. *Experimental psychology: A manual of laboratory practice.* Vol. 2, *Qualitative experiments,* part 1, *Student's manual.* New York: Macmillan.

———. 1905b. *Experimental psychology: A manual of laboratory practice.* Vol. 2, *Qualitative experiments,* part 2, *Instructor's manual.* New York: Macmillan.

Von Knorring-Giorgi, B. 1998. A phenomenological analysis of the experience of pivotal moments in therapy as defined by clients. Ph.D. diss., Université du Québec à Montréal.

Ward, J. 1886. Psychology. In *Encyclopedia Britannica*. 9th ed. Vol. 20. Edinburgh: Black.

————. 1918. *Psychological principles*. Cambridge: Cambridge University Press.

Watson, J. B. 1913. Psychology as the behaviorist views it. *Psychological Review* 20:158–77.

————. 1919. *Psychology from the standpoint of the behaviorist*. Philadelphia: J. B. Lippincott.

————. 1928. *The ways of behaviorism*. New York: Harper & Brothers.

Werner, H., and S. Wapner. 1950. Sensory tonic field theory of perception. In *Perception and personality*, ed. J. S. Bruner and D. Krech, 88–107. Durham, NC: Duke University Press.

Wertz, F. 1982. The findings and value of a descriptive approach to everyday perceptual process. *Journal of Phenomenological Psychology* 13:169–95.

————. 1983. Revolution in psychology: A case study of the new look school of perceptual psychology. In *Duquesne studies in phenomenological psychology*, vol. 4, ed. A. Giorgi, A. Barton, and C. Maes, 222–43. Pittsburgh: Duquesne University Press.

Wolf, T. 1966. Intuition and experiment: Alfred Binet's first efforts in child psychology. *Journal of the History of Behavioral Sciences* 2:233–39.

Wundt, W. 1904. *Principles of physiological psychology*. Translated by E. B. Titchener. London: Swan Sonnenschein. (Orig. pub. German, 1902).

Yin, R. K. 2004. Introduction to *The case study anthology*, by R. K. Yin, xi–xv. Thousand Oaks, CA: Sage.

Zahavi, D. 2000. *Husserl's phenomenology*. Stanford, CA: Stanford University Press.

————. 2005. *Subjectivity and selfhood: Investigating the first-person perspective*. Cambridge, MA: The MIT Press.

INDEX

abstract sciences, 75
Agassiz, Louis, 32
Allport, Gordon, 24–25, 43–46, 50, 53–54
analysis: attitude and, 127–28, 130–37; of descriptions, 125–37, 191–95; of jealousy experience, 145–66, 179–80; of meaning units, 182; reductions and, 118–19. *See also* psychoanalysis
analysis-synthesis, 81–82
anthropology, 72–73
attitude: analysis and, 127–28, 130–37; assuming transcendental phenomenological, 87–88; bracketing and, 91; intersubjective, 136; of participants, 96–97; phenomenological, 181–82; and phenomenological method, 190; of researcher, 184

Bartlett, Sir Frederic C., 24, 41–43, 50–51, 52
behavior, 108, 186–87
behavioral lability, 84–85
behaviorism, 20, 21–22, 28
Binet, Alfred, 18, 47
Bonaparte, Napoleon, 191–92, 194–95
Boring, E. G., 209n2
bracketing, 91–93
Brentano, F., 17–19
Buytendijk, F. J. J., xii

case study method, 198
children, 46–48, 51–53

Cobb-Stevens, R., 204
cognitive perspective, 29
Coles, Robert, 47–52
Combs, Arthur, 25
concrete sciences, 75
consciousness: acts of, 119–20; attitude and, 88; behaviorism and, 20; definition of psychology and, 108; describing essences and, 91; knowledge and, 9–10; meaning and, 81–82; measurement and meaning and, 79–80; noetic-noematic correlation and, 105; of participant and researcher, 182; perceptual sense and, 185–86; phenomenology and, 4–5, 68; phenomenon of, 76–77; psychological views on, 186–87; of researcher, 136–37
constituent, 102–03
constitution, 186

data, 61–62, 64–66, 113–14, 121–25. *See also* description(s)
definite manifold, 76–77
Dennett, D., 136
dependent parts, 115, 120
description(s): analysis of, 125–37, 191–95; of essence, 89; gathering, 96–98, 113–14, 116–17, 121–25; of jealousy experience, 140–43, 145–66, 179–80; of participant, 181; of structure, 104–05, 199–204; vulnerability in retrospective, 117–19. *See also* data
descriptive science, 77–78

229